THE

MERCHANT ADVENTURERS

OF

ENGLAND

THEIR LAWS AND ORDINANCES

WITH

OTHER DOCUMENTS

W. E. LINGELBACH, Ph. D.

" They were powerful and active men, they who broke the ban which lay for long on the commerce of the English, and obtained for the English flag and the English traders a recognized position in the world's affairs.''—Schanz, *Handelspolitik*, I, 327.

THE LAWBOOK EXCHANGE, LTD.
Clark, New Jersey

ISBN-13: 978-1-58477-442-6 (hardcover)
ISBN-13: 978-1-61619-061-3 (paperback)

Lawbook Exchange edition 2005, 2010

THE LAWBOOK EXCHANGE, LTD.

33 Terminal Avenue
Clark, New Jersey 07066-1321

*Please see our website for a selection of our other publications
and fine facsimile reprints of classic works of legal history:*
www.lawbookexchange.com

Library of Congress Cataloging-in-Publication Data

Lingelbach, William E. (William Ezra), 1871-1962.
  The Merchant Adventurers of England : their laws and ordinances,
with other documents / W.E. Lingelbach.
       p. cm.
  Originally published: Philadelphia ; New York : Sold by Longmans, Green & Co.,
1902, in series: Translations and reprints from the original sources of European
history ; 2nd ser., v. 2.
  ISBN 1-58477-442-8 (cloth: alk. paper)
  1. Company of Merchant Adventurers of England—History—Sources. 2. Great
Britain—Commerce—History—Sources. I. Title. II. Translations and reprints from
the original sources of European history ; 2nd ser., v. 2.

HF486.M17L56 2004
382'.0942'0903—dc22   2004040934

Printed in the United States of America on acid-free paper

THE

MERCHANT ADVENTURERS

OF

ENGLAND

THEIR LAWS AND ORDINANCES

WITH

OTHER DOCUMENTS

W. E. LINGELBACH, Ph. D.

" They were powerful and active men, they who broke the ban
which lay for long on the commerce of the English, and obtained
for the English flag and the English traders a recognized position
in the world's affairs."—Schanz, *Handelspolitik*, I, 327.

1902

PREFACE.

THE present volume was first suggested by my studies on the "Internal Organization and the Seat of Government of the Merchant Adventurers."[1] While pursuing investigations in that connection, I came constantly upon facts and conditions which revealed that the activities and influence of the Merchant Adventurers[2] were vastly more widespread and important than is generally supposed. Evidence, proving conclusively the continued existence of the Fellowship down to the early nineteenth century, a date almost two hundred years later than the period with which the studies on the Adventurers usually conclude, was also found. Furthermore, there exist in some of the best secondary writers on English economic history in regard to the Adventurers' Society, statements and theories that are plainly out of accord with the testimony of the sources. Some of these pertain to the essential features of the Society's organization and history, and therefore call for especial investigation. It was to draw attention to these facts, and to assist, in a modest way, in the work of clearing up the history of an organization whose activities have been of such vital importance to English economic and political development, that the publication of this volume was undertaken.

Of the sources for the history of the Merchant Adventurers, Schanz says: "*Die Literatur über die Merchant Adventurers ist ausserordentlich dürftig; die Neuzeit hat dem Gegenstand so gut wie keine Beachtung geschenkt. Alle Nachrichten, die man über disselben gelegentlich findet, sind direct oder indirect aus Flug-*

---

[1] *The Internal Organization and Seat of Government of the Merchant Adventurers*, Transactions of the Royal Historical Society, Vol. XV, pp. 1-45.

[2] This is the form of the name used by the secondary writers. It should be noted, however, that the official name in the charters and acts always has the plural of the word merchant, thus "the Governour, Assistants and Fellowship of the Merchant Adventurers of England." This is true likewise of Wheeler and others of the early 17th century. In connection with the documents of this volume, I have adhered to the old spelling.

und Parteischriften des 17 Jahrhunderts geflossen." [1] During the twenty years that have elapsed since this statement was made, so much admirable work on historical manuscripts and other sources for English history has been done that it needs radical modification. We need no longer be dependent upon the pamphlets of the 17th centuries for our knowledge of the Adventurers. These are frequently prejudiced, and for much of the history of the Society they are at best secondary in character. Within recent years a great deal of new and important material of a primary nature has been found; public and private records have been made accessible and manageable. Many of these, both for England and the Continent, are replete with facts of the life and activities of the Adventurers. In one respect, however, recent investigation and study have proved fruitless. The one great hiatus in the sources for the history of the Society still exists; for nowhere has there been found a definite clue to the existence and whereabouts of the private records of the Fellowship. That these were numerous and very extensive can be shown conclusively, and I have every reason to entertain the hope that ere long some at least may be found. Until this happens, the *Laws and Ordinances* must continue to occupy a unique place among the sources for the history of the Fellowship, and must furnish the chief material for the study of its organization and character.

The only copy of the *Laws and Ordinances* known to be in existence, and of which the text in this volume is a careful reprint, is found among the Additional Manuscripts of the British Museum. It consists of a large folio volume of over 200 pages, on vellum, with the original binding in leather, enforced by heavy brass mountings and clasps. Thus far I have been unable to find any clue to the early history of the manuscript. The Museum bought it on the 19th of March, 1852, at the sale of the stock of Thomas Thorpe, a bookseller, but there is nothing in the manuscript itself, or in the sale catalogue, to throw light on its earlier history.

In editing the document, the manuscript has been followed as closely as possible, the orthography of the original being adhered to throughout. The folio paging of the manuscript has been introduced in the margin of the reprint in order to facilitate com-

[1] Schanz, *Handelspolitik*, Vol. I, p. 332.

parison with the original when desirable. Every attempt at a critical editing of the individual ordinances with reference to the time and place of their adoption, the circumstances that called them forth, and their relation to other ordinances dealing with the same subject, has been scrupulously avoided. Only a very long and intimate acquaintance with the subject would render consistent editing along these lines possible.

The date of the manuscript demands attention. The supposition that it is the original codification made by Wheeler's own hand in 1608 is probably incorrect; for the ordinances of 1611 are in the same handwriting as the main body of the manuscript, and were apparently written at the same time, as, for example, the ordinance on folio 92, "enacted at Middlebroughe the last day of December anno 1611." On the other hand, all ordinances enacted after December of 1611 were added by a different hand. Thus an ordinance on folio 92, " Enacted at a General Court holden in Hambrough the 27th daye of ffebruary anno 1612"—is in a different hand from those preceding it. There is therefore strong reason for the view that the main body of the text of the laws is a copy made in 1611, probably from the original by Wheeler. Ordinances after that date were added in a somewhat haphazard manner from time to time, provision for the additions being made in the document by leaving blank folios at the end of each division or chapter. Some of these were made as late as 1770. Article fifty-two of the first chapter concludes with the words, "these last four articles were transcribed at London the 13th February 1770 by Nehemiah Nisbeth, Secretary."

The other sources published in this volume have been selected partly with the object of presenting, in so far as that is possible in so small a space, an outline narrative of the external history of the Fellowship; of its origin and loose organization during the early centuries of its existence; of its incorporation, monopoly rights and extended activities in the 16th and 17th centuries; and finally, of its gradual decline after the loss of these privileges till it appears as an ancient and honorable Society, but of little importance, in Hamburg at the opening of the last century. If taken collectively, the sources following the longer document of the *Laws and Ordinances* can be made to tell this story in a fairly consistent fashion for a period extending over a much greater length of time than has ever been done. Taken separately, the documents contain a great deal of information bearing upon the internal life and organization of the Society.

The character of the sources, and the fact that they are nearly all available only in manuscript form has made painstaking care a necessity. But despite this, I am conscious of many shortcomings. The history of the Fellowship, on pp. xvii–xli, is based largely on manuscript sources. A great deal of interest and of importance had to be omitted, or if introduced, left standing without support, by illustration or otherwise, for lack of space. Besides the data for much of the subject is still quite fragmentary; a great deal of work remains to be done on special phases of the life of the Society before its history can be definitively written. The "Brief History" as it stands, is the first attempt to carry the story of the Adventurers beyond the opening of the 17th century; much of it is therefore new ground and necessarily far from complete.

A comprehensive bibliography of the sources for the history of the Adventurers, with critical and descriptive accounts of the most important of these, is now well on toward completion, but before publication it is my purpose to subject it to a careful revision by a second direct comparison with the documents in the various archives of Europe.

In conclusion, I am happy at the opportunity of expressing my sincere gratitude and indebtedness to Hubert Hall, Esq., Mr. Joseph G. Rosengarten and Professor E. P. Cheyney for valuable assistance and encouragement while the work was in progress.

W. E. LINGELBACH.

UNIVERSITY OF PENNSYLVANIA.

CONTENTS.

xi

ERRATA.

P. 10, l. 2 from the bottom, *un* instead of *nn* in *grauntes*, and so throughout the first chapter. The *nn* occurs most frequently in the manuscript, but as it is not at all consistent it is apparently *un* that is intended.

P. 5, n. 1, l. 6, *Merchant* instead of *Merchants*, and so throughout the foot-notes to the volume. Cf. p. ix, n. 2.

P. 197, add as a foot-note, " The continuation of the by-law follows on page 257."

P. 221, n. 2, add, " The first six lines of the document as found in Hakluyt are manifestly in the nature of descriptive material by the writer."

THE MERCHANT ADVENTURERS OF ENGLAND.

A BRIEF HISTORY.

THE story of the Merchant Adventurers covers a period of nearly six hundred years. Its beginnings date back to the obscure and unsettled conditions of English commerce of the Middle Ages; its end is not till the present century. In 1805 they were still active in Hamburg, although their Society had long before that time lost its influence and importance. Of this period two centuries are of especial importance; they mark the period of greatest corporate activity of the Society, and extend approximately from the reign of the first Tudor, Henry VII, to the coming of William and Mary, the year 1689 marking the final withdrawal of the Fellowship's monopoly privileges.[1] During this period the Adventurers were thoroughly organized as a society or fellowship, with a well developed constitution and numerous by-laws. Their official name as it appears in the charter incorporating and making them a "body politick," was "The Governour, Assistants and Fellowship of the Merchants Adventurers of England." The central government or authority was vested in the hands of "a Governor, or in his absence, a Deputie, and four and twentie Assistantes in the Marte Towne."[2] The "marte towne" was always a city on the continent, where the Adventurers resided and stapled their commodities. For it should be remembered at the outset that the Merchant Adventurers were engaged solely in the foreign trade, and the centre of their organization was therefore located abroad and not in England, as one might otherwise expect.[3]

The Governor and his assistants were chosen by the Adventurers assembled in congregation or "general court" on the continent. These officers had absolute power to make laws, customs and ordi-

[1] *Statutes of the Realm*, 1 William and Mary, c. 12. Cf. *Extract from the Act*, p. 249.

[2] Wheeler, *Treatise of Commerce*, 25.

[3] Lingelbach, *The Internal Organization of the Merchant Adventurers*. Transactions of the Royal Historical Society, Vol. 15, p. 33 ff.

nances for the rule of members of the Society and the regulation of trade.   Full authority was conferred upon them to enforce the laws thus made and to carry them into execution, both among the brethren of the Fellowship and others "intermeddling" in their trade.[1] As Wheeler writes, they "have jurisdiction and full authoritie as wel from her Majestie as from the Princes, States and Rulers of the Low Countries, and beyond the seas, without appeale, provocation, or declination, to ende and determine all civill causes, questions, and controversies arising betweene or among the brethern, members and supposts of the said Companie, or betweene them and others, either English, or Strangers, who either may or will prorogate the Jurisdiction of the said Companie and their court, or are subject to the same by the priviledges, and Charters thereunto granted."[2]

It was further the duty of the Governor and his assistants not only to watch over the interests of the Fellowship as a body, but to aid and assist the brethren in their private suits, and to defend the rights of each member to the utmost of their power.   The right to impose heavy fines, to confiscate the goods of intermeddlers, or to cast offenders into prison, was guaranteed the Society by its charters, and used by it with telling effect.   A member found guilty of aiding or abetting intermeddling was at once disfranchised.   Violations of the ordinary rules of the Society were punished by money fines increasing with each repetition of the offence, and not infrequently culminating in imprisonment.   Criticism of the judgment of the Court was a punishable offence, and appeal to the civil courts was prohibited.

The membership of the Society early in the seventeenth century consisted, according to Wheeler, of more than 3500 "wealthie and well experimented Merchants, dwelling in diverse great Cities, Maritime Townes and other parts of the Realme, to wit, London, Yorke, Norwich, Exeter, Ipswitch, Newcastle, Hull, etc."[3]   Membership in the Society was by no means easy to attain.   Election to the freedom, to be valid, must take place in a general court at the

---

[1] *Laws and Ordinances*, p. 6.   [2] Wheeler, *Treatise of Commerce*, 25.

[3] Wheeler, *Treatise of Commerce*, 19. To this list of places Gross adds Boston, Bristol, Devizes, Salisbury and Yarmouth. Gross, *Gild Merchant*, I, 151. It should also be noted that the Fellowship had at times local courts or residences at various places on the continent.

Residence in the mart town. Eligibility to election as a "free and sworn brother of the fellowship" demanded the completion of a term of apprenticeship of eight years, or a right based on patrimony, which required that the father must have been free of the fellowship before the birth of the son.[1] Artisans, unfree persons, bastards, bankrupts, criminals, and persons of a disreputable manner of life were debarred, so also all foreigners and even persons whose parents were not both English. If a member married a foreign woman or came into the possession of land or hereditaments abroad, he was by that fact itself deprived of his membership.

Among the members "dwelling in diverse great cities, Maritime Townes and other parts of the Realme," local or subsidiary fellowships were organized. These were under the direct supervision of the main body, represented by the governor and assistants or the "High Court," as it is sometimes called, at the Residence abroad. For "by the said Governour and Assistantes are also appointed and chosen a Deputie, and certaine discreet persons, to be associates to the said Deputie, in all other places convenient, as well within, as without the realme of England, who all hold correspondence with the Governour of the Company, and chiefe Court in the Marte Towne on the other side the seas."[2]

"The parts and places which they trade unto, are the Townes and Portes lying between the rivers *Somme* in France and the *Scawe* in the Germane sea:[3] not into all at once or at each man's pleasure, but into one or two Towns at the most within the above-said bounds, which they commonly call the Mart Towne or Townes; for that there onely they stapled the commodities, which they brought out of England, and put the same to sale, and bought such forreigne commodities as the land wanted, and were brought

---

[1] *Laws and Ordinances*, pp. 34-52.

[2] Wheeler, *Treatise of Commerce*, 25. The election of officers for the *sub posts* by the Court abroad appears also in the by-laws, cf. *Laws and Ordinances*, p. 6. For a more detailed discussion of this question, see my paper on the Internal Organization of the Society, cited above.

[3] The trade of the Adventurers was at first confined to the Netherlands, later it was extended to the boundaries here mentioned, which included also the territories inland, and Germany. Cf. *Laws and Ordinances*, pp. 53, 59 and 134. At other times it was much more restricted, cf. R. O. State Papers, Elizabeth, 130, 33.

from far by merchants of diverse nations and countries flocking thither as to a Faire or Market to buy and sell."[1] The great staple commodity of the Adventurers' trade was "the woollen cloth manufactory of the Realme." For many years they had a complete monopoly of the cloth export of England, though they had had in their early history a more varied commerce, "trading in cloth, kersie, and all other, as well English as forreigne Commodities vendible abroad."

This trade was carefully regulated and organized by a large number of statutes and by-laws. Those of greatest significance are directed towards the maintenance of the monopoly of the Company, the enforcing of the staple, and the control of the "Stint." For within the territory designated in the Charters of the Society, no Englishman, not a member of the fraternity, was allowed to trade; no member could sell his goods at any town but the mart or staple town, and there only in such quantities as had been definitely prescribed for each member by the ordinances.[2] This last was called the "stint of trade." By it was determined exactly how much cloth and other commodities individual members were allowed to export annually. The yearly trade in cloth was limited during the first three years of membership to 400 pieces. After the fourth year it increased year by year till it reached the number of 1000 pieces, which stood as the extreme limit for the cloth shipments of any member for one year.

At certain seasons the Adventurers' cloth fleet, usually in the convoy of several men-of-war, sailed from England for the mart town on the continent.[3] There, the show and sale of goods was carefully regulated. Only brethren of the Fellowship could do business there, and even they were not allowed to do business for non-members. Mondays, Wednesdays and Fridays were "show days" on which goods were exposed for sale. No business could be transacted on other days, and any attempt at forestalling or securing sales prematurely by accosting merchants on the street was prohibited. These rules were enforced with great strictness,

[1] Wheeler, *Treatise of Commerce*, 20.

[2] Cf. *Laws and Ordinances*, p. 68.

[3] The value of a single shipment of this kind often exceeded £350,000. Cf. Br. Mus., Cott. MS, Galba B, XI, fol. 241 ff.

transgressors being punished with well-nigh ruthless severity. The interloper whose daring led him to defy the monopoly rights of the Society soon came to grief; his wares were confiscated, or if these were inaccessible "his body" was "attached and committed to prisone" until the heavy fines were paid, and he bound himself by a solemn oath to desist from his trade. If a merchant, not a member of the Society, failed to fulfil his obligations to any brother of the Fellowship all members were ordered to avoid business relations with him. Members were forbidden to give credit on sales for a longer period than six months, or to offer more than 7 per cent. discount for cash payments.[1]

These are a few of the more important rules of the Company in regard to its trade. Intimately related with them are those regulating the powers and duties of the subsidiary fellowships, their relation to the General Court, the exercise of merchant law, the relations between members, conduct and procedure in the courts of the Society, the life of members in the Residence abroad, etc.

The rights and duties of the local fellowships or courts, and their relation to the General Court of the Society, constitute one of the most important and at the same time one of the most difficult subjects in the history of the Adventurers. Despite the fact that the provisions in the constitution and by-laws are definite and precise on the constitutional relations,[2] there is every evidence that the practice by no means always conformed to the formulated rules. Frequent quarrels and controversies between the subsidiary fellowships and the General Court of the Society occurred. Local jealousy was frequently the cause. More frequently it was due to the fact that the subsidiary fellowships in some of the outlying maritime towns of England had at one time existed independently as a Society of Adventurers, as for example, the Merchant Adventurers of Newcastle, but had later been forced into the General Society because of the control of trade exercised by that body through its exclusive charter rights. These local societies had their own traditions, their own peculiar interests, and in certain cases a degree of independence quite different from the local fellowships in other places where the organization came into exist-

---

[1] *Laws and Ordinances,* p. 105, ff.   [2] *Ibid.,* p. 6.

ence through the activity of the Merchant Adventurers Society itself.[1]

Looking at the internal government of the Fellowship one is impressed with the great centralization of power and the almost despotic authority exercised by the Governor and his Court. The results were far reaching. It not only made possible a very efficient control over the members of the Society and their interests, but it also secured that promptness and authoritative action which characterized the relations of the Adventurers with other organizations or persons, political or private, with whom they had to deal. Victory was nearly always on their side in the numerous conflicts in which they were parties. Furthermore their wealth was enormous, for they had the good fortune of early securing a monopoly of the trade of cloth manufacturing. In proportion as the making of cloth developed, their trade necessarily increased in importance and profit. Hence it is that after the 15th century the company of Merchant Adventurers became one of the most powerful and influential organizations in the State.[2]

To the effective aid of the Adventurers was due, in a very large measure, the success of the commercial policy of the early Tudors. They won English trade from the foreigner, and laid for Englishmen the basis for their later commercial supremacy. But in addition to the influence exerted by the Adventurers upon the commercial and industrial development of England, the Fellowship was a very important factor in the political affairs of the realm, both national and international. It is through the Adventurers' Society that Gresham was enabled to restore the financial credit of the realm and turn the rate of exchange in favor of England at a most critical period. To them must be ascribed to a

---

[1] This phase of the subject can be satisfactorily treated only after the records of a number of the local fellowships are made accessible. The publication of the *Records of the Newcastle Merchant Adventurers*, Surtees Society Publications, Vols. 93 and 101, has thrown a flood of light on the subject, besides affording much valuable material for other phases of the history of the General Society. The best work on this side of the Society's history up to the present are the notes by Gross, *Gild Merchant*, I. Space precludes any attempt at treating the question here.

[2] Many proofs of these statements exist. In 1560 Queen Elizabeth borrowed £30,000 from the Adventurers. *Newcastle Merchant Adventurers*, I, 89.

considerable degree the success of the cause of parliament in the great Civil War, for they contributed heavily to the expenses of the popular party.[1] I have shown elsewhere the part played by the Governor of the Society in the attempt to force the kingship on Cromwell in 1656.[2] These facts will serve to illustrate how far-reaching was the work of the Society even in the field of national politics, though a care must be had not to attribute united corporate action to the Adventurers in every instance, for the acts were frequently due to the attitude of certain leaders only.

In treating the external history of the Merchant Adventurers the historian is confronted at the outset with the usual difficulties associated with the origins of institutions whose foundations are laid in the Middle Ages. There is a consensus of opinion as to the main lines of the early development, but none as to the details. The representatives of the Society in the 17th century claimed that the Fellowship originated among "some few mercers of London" called the Brotherhood of St. Thomas à Becket of Canterbury; that thus organized they received special privileges of trade from John, Duke of Brabant, in the 13th century; that Edward III confirmed the same, and in 1399 Henry IV "gave to the Company a very beneficiall and ample Charter of Privileges."[3]

The presence of a large number of Mercers[4] among the Adventurers during their early history is well established; not so, however,

---

[1] As an actual example of this, the following may be cited: "An order representing the re-payment of £30,000 lent by the Merchant Adventurers, May 5, 1642" (L. J. 5, 47); "a draft order for securing re-payment of £10,000 to the Fellowship of Merchant Adventurers, Dec. 24, 1644" (L. J. 7, 112); "a draft ordinance for reimbursing and securing to the Fellowship of Merchants Adventurers certain moneys disbursed by them for public use, Dec. 1, 1647 (L. J. 11, 562), and "an order to secure the re-payment of £10,000 lent by the Merchant Adventurers for the use of the navy, Oct. 27, 1648" (L. J. 10, 567).

[2] Paper cited above, Transactions of the Royal Historical Society, Vol. XV, p. 22; Thurloe, *State Papers*, VI, 74.

[3] Br. Mus., Stowe MS., 303. fol. 99; also *Statutes of the Realm*, 12 Henry VII' c. 6.

[4] The preponderance of the Mercers in the Merchant Adventurers Society appears repeatedly. Cf. Schanz, *Handelspolitik*, I, 341; Gross, *Gild Merchant*, I, 152. Gross also brings out the composite character of the membership of the Society; the residence of the Adventurers at Exeter, for example, "con⁻ sisted of three separate fraternities: the Mercers, Drapers and Boothmen or

their claim that they were early organized as a Brotherhood of St. Thomas à Becket, or that the grants by the Kings of England and the princes of the Low Countries were exclusively to them. The evidence for the existence of a trading Brotherhood of St. Thomas à Becket is only meagre,[1] and none whatever has come to light in favor of the claim that they alone were entitled to the privileges and grants to Englishmen on the continent. On the contrary, the spirit and wording of the grants themselves, as well as the contentions of other merchants, not of the Fellowship, seem to prove that the special rights and privileges granted by the lords of the Low Countries and the Kings of England in the 14th and even early in the 15th century were very general, and were meant to extend to all Englishmen beyond the seas. In the charter of 1505 the privileges are for the first time limited to a special group of merchants. In this charter "our subjects called Merchant Adventurers" are especially designated as the recipients of the grant, and all other merchants are enjoined to enter the fellowship.[2] Some years before, in 1497, they had been officially, though indirectly, recognized by act of parliament.[3] From the preamble of the act it appears that complaint was made against the high-handed action of the Merchant Adventurers in compelling all who traded to the parts of "Flanders, Holand, Seland, Brabant and the other places thereto nygh adjoining" to join their society, and pay the fine of £20 sterling. The act does not abolish the fine; it merely reduces it to ten marks sterling, and decrees that no other fine shall be levied "to the use of the said fraternitie or feliship, or of any other like, excepte only x marc sterling." This concedes the legal right of the Society to levy fines, and is therefore an indirect recognition of the organization.

Corn Merchants." From a Star Chamber decree of 1516, it appears that mercers, drapers, boothmen and spicers composed the Gild Merchant, or the nucleus out of which the Newcastle Society of Merchant Adventurers arose. Gross, II, 380, sets out the decree almost in full. It is also worthy of note that the records of the London residence of the Merchant Adventurers were, until 1526, kept in same book as those of the Mercers Society.

[1] See page 199, n. 1.

[2] Br. Mus., Cott. MS., Tib. D. VIII, Vol. 37, published by Schanz, *Handelspolitik*, II, Urk. Bei., 121. The instrument also speaks of "the hoole fellowshipp."

[3] *Statutes of the Realm*, 12 Henry VII, c. 6, p. 204, of this volume.

This is only one of many facts which show conclusively that a fellowship or fraternity existed among the Adventurers long before we find them so spoken of in the official instruments of the political powers. In other words, the nucleus and first organization of the earlier society was not created from above. It was the out-growth of conditions and necessities confronting English merchants trading to the Low Countries.

English commerce in the thirteenth and fourteenth centuries was in the hands of foreigners,—the Italians and the merchants of the Hanse League,—and the Staplers. During the fourteenth century, however, there developed outside of the monopoly of the foreigners and of the merchants of the Staple an extensive trade among native merchants, who traded where they would, and at their own risk. The name "Adventurers" was early attached to them, though it was at first applied to all merchants not Staplers irrespective of the places or the commodities of their trade. Thus, there were "Adventurers to Iceland, to Prussia, to Spain, Italy,"[1] and other places. But as the great bulk of English commerce was to the Low Countries, the "Adventurers" trading to Holland, Zealand, Brabant, etc., were the most numerous and important, and the name became gradually associated with them. For purposes of protection and mutual advantage in trade they often combined and rapidly made for themselves a place and a reputation in the commerce of the North Sea. Whenever the Staple town was changed we find them promptly concentrating at the abandoned mart, and making common cause with such of the Staplers as were left behind. Combination and the acquisition of privileges from the civil and political authorities is a distinguishing feature of the medieval industrial organization, and the "Adventurers" were not behindhand in this respect.

During the thirteenth century, whether in 1216, 1248, 1286 or 1296[2] has not been finally settled, trading privileges were granted by the princes of the Low Countries. These privileges were quite general in character, securing to Englishmen and others at Antwerp, "omnes et singuli mercatores regni Anglii necnon cuiuscun-

---

[1] Compare, "the seid marchauntis venterers," *Statutes of the Realm*, 25 Henry VIII, c. 4.

[2] All four dates are given by the writers of the 17th century.

que regni seu terre.'', the right of choosing a governor to settle difficulties among themselves, and of appearing before the courts of the Low Countries against the natives. In 1305 and 1315 the previous privileges were renewed and additional articles added. These also are quite general, but they show an intimate relation between the Staplers and the Adventurers of this period, as the commodities of trade mentioned are mostly those of the Staple.

In 1359, after the removal of the English staple to England, similar privileges[1] were granted by Louis le Male to a group of English merchants at Bruges, and confirmed in the same year by Edward III.[2] The articles of the grant reveal a group of merchants organized on lines very similar to those found later among the Merchant Adventurers, and as the differentiation between the trade in raw commodities and woollen cloth had not yet been made, I am inclined to look upon the merchants at Bruges as typical Merchant Adventurers of this period. The removal of the Staple to England doubtless furnished a definite occasion for the organization of English merchants in the Low Countries. Up to that time they could look to the Staple Society and its Mayor for the protection of their interests. With the removal of the authorities and officers of the Staple this was no longer possible, and the need for an organization to take up the functions abandoned by the Society of the Staple made itself felt.

The charter of 1407, called by Schanz "*die Consulats Charte*,'' has come to be regarded as marking the beginning of the later Society. The reason for this is not well founded, for this charter is no more specific in its terms than the earlier grants. It is addressed to ''the merchants of our kingdom of England and of our other dominions, in the regions of Holland, Zealand, Brabant, Flanders and other parts beyond the sea which are in friendship with us.'' The right granted by the charter to organize and govern the affairs of Englishmen living and trading in the parts mentioned was not confined to any particular place nor even to any particular group of merchants. Indeed there is evidence that there were local

---

[1] Varenbergh, *Histoire des Relations diplomatiques entre la Flandre et l'Angleterre*, 1447.

[2] The instrument is published by Cunningham, *English Industry and Commerce.* I, Appendix, C. 4.

bodies of English merchants organized on the lines of the Charter in various towns at the same time during the 15th century.

Early in this century, however, Antwerp rapidly attained a special importance, far beyond that of any other city, as the great mart town of the Netherlands. Bruges was gradually abandoned, and the English merchants gathered at Antwerp. Here they obtained a house for their use in 1407. Cloth instead of wool and other raw products was fast becoming their commodity of trade, so that both the character of their trade and the greater distance from the Staple mart, now at Calais, very soon developed a dividing line between the Adventurers at Antwerp and the Staplers Society. The practical need of a strong organization among the Adventurers became apparent, and because of the growing prosperity of their trade at Antwerp and their increasing numbers, they naturally developed most rapidly at that place. Increased trade and numbers brought with them power and influence, and the Society at Antwerp may well be conceived of as gradually bringing under its control the English merchants still trading, individually or in groups, to Bruges and other towns.[1] No evidence exists of any single organization during this period. Such a society may have developed very early, as is claimed by the defenders of the Fellowship in the 17th century, but so far as the testimony of the sources goes, only the first stages of organization had been accomplished, and the basis laid for the future.

In 1462 a charter from Henry IV appointed an Englishman named Obray governor, and provided for the election of twelve assistants to aid and advise him in the government.[2] A society or fellowship clearly appears. Certainly before very long the process of centralization was thoroughly under way, and the Adventurers began to use coercive measures to force all Englishmen trading to the Low Countries to pay fines, and acknowledge their control by paying entrance fees to their organization. These were at first small, "an old noble sterling," but they were gradually increased

[1] I have come across a number of instances indicating local fellowships in towns other than the great mart town. In the charter of 1505, after the removal of the mart to Calais, the 24 assistants are to be " of the most sadd discreet and honest persons of divers *Fellowships* of the said Merchant Adventurers." R. O. State Papers, Dom. Chas. II, 27, fol. 6.

[2] Hakluyt, *The Principal Navigations, Voyages*, etc., I. 209.

to the sum of 20 pounds. In the preamble of the Act of 1497 they arrogated to themselves the exclusive right to trade in the regions specified by the old Charter, and effectively stopped those unwilling to pay the exorbitant fine of 20 pounds from trading in those parts.[1] The Act, as we have seen, ordered the reduction of the fine, but supported the right of the Adventurers to levy it, by ordering all merchants trading to the Low Countries to enter the freedom of the Fellowship.

Henceforth the Merchant Adventurers were firmly established in their control of the trade in woollen manufactures to the coast of the North Sea. Henry VII, seeing in the Society an instrument ready at hand to carry out his policy of nationalizing English commerce, lent it his active support.[2] In 1499 he granted the Society a private coat of arms; two years later he confirmed the previous charter, and in 1505, when the disputes with Burgundy led to the removal of the English to Calais, he gave the Company a new charter. This charter provided for the election of "a governor or governors" and "24 of the most sadd discreet and honest persons of divers Fellowshipes of the same Merchant Adventurers." The governor and his "assistants" were given jurisdiction over all members and power to make statutes; to appoint officers both in England and in Calais; to levy fines and to imprison offenders, and to call the Fellowship together in London or elsewhere as they saw fit. All members duly notified were obliged to be present on pain of a heavy penalty. Resolutions and decrees became valid through the support of the majority of the Court of Assistants. The court also had power to punish at its discretion all violations of the Statutes, and to compel all who used the trade of the Society to enter the freedom.[3]

[1] See text of the Statute, p. 204.

[2] The policy of the crown during this period reveals remarkable insight into the true state of trade. Besides supporting the Adventurers in their efforts to nationalize England's commerce, Henry VII also protected the Society from the control of a "ring of London monopolists" who were attempting to replace the wider association of merchants by a "narrow and exclusive corporation." This attempt on the part of the richer merchants of London, and the dangers therefrom to the rising commerce of the English, are set forth by Busch, *England under the Tudors*, I, 244.

[3] R. O. State Papers, Dom. Chas. II., 27, 6; also Br. Mus. Cott. MS., Tib. D. VIII, fol. 27, published by Schanz, *Handelspolitik*, II, Urk. Bei., 121.

More important, however, than the charter was the consistent support of the Society's authority by the Crown during this period. For, thus strongly organized and supported, the Adventurers quickly assumed the direction of the English trade with the Netherlands when those regions were again opened to them, and soon exercised a most vigorous control over all its details. If prices fell too low, they regulated the export in order to raise them again, if the Society's privileges or the rights of the individual members were violated, redress was promptly demanded, and in case it was not forthcoming reprisals in the form of diverting trade to other ports, or of leaving the place altogether, were resorted to to bring about the desired effect.[1]

Another result of this strongly centralized authority of the Society and the support of the Crown manifested itself very early in conflicts with the two other great trading organizations of the 15th and 16th century, the Ancient Society of the Staple, and the Hanse League.

The strife between the Adventurers and the Staplers began when the former demanded the payment of their membership fee from all Staplers trading in cloth. The pride and dignity of the Staplers, for many years the foremost men of English commerce, naturally rebelled against submitting to the demand. Disputes and quarrels arose. Henry VII and Henry VIII maintained a careful balance between the two societies. But after that the royal power was exercised with less care, and the natural advantages enjoyed by the Adventurers through their control of the steadily increasing cloth export, soon gave them the victory over the older society whose trade in wool and other raw materials must necessarily have diminished in importance with the development of the manufacturing industry. It would require too much space to give even a brief account of the long quarrel between the two societies. A few landmarks only can be mentioned.

The first of these appears in the persistent arrests of the Staplers trading in cloth. In 1505, the year in which the Adventurers secured their charter from Henry VII, the disputes were laid before the Court of Star Chamber. The judgment favored the Adventurers. The decree ordered that the members of one Society

---

[1] Schanz, *Handelspolitik*, I, 343.

should be obliged to aid in bearing the expenses of the other if they took part in its trade.[1] This was interpreted by them to mean that the Staplers in order to take part in the trade of the Merchant Adventurers must first pay the fines of admission to the Adventurers' Society. But Henry VII refused to support them in their interpretation, and ordered that only the usual duties on cloth should be collected from the Staplers. His successor con- tinued the policy.

In spite of this, however, the Staplers were being sorely pressed. Mere decrees availed little against the strong vantage ground held by the Adventurers. Their relations to the development of the great cloth industry of England carried them rapidly forward and upward, while the Staplers were being left behind. By the open- ing of Henry VIII's reign 73 Staplers, among them 14 mayors of the Staple, had joined the Adventurers' Society.[2] Quarrels and dis- putes continued during the 16th century, but no definite settlement was reached. The outcome of the struggle is apparent, even though the detailed facts have not been discovered up to the present. The Staplers succumbed, as they were doomed to do from the first, not because of any essential weakness in their organization or in the government support offered them, but because the economic basis on which their existence rested was being broken up.

The Hanse League was a more determined and in every respect more formidable rival. The issues involved were of greater signi- ficance. The struggle was transferred from the sphere of domestic rivalries to the domain of foreign and international politics. The rivals represented not merely the interests of two trading organi- zations; they are the exponents of great national interests and the representatives of rival civilizations, political as well as industrial. It was a struggle between the representatives of the medieval orga- nization and federative system of the Hanseatic League on the one hand, and exponents of the growing nationalism and the central- ized monarchy of England on the other.

In the 14th and 15th century the Hanse controlled the commerce

[1] R. O. Rot. pat. 20 H. VII, p. 1, m. 24, also Br. Mus. Sloane 4618. No. 55, pub- lished by Schanz, *Handelspolitik*, II, Urk. Bei., 119 and 133.

[2] Schanz, *Handelspolitik*, I, 346.

of the North Sea, and strongly intrenched behind special grants[1] from the various princes and municipalities, their position seemed impregnable. The increasing strength of the Adventurers, however, made a determined attack inevitable. Even before the reign of Elizabeth, when the struggle was finally fought out, the English merchants, supported by the steadfast policy of the early Tudors, had seriously weakened the position of the Hanse in England.[2] In Elizabeth's reign, however, after the Diet of the Hanse Towns at Lübeck had in 1557 decreed in favor of a commercial war against England, their privileges in England were made dependent on their not carrying to the Low Countries any cloth, but only the commodities of their own lands. But the Adventurers did not stop the war with their success at home. They invaded the territory of the Hanse itself, and that at the invitation of one of the principal Hanse Towns. Hamburg had suffered severely from the decree which resulted from the religious troubles on the continent, prohibiting the export of English cloth, and the Senate of the city addressed an invitation to Elizabeth offering to the English merchants the right to trade in Hamburg on the same basis as did the burghers.[3] The Adventurers accepted, and this reception of the Fellowship at Hamburg became the entering wedge which contributed so largely to the breaking up the League of the Hanseatic Cities. The members of the League bent every energy to expel the intruders, and from 1572 till 1611 the Hanse Cities led by Lübeck brought every influence in their power to bear on the burghers and Senate of Hamburg. In 1578 the pressure became so great that the city was forced to yield, and in the "*Hamburger Decret*"[4] of this year the English were notified that their privileges would not be continued. Commerce with the Hanse Towns fell off rapidly, but the Netherland trade had re-opened and the Adven-

---

[1] Those granted by Edward IV in the Treaty of Utrecht in 1473, for the services rendered him by the Hanse, were very extensive and of great value.

[2] The trade of the League was still very considerable; in 1550 they exported 43,000 unfinished cloths, exceeding the value of £200,000, besides great quantities of other merchandize and raw products. Ehrenberg, *England und Hamburg*, 51.

[3] R. O. State Papers, For. Elizabeth, Vol. II. fol. 68, published by Ehrenberg, *England und Hamburg*. *Urkunden*, I. The letter is dated March 17, 1564.

[4] Ehrenberg; *England und Hamburg*, 141.

turers again found a market for their goods at Antwerp. Besides, intermittent trading had been carried on with Stade. Hamburg was again the principal sufferer, and the city again threatened to break with the League. In 1581 she refused to carry out measures of reprisal against the English, notwithstanding the severe measures taken against the Hanse Merchants in England. Nor did the agitation of the League in the Imperial Diet and with the Emperor change her attitude. Negotiations with the Adventurers were opened, secretly at first and then openly. In 1587 intercourse was resumed. Again the pressure from the League led by Lübeck made the continuance of the rights extended by Hamburg to the Adventurers impossible. The Adventurers, weary and angry at the delays, turned to Stade, where they established their staple. At the same time they secured from the home government the adoption of a policy of extreme severity against the commerce of the Hanse. From 1587, the year before the Armada, till 1611, the trade of Hamburg and the Hanse was nearly ruined by the English. The aid of the Emperor was solicited, and in 1597 an imperial edict was issued forbidding all imperial cities from allowing the Merchant Adventurers to settle in their jurisdiction. The decree also forbade all subjects of the Empire to trade with them. These were drastic measures, but the Company was equal to the emergency; it promptly dissolved, so far as the outward signs of their organization at Stade were concerned,[1] and after a time resumed its trade as "interlopers" at Stade and Emden. Moreover, the edict was plainly opposed to the economic interests of the Empire, and could not be strictly enforced. The commercial interests of upper Germany protested, Hamburg was divided between her material needs and her loyalty to the League. Finally loyalty again gave way, and on June 28, 1611, the Senate offered the Adventurers a grant of special privileges based on those of 1567, having previously secured permission from the Emperor, notwithstanding the opposition of Lübeck. This grant marks the conclusion of the long period of conflict. The strain had been severe, but the triumph of the Adventurers was complete.[2]

[1] For text of the edict and the results, see Wheeler, *Treatise of Commerce*, 80 ff.

[2] A document among the State Papers, R. O. Dom. James I, Vol. 67, No. 80, reveals this feature of the struggle ; the great sums needed for the ambassadors and plenipotentiaries, bribes, etc.

"*Für die Hanse,*" Ehrenberg rightly says: "*War die Wieder-aufnahme der Engländer in Hamburg ohne Zweifel einer der letzten Nägel zu ihrem Sarge.*"[1] For Hamburg, on the contrary, the greatest good resulted, and it is to the presence of the English Staple that the steady development of the commerce of the city and its importance as the great distributing centre for the international commerce of the North Sea in the eighteenth century must be attributed.[2]

Long before the final triumph over the Hanse, important events in the history and development of the Merchant Adventurers had occurred. After Henry VII their charters had been confirmed in turn by Henry VIII, Edward VI and Elizabeth. In 1564, the sixth year of Elizabeth's reign, the great step in advance was taken. In that year the Fellowship was formally incorporated as the "Governor Assistants and Fellowship of Merchants Adventurers of England," with very extensive rights and privileges. These have been defined in general terms above.[3] This charter and the one of 1586, which is a repetition of the earlier one in all but the additional articles regarding the subsidiary Fellowships, mark this period as the high water mark of the organization of the Society, and of its recognition by the State.

Their monopoly rights were secured, and the control over the admission of all merchants to the privileges of their Society guaranteed. The Fellowship became in every sense of the word a trading monopoly, and the violent opposition against monopolies in the early 17th century made the Society a chief point of attack. Staplers, "interlopers," and cloth makers, vie with each other in denouncing the monopoly rights and the practices of the Company. Parliament was besieged with petitions, and the Council is never quite through with the vexatious business of hearing and settling causes between the Merchant Adventurers and their numerous opponents. An entire literature on the subject sprang into existence. The Adventurers suffered severely, but the Com-

---

[1] Ehrenberg, *England und Hamburg*, 230.

[2] Much the best account of the relations between the Hanse and the Merchant Adventurers Society during the 15th and 16th century is found in Ehrenberg's *England und Hamburg*, Chapter I-V. Cf. also Wheeler, *Treatise of Commerce*, 62 ff.

[3] Compare *Extracts from the Charter of 1564*, p. 229 ff.

pany was not destroyed as was the case with other organizations. James I confirmed their charters in 1605 and again in
1607. In 1608, however, the tide turned; the well-known patent
to Cockayne was issued for the finishing, dyeing and export
of woollen cloth.[1] The privileges seriously interfered with the
rights of the Adventurers. But their efforts to secure the withdrawal of Cockayne's patent were fruitless. Indeed in 1614 a
royal proclamation declared all licenses to export undyed and
undressed cloth—the great staple of the Adventurers—void.
The Adventurers were forced to hand in their charter, notwithstanding their offer to make increased payments to the Crown. A
new company promoted by Cockayne was formed.[2] But none of
the many expectations in regard to it were realized, and the trade
became very much demoralized. In 1616 overtures to the old
company were made, but they refused to accept the terms, which
were very much like those under which Cockayne's company
operated. The condition of the woollen trade became daily worse,
and all sorts of remedies were tried.[3] Finally after a trial of three
years with the New Company, the Old Society was restored to its
former privileges.[4] But it was many years before the Society
was able to regain its former trade. The licensing of "intermeddlers" made serious inroads on their membership and weakened
them. Besides the provision to export only finished woollen cloths,
had driven many of the industries on the continent for dyeing and
finishing, formerly dependent on the white cloths of the Adventurers, to manufacturing cloth themselves. But the foreigner

[1] For an account of Cockayne's patent and the circumstances which called it
forth, see Dr. Cunningham, *Growth of English Industry and Commerce*, Vol.
II, p. 165,

[2] The arguments for and against the attempt to bring the whole process of
making and finishing cloth into the hands of English workmen, and of abol-
ishing the rights of the Old Company, are found in the Br. Mus., Lands. MS.,
152, fol. 282; cf. also R. O. State Papers, Dom. 187, 29 and 35. Much was expected
of the New Company, but it failed miserably.

[3] As an illustration, may be cited Bacon's scheme forbidding any Englishman
to wear during the six months after September 13 any silken stuff which did
not contain a mixture of wool. *Letters and Life of Lord Bacon*, V, 74.

[4] *Proclamation*, Aug. 12, 1617; R. O. State Papers, Dom. 187, 50. Compare also
the following: "affore a° 1614 the ffellowship were dissolved to make way for
Sir William Cockayne's project of dyeing and dressing all cloths of this land

had not taken kindly to the English finished cloth, and the market for the excellent white woollens of the English was not entirely destroyed. By the end of the reign of James I the Society had again become well established in its trade.

In the troubles between king and parliament during Charles I's reign, the Adventurers naturally played a prominent part. The plans adopted by the king to raise revenue affected their interests in almost every instance, and it is not at all strange that we find them on the side of parliament. When that body refused to give its consent to the tonnage and poundage imposed by Charles, the Adventurers unanimously supported the cause of parliament; they refused to buy or sell cloth, and, according to the Venetian ambassador, if any brought goods into the customs house they were hooted at as traitors by the crowd.[1] He narrates further that a deputation from the Adventurers, "the great Company which had in its hands the exportation of cloth, was summoned before the council," and that when asked why trade had ceased, they finally answered that they were afraid of the protestation of parliament. They were ordered to summon a court of the Company, but the court, "not a hand against it," decided not to export cloth.[2] The anger of the king was so great that he thought of dissolving the Fellowship in order to substitute for it a body of noblemen and courtiers who would make no difficulty about paying the duties.[3] But nothing came of it, and in 1634 the Society was still further established in its rights by a proclamation for the

before exportacion, the stranger did first prohibit all dyed and dresst clothes which still they maintain vigorously, and next put themselves forth on the making of cloth in their own countries, so that after an essay of almost two years the ffellowship was restored to the ancient Charters and privileges they found the vent of their English draperies in Germany and the Low Countries so fallen that they could not export in all woollen manufactures above 40,000 clothes yearly. And although upon their restitucion 15 Jacobi their Charters were much enlarged . . . yet all, for want of the assisting hand of the State was fruitles . . ." Br. Mus., Stowe MS., 303.

[1] R. O. Venetian Transcripts, Contarini to the Doge, March, 1629.

[2] Tanner MS., 71, fol. 1,

[3] Many interesting facts on the Adventurers are found scattered throughout Mr. Gardiner's great work on the 17th century. For the reign of James I the Alexander Prize Essay for 1898 by Miss Hermia Durham, entitled, *The Relations of the Crown to Trade under James I*, is excellent.

better ordering the transportation of cloth and other woollen manufactures into Germany and the Low Countries.[1] Its exclusive rights to export the woollen manufacture were continued, but the Company was enjoined to admit all such of the king's subjects dwelling in London and exercised in the profession of merchandise, and not shopkeepers, as shall desire the same for the fine of £50 apiece. The admission fine for merchants from outlying districts and towns was fixed at £25. All other subjects were inhibited from intermeddling in the trade of the Adventurers. By what means the Society secured the royal support may be inferred from the chronic deficit in the treasury and the wealth of the merchants. In 1640, when the king seized the Spanish bullion in the Tower amounting to £30,000, the Company took the lead in protesting, fearing reprisals on the continent. To bring about a compromise, the Society was forced to make a loan of £40,000 to the Crown.[2] In 1643 an Ordinance by the Lords and Commons confirmed the charters of the Company,[3] and during the period of the Civil War and the Protectorate the Fellowship continued its monopoly in spite of the fact that the Ordinance of 1643 was vigorously opposed. The maintenance of its authority, however, was only accomplished by dint of the most active and aggressive measures on the part of the Society before parliament and the Committee on Trade[4] till a new proclamation in their favor was made in 1656.[5] In 1658 we find them them petitioning Parliament for "a like proclamation as was issued May 30, 1656."[6] After the Restoration their rights were continued,[7] and in 1661 their former charters confirmed. But the frequent demands upon the resources of the Society and the heavy expenses it incurred involved the Adventurers in serious financial embarrassment.[8] They were no longer able to repel the

[1] State Papers, Dom. Chas. I, *Proclamations*, 185.

[2] Rushwood, *State Papers*, III, 1216; Montreuil's Despatches, July 9-19, 16-26, 1640, Bibliothéque Nationale, Paris, 15, 995, fols. 97 and 99.

[3] Br. Mus. Pamphlets, p. 69, f. 7(50), published on page 247 of this volume.

[4] R. O. State Papers, Dom., Int. March, 1649. Br. Mus. Pamphlets, 7129,9,16/2.

[5] R. O. State Papers, Dom. Int. Vol. I, 78, 618-627.   [6] *Ibid.*

[7] This grant is the last of the Company's Charters in the *Inspeximus* in the volume of the Record Office, State Papers, Dom. Vol. 27.

[8] The liabilities of the Company "for money lent at interest upon bonds under their common seal" amounted to £80,000. A petition "by many or-

attacks made upon them. With the coming of William and Mary the Society was deprived of its monopoly of the export of the woollen manufactures and its trade thrown open to all English merchants.[1]

But the act of William and Mary by no means marks the end of the activities of the Merchant Adventurers Society. It is true that they were no longer able to prevent others from sharing the cloth trade with them; and the abrogation of their rights in England seriously damaged their prestige abroad. But it should also be remembered that most of the cloth trade was in their hands, and the extensive privileges which they enjoyed at their mart town and which were retained during the 18th century, together with their excellent organization, gave them a decided advantage over the individual merchant. The basis for the continuance of the Fellowship, although less extensive than before, still existed, and the Society continued to carry on an energetic trade with the continent for another hundred years. Its life naturally became more and more identified with the privileges and grants abroad, and during this later period of their history the story of the Merchant Adventurers is almost entirely associated with their foreign Residences.

A thorough knowledge of these Residences or "factories" and the life of the Adventurers on the continent, both for this and the earlier period, is very essential to an adequate appreciation of the history of the Society. Unfortunately no attempt to work out this side of the story of the Fellowship has been made, and it is impossible here to do more than trace in the barest outline the external history of the Society in its relation to the Residences on the continent.

Of the early Residences at Bruges and other places scarcely anything is known. More definite facts appear in connection with the concentration of the Adventurers at Antwerp in 1407. The chief Residence of the Fellowship remained at the latter

phans, widowes, and others, creditors of the Merchant Adventurers of England" called forth a bill before parliament to make the Adventurers individually liable.

[1] *Statutes of the Realm*, I William and Mary, c. 32. For the section of the act relating to the Adventurers, see page 249.

place during most of the 15th century. In 1446 the city granted special privileges[1] to the Society which it enjoyed till the decree of Philip expelling all English woollen cloth from the Brabant and Flanders in 1464.[2] The consequence of the decree was the removal and assembling of the Adventurers at Utrecht, where they resided till 1467.[3] From this time on till the removal to Calais in 1505 they resided at various places, as for example, Bergen, Middleburg, Antwerp, etc.; the list of privileges shows grants from John Duke of Brabant, John Count Palatine, Albert Duke of Saxony, and others.[4] When friendly relations were again restored with the Netherlands, the Adventurers returned to their old marts, where they remained till the period of the religious troubles, enjoying privileges from a number of cities, principally Antwerp, Bergen and Middleburg. The outbreak of the religious wars in the Netherlands caused the removal of the Adventurers to Germany.[5] In 1567 they were granted special privileges for a period of ten years by the city of Hamburg, and the Company established its mart and Residence there.[6] But as we have seen, the opposition of the Hanse League had been aroused and at the conclusion of the ten years the Senate found itself under the necessity of discontinuing the privileges. Active commercial warfare followed, and the position of the Adventurers in Germany became steadily worse. As a result they were very ready to take up the invitation of Middleburg in 1582 to return to the Netherlands. But the dangers from the Spanish power were still too great, and not till several years later did any marked concentration of the members of the Company at Middleburg take place. By 1587, however, the centre of the Society for the Netherlands was defi-

---

[1] Schanz, *Handelspolitik*, II, Urk. Bei., 133.

[2] Gachard, *Collection des Documents inédits*, II, 196.

[3] Stein, *Die Merchant Adventurers in Utrecht*, Hänsische Geschichtsblätter, Vol. IX, p. 179.

[4] R. O. State Papers, Dom. Chas. II, Vol. 22, fol. 6. Cf. page 218 of this volume, also Br. Mus. Sloane, MS. 2103, fol. 2, published by Schanz, *Handelspolitik*, Urk. Bei., 133; also Thurloe, *State Papers*, I, 220.

[5] R. O. State Papers, Dom. Elizabeth, Vol. 49, No. 30.

[6] The date given in the list of privileges, R. O. State Papers, Dom. Chas. II, Vol. 22, fol. 6, is 1566.

nitely established at Middleburg, where it remained till 1621. But they had not entirely abandoned Germany, for in 1587 the town of Stade likewise granted them a set of privileges, and for some years, till the "Imperial Decree" of March 26, 1597, banishing the Merchants Adventurers from the Empire, Stade remained the Residence of the Society for Germany. During this period Middleburg was the chief Residence of the Society and the seat of their government. It is the period of the greatest activity of the Fellowship, the time of its most perfect organization.

In 1621 the Residence for Holland was removed from Middleburg to Delft, where it remained till 1635.[1] In that year Rotterdam secured it, and for the next twenty years, till 1655, the court was located there.[2] From Rotterdam the Fellowship went to Dort, after hesitating for a long time between the tempting inducements offered by different towns.[3] The privileges offered by Dort were set forth in a Concordat of 58 articles and were to continue for a period of 15 years.[4] The wars which followed broke up the agreement for a time, but it was successfully renewed and the Residence of the Society remained at Dort for the remainder of its existence in the Netherlands. In 1751 the last survivors of the Court were allowed a special dispensation exempting them from the newly imposed taxes, but the Residence had long before lost all importance.[5]

This was not the case with the Residence at Hamburg, however. Early in the 17th century the court at Hamburg became the chief Residence and "High Court of the Society," and long after the commerce to the Netherlands had dwindled to insignificance the Fellowship at Hamburg was in control of a large and prosperous trade. There the Adventurers contributed largely to the rapid rise of Hamburg in the 17th century to the foremost rank among

[1] Stadtarchiv, 'Skragenhage, *Resolutien van Holland*, Jan. 6, 8 and 9; Mar. 9; Apr. 23; May 2, 28, and Sept. 18, 1621.

[2] *Ibid.*, Dec. 26, 1634; Mar. 8, 10, 22 and 28; Apr. 2, and May 22, 1635.

[3] R. O. State Papers, Dom. Chas. II, Vol. 280, No. 70. Also note following.

[4] Stadtarchiv, 'Skragenhage, *Resolutien van Holland*, May 4; July 31; Aug. 12; Sept. 14 and 22, 1655. An abstract of the privileges is found on p. 240.

[5] Stadtarchiv, Dordrecht, *Resolutien von den Oudraad*, Jan. 5, 1751. For a translation of this letter from the States General to the Oudraad at Dort, see p. 253.

the sea-ports of the North Sea, a position it continued to hold throughout the next two centuries. Hamburg became the great commercial city of North Germany, serving in a sense as a distributing centre for the international trade of northern Europe. Here the Adventurers were highly favored by the burghers and the authorities after the city's final defection from the Hanse League. The privileges of 1611 were unusually liberal, so that despite the freedom of trade at home, the English traders to Hamburg, at least, still found it of very material advantage to belong to the old Fellowship. The details of the Company's history for this late period both at Hamburg and in England are still quite unknown! Towards the end of the 17th century the name "Hamburg Company" began to supplant the old name of "Merchants Adventurers of England," but the latter was retained by the Society itself in its official documents. During the 18th century the Adventurers do not appear to any extent in history. In the Treaty of Hamburg in 1719 there occurs a reference[1] to them as "the laudable English Company."

Maitland[2] in his History of London in 1756 states that the trade of the London Company had fallen off almost completely, and in a few years, he estimated, the old society would doubtless cease to exist. But Maitland failed to realize that the Society then as formerly was not a London Company, but an English Company, with headquarters abroad. The fact that Hamburg had absorbed nearly all the trade of Great Britain with the continent is to him an indication that the Adventurers are no longer active, whereas it really points to an increased activity. Anderson possessed a much clearer knowledge of the facts when he stated that in 1763 the Merchant Adventurers were still carrying on a great commerce. On the other hand, it must be remembered that the numerous wars and the consequent insecurity of trade during the 18th century gradually drove the English merchant into other channels of commerce, and the trade with the continent gradually fell into the hands of the foreigner.

Of the life of the Adventurers at their Residence in Hamburg,

[1] Anderson, *Annals of Commerce*, III, 90.

[2] Maitland, *History of London*, 1256.

and the vicissitudes of the Fellowship during the 18th century, little is known as yet. Much that is of interest and some points of considerable importance rewarded my labors among the uncalendared papers of the Home Office. Some of these will be found among the letters and papers published in this volume. The Thornton Correspondence of 1805, and the paragraph in his Instructions, give clear and positive evidence of the existence of the Company at the opening of the century.

The Lawes, Customes and
Ordinances of the ffellowshippe of
Merchantes Adventurers of the
Realm of England Collected
And digested into order by
John Wheeler Secretarie to
the said ffellowshippe
Anno Domini
1608
And Sithence continued according
to the further orders from
time to tyme made for
the gouernement of the
said ffellowshipp.

Reddite cuique quod
suum est.[1]

[1] Br. Mus. Add. MS., 18913.

CHAPTERS OF THIS BOOKE.

GOVERNMENT AND COURTES.

Caput Primum.

Accordinge to the Auncient Custome there shalbe folio 3. yearly Chosen by the Brethren of the ffellowshippe of Merchantes Adventurers of the Realm of England or by the most part of them one this syde the Seas,[1] lawfully and accordinge to the Priuileges of the said ffellowshippe orderly Assembled one Governour of all the said ffellowshippe, which Governour or his deputie or deputees and ffour and twentie Assystents or the greatest part of them, to bee Chosen martly[2] or as occasion shall serue from tyme to tyme by the brethren of the said ffellowshippe or by the most parte of them one this syde the Seas, shall duringe the said ffellowshippes pleasure or martly haue ffull power and

One gouvenour or his Deputye or Deputies and 24 Assistents shall bee chosen on that side the seas brethren of the fellowship of Merchants Adventurers of England, or by the most parte of yem.

---

[1] "On this syde the Seas." This phrase is constantly employed in the ordinances in the sense of "on the Continent," as opposed to "England," cp. fol. 3, "and the same (laws and statutes) to put in execution as well in England as on this syde the seas," *ibid.*, "whether one this syde the Seas or in England," fols. 5, 13, 33 *et passim*. The seat of government of the Merchants Adventurers of England was located abroad, hence the phrase "on this syde the seas," meaning on the Continent, throughout the Laws. (For a full discussion of this basic question in the history of the Fellowship, see the paper read before the Royal Historical Society, November, 1901. Transactions of the Royal Historical Society, Vol. 15.)

[2] "Martly" is at the time of the mart or days of sale, when the large shipments of cloth to the continent were exposed for sale by the Fellowship in its resident, or as it is more frequently called, mart town. The marts occurred four times a year. An ordinance on folio 31 speaks of them as the Pasche, Sinxon, Balms and Cold Marts.

I

Their authoritye. Authoritie (so ffarre as the Priuileges and orders will permitte) in all thinges lawfully to Governe and rule the foresaid fellowshippe, accordinge to the Lawes Statutes Actes and Ordinances of the same made or to bee made, Disobedient persons and transgressors accordinglye to correct and punishe, by fynes Imprisonment, or otherwise, Taxes Lones Cessements and Impositions to sett and Leuye vpon the persons and goodes as well of Brethern of the ffellowshippe as of other Englishe subiectes hauntinge or vsinge the Trade of a merchant Adventurer in the places or countries where the ffellowshippe ys priuileged. And to Enact Lawes Statutes and Ordinances ffrom tyme to tyme, and the same to put in execution as well in England as one this syde the Seas. And the said Lawes Statutes and ordinances to reuoke and alter at their pleasure, ffor the better Government as well of themselues and the whole ffellowshippe, as also of all other Englishe subiectes now or hereafter Intermedlinge with or by any meanes vsinge the Trade of a merchant Adventurer one this syde the Seas where the ffellowshippe ys or shalbe Priuileged. And ffurthermore wheresoeuer anie parte of the foresaid ffellowshippe ys or shalbe dwellinge abydinge or Resident in Competent nomber, whether one this syde the Seas or in England, there shalbe yearly or otherwise as need shall Requyre Chosen by the abouesaid Governour or his deputie or Deputees, Assistents and ffellowshippe, or by Authoritie ffrom them to that Intent giuen and grannted, One Deputie and so many honest and discreete persons as shalbe thought meet and Convenient from tyme to **Deputye and Asso-** tyme to bee Associates to the aforesaid **ciates their office.** Deputie in euerie one of the foresaid places —which Deputie and Associates or the

N° 1

most parte of them shall have ffull power and Authoritie
to put in execution as need shalbe the Lawes Statutes
and Ordinances of the ffellowshippe made as aforesaid
and to bee made, and accordinge to the same to Correct
and punishe disobedient persons and offendors and to
decide and end all Ciuile Questions stryfes or debates
arysing either amongst the Brethern of the said ffellowshippe or between them and other persons submittinge
themselues to the Lawes, Statutes, Ordinances, Orders
and Sentences of the said ffellowshippe.

No Bankrupt or other Infamous persone or iustly folio 4.[1]
attainted or suspected of anie notorious Bankrupt, Infamous
Cryme shalbe Chosen to anie Office of person or attaynted or
Government in Court or shalbe Assistent suspected of any in-
or Associate in this ffellowshippe. And famous crime shall
to the Intent that suche persons may bee not be chosen to any
the better knowen, there shalbe once a office of gouerment.
year dilligent enquyre made and notice taken of all that
shall Bankrupt, or Comitt anie notorious offence or Cryme 2
and yf anie bee found their names shalbe written in a
table and publikely hunge up to the view of euerie one.

Whatsoeuer Office Charge or busynes anie brother of
this ffellowshippe shalbe chosen vnto or appointed by the
Court, where he ys abydinge he shall not No man shall refuse
refuse to take vpon him and performe such to take upon him the
Office, Charge or busynes vpon pain of office Chardge or bus-
tenn poundes sterlinge for euerie suche ines committed vnto
refusall or none performance except there him by Court, pena, x[ll].

---

[1] The folio pages given in the margin throughout this volume
mark the beginning of a new page in the original manuscript, the
numbers corresponding to those of the table of contents. The
actual paging of the manuscript is double, $e.$ $g.$, $\dfrac{f.\ 2^b}{[p.\ 4]}$, the lower
number being that used as the folio page in the table of contents.

3 shalbe reasonable Cause to the Contrarie, and so accepted of by the Court, Provided that yf anie persone be Chosen Treasurer and refuse and doe not serve the place, he shall forfeict ffyftie poundes sterlinge to the vse of the ffellowshippe.

The Treasurer chosen and refusing to serve shall forfeit fiftye poundes.

Yf anie brother of this ffellowshippe shall by order of the Governour or his deputie Assystentes and Generalitie of the said ffellowshippe bee chosen and called ouer by letters vnto him directed from the Court, to be Treasurer or to bee Assistent or Associate one this syde the Seas, he shall not fayle yf wynde and wether serue to appear in persone at the tyme and place appointed, and serue his full terme ex-
4 cept he haue leaue of a Generall Court to depart before, vpon pain of ffyftie poundes sterlinge to the vse of the ffellowshippe without fauour or pardone reasonable cause or excuse in dew tyme made to the satisfaction of the Court alwayes excepted, as in the Ordinances the choice and charge of the Treasurers and Assistentes one this syde the Seas, ys more particularly sett downe and expressed.

He that is chosen to be Treasurer Assistent or Associate on that side ye seas he shall appeare opon paine of fiftye poundes.

The Governour or his deputie and deputees, shall accordinge to oath to the vttermoste of his or their power supporte and mainteyn the ffellowshippe of merchantes Adventurers, and the Priuileges of the same. And shall Indifferently and vprightly execute the Statutes, Lawes and Ordinances of the said ffellowshippe, Correctinge the breakers and Offenders thereof accordinglye, he or they shall not bringe in or make anie new Customes Lawes or
5 Ordinances without the aduyce and consent of the As-

What ye Gouuernor or his Deputye, or Deputies ought to doo, and what not doo.

sistentes or the greatest parte of them, neither shall he or
they bynde or charge hym or themselues or enter into
and processe sewt or busynes in the name of the ffellowshippe, without the lykinge and agreement of the same,
vpon pain to bee deemed and holden insufficient , and
vnworthye of the place of Government in the said ffellowshippe.

An Assistent or Associate accordinge to
oath shalbe Indifferent and equall between
all manner of parties and shall giue his
best aduyce and Counseill supportinge and maynteyn-
inge the Comon weale of the ffellowshippe of merchants 6
Adventurers, And settinge apart all priuate respectes of
Love or dread, favour or meed And so shall effectually
Assist the Governour or his Deputie or Deputees, in execution of the Lawes Statutes and Ordinances of the
foresaid ffellowshippe agreable with equitie and conscience, vpon pain to bee held as a persone vnworthy to
occupie the Place of an Assistent or Associate.

The Governour or his Deputie and Deputees and all
other officers of the ffellowshippe, shalbe alwayes helpfull
to anie brother or persone of the said ffellowshippe with the Entercourses, Priuileges, Compositions and other prouisions,
(suche brother or persone not havinge
willfully run into danger or trouble) and
shalbe redie to defend him as far as
reasone requyreth, at his Costes & charges. And yf the
Court so thinke good in his particular or priuate name to 7
pursue his cause to the end, he requyringe the same and
payinge the charges as aforesaid.

Whensoever anie brethern of this ffellowshippe shalbe
appointed by Court for the doeinge of anie busynes

The office of an Assistent or Associate.

folio 5.

Helpe to be geuen to anye person of the fellowship by the officers of ye same with ye entercourses, priuileges, etc.

matter or Comission generall or particuler, either one this
syde the seas or England, he or they shall
doe all that in hym or them lyeth, to performe and finishe the same, within or at
suche tyme as to him or them shalbe sett

Committies appoint-
ed by Court not doing
their office to pay XL
sh. sterling.

8 or limited upon pain of ffourtie shillings sterlinge, to be
forfeicted and paid by him that shalbe found in default in
the premisses, neither shall he or they depart the Towne
or place where suche busynes ys to bee donne without
licence of Court, vpon iust occasion, the said busynes not
beinge finished vpon the lyke penaltie.   And whoesoever
Chosen and appointed to anie busynes or comission beinge
warned by an officer or beadle to appear
maketh default, he shall forfeict and pay
for eache tyme 6 sh. 8 d. sterlinge.

And not appearing
upon warning geuen.
vjs. viij d.

Yf anie subiect of the Kynges Maiestie or of his successors Intermedlinge with the trade of a
merchant Adventurer one this syde the
Seas shall comitt or doe anie offence
against anie the Lawes, Statutes, Actes, or
orders, of the ffellowshippe and beinge
Lawfully convict and condempned for the
same, shall upon orderlie demannd refuse

Act against viola-
tors of the Companyes
Priuiledges Charters,
graunts, or any the
lawes, statutes or or-
dinanees of ye fellow-
shippe.

to pay or shall not pay suche fines, Amerciamentes, Impositions and sommes of monie as shalbe laid upon him
9 or upon his goods or merchandises, or shall attempt by
anie meanes directly or Indirectly by way of Complaint
cautele devyce Confederasie or Intelligence with anie
foreign Prince Potentate or magistrate, or shall with anie
stranger borne cause to bee attempted or goe about to
violate, break, offend or make void the force of anie of
the priuileges, Liberties or granntes giuen to the ffellowshippe or anie part of them, suche persone so offendinge

refusinge attemptinge or Causinge to bee attempted, shall
for the first tyme forfeict one hundred pounds sterlinge
for the second tyme two hundred pounds sterlinge for the
third tyme three hundred pounds ster: and for euerie
tyme after lyke fyne of 300 l. str: And wheresoeuer his
bodie may bee found the same shalbe arrested and Comitted to prisonne, till he haue fully satisfyed & paid the
penalties and ffines aforesaid. And yf anie brother of
the ffellowshippe shall comitt, offend, refuse attempt or
cause to bee attempted as aforesaid and namely shall
labour procure, sollicite or Instance, priuily or openly by   folio 6.
Couen Colour fraude or malengine by himself or by anie
other persone or persons, shall help, aid, counseill or
Assist with any goodes monie or reward offer or promise,
or shall attempt or doe anie thinge in woord or deed to
the breach preiudice disanullinge or makinge void of the
Priuileges, ffreedomes, Charters or grannts to the ffellowshippe of merchantes Adventurers by his maiestie that
now ys, or by anie other his Noble Progenitors or by anie
other Prince Potentate State or Comonwealth whatsoever heretofore grannted or hereafter to be grannted, by
his said maiestie or his heires or successors, or by anie
other Prince Potentate or Comonwealth whatsoeuer,
suche persone so doinge or Attemptinge against the said
priuileges, charters, ffreedomes or grannts to the violation
or derogation of them or of anie Article point or clause in
them or anie of them conteyned, shall bee held a periured
persone and bee disfranchised and banished from the
liberties of the said ffellowshippe for ever.

If anie brother of this ffellowshippe shall
aduisedly and stubbornly comitt or doe
anie trespasse against his oath to the said
ffellowshippe taken, or any parte thereof,

Against Brethren of
the fellowship violat-
ing their oath, con-
uicted for any enor-

mous offence, etc., or shalbe conuict of some other great or
shall be excluded enormous offence trespasse Contempt or
from the liberties of abuse against the Lawes Statutes, Actes,
the sayd fellowship. orders or Ordinances of the said ffellowshippe made or to be made, or shalbe iustly attainted of
10 cooseninge, felonie or other heynous or Capitall Cryme,
he shalbe utterly excluded of and from all the libertyes
of the said ffellowshippe.

When sentence of disfranchisement ys to be passed or
Disfranchizement, pronounced against anie person whatso-
aud readmittance of ever, the same shalbe donne at a General
disfranchized persons Court by the Governour or his Deputie
to be done by xxtie and twentie Assistents thereat present and
of ye Assistents. Assembled. And the same order shalbe
11 observed at the receivinge again into the ffreedome of the
ffellowshippe anie persone disfranchised which by the
ordinances may bee received in again.

12   Yf anie persone subiect to the Government of the ffellowshippe, either by subbornation vnlawful procurement,
persuation or sinister means of anie other or by his owne
Act, consent and agreement, shall wittinglye and cor-
ruptly comitt willfull periurie by his depo-
Periurye, and false sition vpon oathe ministred by order of
witnes losse of ten Court, or beinge examined to bear records
pounds and disfran- of a truthe, or shall procure anie wyttnesse
chisement. or wyttnesses by reward promises or vnlawfull means, or labour, or shall cause anie other persone
in anie sorte or manner whatsoeuer to comitt willfull or
corrupt periurie in anie matter or Cause waightie whatsoever, concerninge the foresaid ffellowshippe or orders of
the same, such persone so offendinge and thereof dewlye
Convict, shall forfeict tenn pounds sterlinge to the use of
the ffellowshippe and further bee disfranchised & deprived

of and ffrom all the Liberties and Rightes of the said
ffellowshippe.

Yf anie persone subiect to the Government and orders folio 7.
of the ffellowshippe whether at Court or out of Court 13
shall vnreverently or vndewtifully behave himself in
woord or deed, wrytinge or gesture or shalbe contentious
and vndecently holde argument against the Governour or
his Deputie, he shall forfeit and pay fourtie   Unreuerent cariage
shillinges sterlinge; And yf he will not bee   towards the Gouv-
quieted so, but eftsoons reneweth or con-   ernor or Deputye.
tinueth suche his disorderly behauiour, he   Penaltie   XLsh   for
shall forfeict and pay four poundes ster-   wilfull   continuance
linge. But yf then also beinge comannded   therein iiijli.
to cease, and admonished of his dewtye and the dannger
he runneth into by his misdemeanour or after that this
Act (yf the matter fall out in Court) shalbe read unto
him, he not withstandinge will not bee ruled reclaymed
or take annswer, but replyeth against or   Yf he will not be
provoketh the Governour or his Deputie,   reclaymed but troub.
or otherwise troubleth or abuseth the   leth and abuseth the
Court and ministers thereof he shall for-   Court—ten poundes
feict and pay tenn poundes sterlinge to the   sterl: and imprison-
use of the ffellowshippe, and his bodie   ment.
shalbe comitted to prisone to abyde the further order
of the Court, And no brother of this
ffellowshippe shall abette or favour anie   No man shall fauour
such unruly persone in his misdemeanour   any such vnrule per-
upon the like penaltie.   son upon like penaltye.

Act or determination of Court beinge plainlie passed 14
and sett downe, concerninge anie matter or question
whatsoeuer handled before the Court, yt shall not bee
lawfull for anie particular persone to Controlle, speake or

No replye after an Act is past pena ten poundes sterl. nor appeale from ye determinacion of Court vpon like penaltye and Imprisonment.

replye against the same, vpon pain of tenn poundes sterlinge, Likewise when Sentence by Agreement of Court ys pronounced by the Governour or his deputie, and by order recorded, no persone of the ffellowshippe shall reply or speake against the same, Neither shall attempt anie further provocation or appele, but submitt himself to suche sentence, vpon pain of tenn poundes sterlinge and Im-

Yet by peticion to the Court to seeke redresse is allowed.

prisonment thereto abyde the pleasure of the Court, Nevertheles yt shalbe lawfull by way of petition to seek redresse or grace at the Courtes handes, in quiete and dewtifull manner without Incurringe anie penaltie therefore.

15   No persone of this ffellowshippe or other shall vpbrayd

Vpbrayding any person for any matter for which he hath bene called in question before the Court etc pein ten poundes sterl for ye first time and twenty for the next.

or contumeliously Charge any other persone, with anie matter or cause for the which he hathe been called in question and convented before the Court, and abidden the order & determination of the same, Neither shall speak reporte or spread abroad anie woord or matter tendinge to the reproch or defamation of anie suche persone for cause aforesaid, vpon pain of tenn pounds sterlinge for the first tyme & twentie pounds for the second tyme herein offendinge to the vse of the ffellowshippe.

16   No persone or supposte of the ffellowshippe shall by

For speaking writing or doing whatsoeuer to the reproach of ye Gouuernour Deputy or Court. Pena Imprisonment.

woord wrytinge or ryme advisedly falsely or of malicious Intent speake declare or giue out in wrytinge or otherwise anie thinge whatsoeuer tendinge to the reproch Contempt, slannder or defamation of the

Governour or his Deputie or of the Court, vpon pain of Imprisonment or other punishment at the discretion of the said Court.

Yf anie persone of the ffellowshippe for anie cause folio 8. whatsoeuer, concerninge the orders of the said ffellow- 17 shippe, pretended either against him or against some other for whome he hathe to doe, or for anie cause question quarrell, stryfe Action or debate betweeu hym and some other shall bee called and dealt with all before the Court, after suche matter cause etc There handled [ended] and discided. Yt shall not bee lawfull for suche persone at anie tyme after by woord or wrytinge to speake or declare or to doe anie thinge tendinge to the re-   Reproach brought proache or defamation of the Governour or   upon ye Gouuernour his Deputie and Assistentes or Associates   Deputy or Assistents or of anie of them, for anie thinge by them   for matters passed in or by anie of them spoken or donne in   Court. Pena: XXII. that cause or matter, vpon pain of tenn poundes sterlinge for the first tyme and twentie poundes sterlinge for the second tyme or other arbitrarie correction at the discretion of the said Governour or his Deputie and the Court: Neverthelles yt shalbe lawfull by way of Petition to sue for anie reasonable remedie or relief, givinge and vsinge decent woordes and behaviour towardes the Court and euerie member thereof.

The Governour or his Deputie and Deputees shall and 18 may at all tymes lawfull and Convenient, warne and call together the Brethern of this ffellowshippe wheresoever anie parte thereof ys Resydinge, to Courtes Congrega- tions, Assemblyes and meetinges, for the Generall or par- ticulare busynes and affaires of the said ffellowshippe. And whensoever anie Court Congregation Assemby or meetinge shalbe warned as aforesaid, whatsoeuer persone

of the ffellowshippe shalbe absent or beinge warned shall
not giue attendance at the tyme and place appointed, yf

Absence from Courts and meetings.
he bee an Assistent or Associate one this
syde the Seas, he shall forfeict and pay 6
sh. 8 d. fflemishe, and yf he bee of the
Generalite 3^{sh} 4^d fflemishe, yf anie persone bee absent
three Generall Court dayes together he shall forfeict and
pay 20^s fflemishe. And whosoeuer shall

Late comming or departing before the Court break up.
come late to Court warned, that ys after
three strokes with the hammer given by
the Governour or his Deputie, or shall depart and not return again before the Court break vp and
ryse, he shall pay halfe of the aboue-written penaltie for
absence to wytt 3^s 4^d all the aboue said penalties to bee

Th' employment of ye penalties.
applyed twoe thirdes to the vse of the Poor
and one third to the Beadles collectinge
the same, And yf the Beadle or other
officer theretoappointed shall neglect to leuye the abouesaid penalties, or shall suffer anie to depart without leaue
or pawne sufficient giuen to return in dew tyme, he shall
himself doe good the said penalties without favour or
pardone, And whosoeuer beinge demannded by the
Beadle or officer therto appointed, shall refuse to make
payment of the abouewritten penalties he shall forfeict
and pay the doble of that he ought to haue paid by this
Act, leaue or iust Cause in this and all the former Cases
alwaies excepted.

folio 9.
19 The Assistentes or Associates beinge absent, so that
the Governour or his Deputie and those present cannot
keep Court but break vp for want of dew appearence,
suche persons are to bee accompted as absent the whole
Court, and shall pay the fyne of 6^s 8^d fflemishe for suche
absence.

When anie Court Congregation or Assembly shalbe 20
lawfully warned, and that anie persone shalbe sent for
and Charged to come and appear before the Governour
or his Deputie at suche Court Congregation or Assembly
or when Comanndment shalbe giuen by the said Governour or his Deputie or Deputees to the Brethern of the
ffellowshippe Generally or particularly to give attendance
or otherwise to doe anythinge reasonable and lawfull In
Court or out of Court vpon pain of disobedience whoesoeuer without leaue or iust Cause shall not
appear or giue Attendance, or appearinge
shall depart before he bee orderly dismissed, or shall willfully neglect or refuse

Warning geven to
Courts and meetings
vpon disobedience.

to doe or performe accordinge to suche Comanndment as
aforesaid, he shall forfeict and pay for the first tyme
ffyve pounds sterlinge for the second tyme tenn poundes
sterlinge and faylinge the third tyme he shalbe Comitted
to warde, there to abide the further pleasure of the Court,
And whoesoeuer beinge warned by the Officer to appear
by an houre or tyme prefixed before a Court of Assistentes
or Associates, shall without leaue Omitt so to doe, or
appearinge shall depart before he bee dismissed by the
Court (yf suche warninge were not giuen vpon Disobedience) he shall only pay for euerie suche default 6ˢ 8ᵈ
fflemishe, And yf he Come after the houre and tyme sett
he shall pay 3ˢ 4ᵈ fflemishe twoe thirds to the vse of the
poor the rest to the officers.

Yf anie persone of this ffellowshippe shalbe found and 21
prooued to have disclosed to anie persone Englishe or
other vnffree of the said ffellowshippe, anie secret or
matter passed in Court, or shall to the hurt or displeasure
of anie brother of the ffellowshippe open to anie persone
whoesoeuer anie thinge passed or spoken in Court, he

Discouerye of matters done in Court.
shall forfeict and pay for the first offence ffyue poundes sterlinge, and for the second offence tenn pounds ster: and for the third offence twentie pounds ster: And yf the secret or matter uttered to anie other then a ffree brother shalbe suche and of that Importance or qualitie as might or was likely to have turned to the displeasure hurt or preiudice of the ffellowshippe or of some member thereof, then the offendor Convict, by sufficient proofe, confession or wyttnesse, shall abyde suche penaltie or punishment with all severitie of the Court shall deem meet and Convenient for suche an offence.

22   In the absence of the Governour or his Deputie, yt

The Treasurer or Secretarye may assemble the ffellowship in the absence of ye Gouuernour or Deputye.
shalbe lawfull for the Treasurer for the tyme beinge or none beinge, for the Secretarie, to call and Assemble those of the ffellowshippe together, and unto them or the said meetinge or Assembly to propound sett foorth and handle suche matter or matters as as are to bee sett foorth propounded or handled concerninge the busynes Causes and auayle of the said ffel-

folio 10. lowshippe, And to requyre and take the voices, myndes aduyce and Resolution of the Assistentes or generalitie or of bothe together one that behalfe, keepinge dew note of that which passeth ys concluded or resolued to the end that the same may be confirmed or Reformed, yf occasion serve by the Court, at some other Convenient tyme. And yf anie man shall not appear and bee absent without reasonable or lawfull cause or excuse upon warninge of suche meetinge or Assemby after the accustomed manner he shall forfeict and pay as in case of absence or none appearance at Courtes or Assemblyes warned by order of the Gouernour or his Deputie.

Yt shall not bee lawfull for anie brother of the ffellow- 23
shippe to Interrupt another in his speeche
vnto the Court, or to speake when another
is speakinge, or to direct his speeche to
Interruption whilst another is speakinge.
anie particular man or persone that spake last before
him, but he shall direct the same to the Governour or
his Deputie annswearinge only to the matter propounded
or in handlinge, without naminge anie man that spake
before hym vpon payn of 12^d fflemishe for euerie tyme
that he shall offend in the premisses to the vse of the
poor.

When anie persone shalbe before the Court to make 24
suite or to shew declare or annswer anie matter or Cause
whatsoeuer, no brother of the ffellowshippe shall Interrupt
or lett help prompt or aydd anie suche
persone in his speeche or talke, neither
shall he speake openly anie thinge touchinge the matter or Cause while the partie
Prompting or ayd- ing another in his speech.
ys present, vpon pain of twentie pence fflemishe, except
he shall bee Requyred to speake or shew his aduyce or
knowledg by the Governour or his Deputie.

Silence beinge comannded or signifyed by a stroke of 25
the hammer, no persone shall speak loude
or holde talke with another, but beestill
Silence.
and silent vpon pain of 6^d fflemishe to the poor.

When anie matter shalbe handled or fall in question 26
Concerninge anie persone of the ffellowshippe present he shall himself auoyd the
Court, lykewise the brother, partner, factor or servant of suche persone or anie
other in question or whose cause ys
handled, yf there bee anie suche in Court.
He whose cause is handled, his brother, partner, factor or ser- uant shall auoide the Court.

No dishonest fowle or vnseemly language or gesture 27

shalbe vsed in tyme of Court by anie one
Dishonest language, persone to another but the vser thereof
etc. shall forfeict and pay tenn shillings fflemishe to the poor.

When anie matter shalbe handled or propounded in
Court, yt shalbe lawfull for euerie ffree brother to deliuer his mynde and declare his opinion Concerninge the
said matter at large, three seuerall tymes and no more
vpon pain of 3ˢ 4ᵈ fflemishe doeinge otherwise, except he
bee comannded by the Governour or his deputie.

folio 11. The Assistents Associates and ffreemen of the Com-
29 panie or ffellowshippe shall not sytt among the apprentyces but in suche place and places as for them ys properly
appointed in Court, vpon pain of 12ᵈ fflemishe, neither
shall anie Covenant servant or ffreeman or he that ys his
maisters Atturney sytt amonge the said apprentyces,
vpon pain of 6ᵈ fflemishe.

30 Apprentyces except they bee their maisters factors and
Apprentizes shall Atturneyes shall haue no voice nor hand
have no voyce nor in Court, neither shall they sitt out of the
hande in Courts except foormes or place for them appointed, vpon
they bee their mas- pain of 6ᵈ fflemishe, Notwithstandinge yt
ters' factors and at- shalbe lawfull for anie apprentyce havinge
torneys. occasion to deliuer his mynde, speake or
make anie sewte or motion to the Court to present himself and Come foorth of his place before the Court with
dew Reuerence, and so to speake deliuer his mynde and
to make his suite or motion, for himself or anie other as
occasion shall serue.

31 The Treasurer for the tyme beinge shall collect the
The Treasurer shall Broakes for late cominge and for absence
collect the Broakes for from Courtes of Assistentes or Associates,
late coming and ab- which yf he neglect to doe he shall forfeict

and pay the doble thereof himself to the sence from Courts of Assistents. vsse of the poor.

The Beadles shall collect the forfeictures or Broakes for 32 late cominge to Generall Courtes and absence from them, and shall hand a third parte thereof for themselues the rest to bee to the vse of the poore, vpon pain of payinge the said forfeictures and brokes themselues yf they bee remisse and negligent in the Collection thereof, And at the end of euerie Generall Court, they shall giue the Treasurer a note of absentes from the said Court, and whoe haue paid for absence from former Courtes, before they receiue of the said Treasurer the third part of that Collected.

The Beadles shall collect the Broakes for absence & late coming to Generall Courts.

All the abouewritten Penalties broakes or forfeictures, 33 to wytt for cominge late to Courtes absence and all other matter of that nature or thereone depending. Likewise for sittinge out of order, speakinge loude, and when silence is comannded, speakinge oftener then three tymes in one Cause, speakinge while the partie ys present in Court, promptinge or Interruptinge anie man in his speeche, and all other the lyke abuses and offences above-mencioned, shalbe levyed and paid to the vse of the poor, savinge to the Beadles or officers one third parte thereof ffor their paynes, And whoesoeuer shall Refuse to pay the said penalties, Broakes, and forfeictures, he shalbe Compelled to pay doble ffor the first tyme, and for the second offence or denyall shalbe punished at the discretion of the Governour or his Deputie.

What Broakes shall be leuied to ye vse of the poore: and the Beadles to haue one third of yem.

Yf anie man shalbe presented to the Treasurer in the folio 12. Beadles note for absence and beinge demannded payment 34

2

shall notwithstandinge departe the marte Towne, without makinge orderly payment, the doble of the said broake shalbe levyed of his factor or seruant or goodes, but yf he were not demannded the same he shall pay but the single.

35   Yf anie brother or persone of this ffellowshippe beinge examined by order of Court vpon his oathe, Concerninge anie matter Cause or offence, which oathe he or some other whoe he serueth or hathe to doe for standeth pre-

He that shall he sented or charged to haue donne or Comitt
examined vpon oath or against anie the Lawes, Statutes, Actes or
otherwise shall refuse Ordinances of the said ffellowshippe, shall
to answer; shall bee refuse to make direct answear or to depose
holden condempned. in manner and forme as shalbe to hym
enioyned by the Governour or his Deputie, he shalbe holden faultie and condempned as guiltie in suche fine or fynes as by the Lawe, Statute, Act or Ordinance (vpon which he refuseth to be examined or deposed) ys prouided against the broakes thereof, And yf anie brother of this ffellowshippe or other persone subiect to the Orders thereof shalbe Comannded by the Governour or his Deputie to vtter and declare vpon oath suche thinges as lawfully may and ought to be knowen, in matters of doubt or in causes of difference or variance between partie and partie, or for to giue Evidence and testimonie of that which he hathe seen or heard, or finally shalbe charged to say or deliuer a truthe in a matter or Cause Concerninge the ffellowshippe, or otherwise suche brother or persone shalbe holden and not refuse to declare, giue evidence and testimonie or to say or deliver a truthe vpon pain of ffyve poundes sterlinge for his disobedience and neuertheles to abyde the further Order and Censure of the Court, at the discretion of the Governour or his Deputie

and the Assistentes or Associates. And yf anie persone
or persons shalbe found periured (which God forbidd) for
anie cause waightie or of willfull mynde to fayne or glose
with Colourable woordes, hydinge fraudulently or not dis-
coveringe the plain truthe or verie substance of the matter
whereby Right and Justice the sooner and
better might bee administred, he shalbe   Conuicted of Peri-
held suspect, and for his periurie shall   urye penaltye X^{li} and
forfeict tenn poundes sterlinge to the vse   disfranchizement.
of the ffellowshippe, and further from thencefoorth stand
clearly dismissed depriued and put out of the ffellowshippe for euermore.

    Yf the ffellowshippe shalbe indebted or owe vnto anie 36
brother of the same, somme or sommes of
monie suche brother shall not therefore   No retayning or
retayne or stop in his handes anie matter   stopping of any matter
of dutie whether yt bee pledge or securitie   from the Comp^a vnles
ffor another or his owne proper debt or   it bee for fee or ex-
dutie vpon pain of payinge the doble of   penses allowed by
that which he shalbe found to owe, to bee   Auditors, or warrant past.
indebted or to haue in handes of the ffellowshippes.
Nevertheles yf the ffellowshippe shall owe vnto anie
persone for ffee or reward or for expenses or charges laid
out about the busynes of the ffellowshippe by order of
Court, And that yt bee so found and allowed by Auditors folio 13.
thereto appointed, or that by Act of Court warrant bee
passed for payment, yf suche persone bee Indebted to the
ffellowshippe for himself or anie other, yt shalbe lawfull
for him to retayn the said debt or so muche thereof, as ys
dew for his ffull satisfaction. But in case suche dutie or
duties beinge owinge vnto anie persone, and that notwithstandinge for some Consideration or Cause the Court
therevnto movinge, respyte or deferringe of payment

shalbe taken for a tyme, he or they shall not arrest, vexe, trouble, or cause to be arrested vexed or molested the persone goodes shippe or shippes of anie brother of the ffellowshippe, laden for or to the partes one this syde the Seas, in anie Porte or place within the kynges dominions, vpon pain to forfeict vnto the ffellowshippe his whole demannd debt or dutie, And further yf suche persone or persons shalbe ffree of this ffellowshippe, he or they shalbe disfranchised except the matter have been declared before the Court and licence been grannted so to doe.

37 Yf anie brother of the ffellowshippe or Officer of the same, shall disburse or lay out monie for

He that shall disburse any mony for the fellowship shall bring in his Byll to the Treasurer for the same.

or in the affaires of the ffellowshippe, he shall bringe in his bill to the Court, or to the Treasurer for the tyme beinge and demannd payment accordingle, yf one this syde the Seas within the same marte that he shall disburse the said monie in, and yf in England in the verrie same marte or in the next marte ffollowinge at the furthest, vpon pain in vsinge anie further delay or after he shalbe warned by the Treasurer to bringe in his disbursements to the said Treasurer or to the husband to loose his demannd or pretended charges laid out, and the ffellowshippe shall not bee bound anie tyme after to answer the same, And for all suche as haue anie monie in their handes of the ffellowshippe, to be laid out or disbursed to the use thereof they shall bringe in the remaines within lyke tyme as aboue ys sett downe, vpon pain to forfeict the doble of that which shalbe proued to bee restinge in his or their handes vnlaid out, or not disposed of except the Court shall otherwise see good and determine.

Yt shall not bee lawfvll to giue away anie monie aboue 38
the somme of fourtie shillinges sterlinge
out of the Sinxon Marte, except by the No mony to be
Generalitie yt shalbe found that the monie geuen away (out of
or gifte to bee giuen away or bestowed ceeding XL^s except by
dothe or may tend to the proffytt Credyte order of ye Gen-
seruyce or behoof of the ffellowshippe in eralitye.
which Cases or anie of them, yt shalbe lawfull for the
Generalitie at all tymes to giue or bestowe suche somme
or sommes of mouie as they shall thinke meet and Convenient vpon anie persone whatsoever.

Everie persone of this ffellowshippe shall at his first folio 14.
cominge to the Marte Townes, or Imediately after his 39
Admission procure from the Secretarie or sworn Clerk of
the ffellowshippe copie of the Taxations and dutyes
payable by the Priuileges, Concordates, or agreementes in
the place ffor Tolle Cranage, way monie
labourers hyre, and all other, and shall The Tole or Taxa-
not for anie cause by way of reward or for ceeded.
his sooner dispatche presume to exceed
the Rate of the said Taxations or duties, vpon pain of
ffyue poundes ster. And yf anie person shalbe found to
Continew suche disorder or abuse he shalbe further punished at the discretion of the Court as a willfull contemp-
ner and violatour of good orders.

No brother or other persone of the ffellowshippe shall 40
withhold embesell or keep by him anie
letters Request or writinge directed or sent Deteining of writ-
or otherwise pertayninge to the ffellow- fellowship.
shippe, but shall foorthwith after the receipt thereof or that the same Cometh to his handes,
make deliuerie and present the same to the Governour or
his Deputie or in either of their absences to the Secre-

tarie vpon pain of ffyue poundes sterlinge. And yf the
Governour or his Deputie for the tyme beinge shall
retayne any letter request or wrytinge directed as aforesaid, and doe not the same to be read openly at the next
Court or Assembly after the receipt thereof he shall forfeict tenn pounds sterlinge. Except it bee a libell or
wrytinge tendinge to euill purpose and to rayse stryfe,
Contention or Comotion against the ffellowshippe, the
Authors Whereof are to be seuerly punished to the example and terrifyinge of others at the discretion of the
said Governour or his Deputie and the Court or accordinge to the Orders.

41   Whatsoeuer shalbe passed or enacted at anie Court
shalbe read at the endinge of the said
Court or at the begyninge of the next, to
the end that the same vpon the second
readinge may be Confirmed, or yf need bee
bee reformed or repeeled vpon pain of twentie shillinges
sterlinge yf the fault bee in the Governour or his Deputie,
and tenn shillinges ster: yf the fault bee in the Secretarie
to the use of the ffellowshippe.

Reading of that which passeth at the Court.

42   At the begyninge or endinge of Courtes and otherwise
as tyme and leisure will permitte, one or
more of the ordinances shalbe openly read,
except the Court for good cause or lett to
the contrarie vpon pain of 6^s 8^d fflemishe, to bee forfeicted
by the Governour herein makinge default, 3^s 4^d by the
Deputie, and 20^d by the Secretarie to the use of the
ffellowshippe.

Reading ye ordi-nances.

folio 15.   To the ende that Brethern and members of the ffellow-
43   shippe one this syde the Seas tradinge in tollerated place
or places out of the marte Towne may be concernd as
they ought to bee euerywhere vnder the due obedience

of the Governour or his Deputie and Assistentes and of the good lawes orders and Constitutions of the said ffellowshippe alredie made or to bee made for the quiete and orderly rule and government of the foresaid ffellowshippe and of the Brethern and members thereof, wheresoeuer abydinge. Yt ys therefore ordeyned and enacted that no persone or persons of the said ffellowshippe shall take upon him or themselues to sue in his or their name or names, or in the name of the ffellowshippe either in England or out of England for the obtayninge or Augmentinge of anie licence, graunt, Charter or Priuilege to his or their owne particular, or priuate vse benefyte or comoditye, but to the vse benefyte or comoditye of the whole ffellowshippe of Merchantes Adventurers of the Realm of England.

No man shall sue for any license, graunt, charter, or Priuiledg for his owne use.

And yf anie persone whether he bee in companie with others or out of companie of himself aparte, or jointly with another shalbe found to transgresse against this ordinance or anie branche or Article thereof (for which no penaltie ys alredie‧ provided) or shall giue his ayde connseill or consent to the breach or violation of the same, he and euerie one so offendinge shall forfeict and pay to the vse of the ffellowshippe the some of twoe hundred poundes sterlinge without favour or pardone one third parte to the vse of the presenter makinge dew proofe thereof as appertayneth.

The ordinances alredie made or hereafter to bee made 44 by Authoritie of the ffellowshippe shalbe understood to bee of force, and shalbe of force in deed not only for and in the Countries of Holland, Zeeland, Brebant, Flanders and other the Provinces of the Neth-

The ordinances shall bee of force in all places where the Company is Priuiledged.

erlands, but also for and in all other countryes one this
syde the seas where the ffellowshippe by the Charters and
Priuileges of the same ys or hereafter shalbe Priuileged.

45 Where there ys no expresse custome order, statute or
ordinance for any matter cause or thinge

Sic. Where there is no ordinance in the ffellowshipp, the lawe of England shall take place.

fallinge out in the ffellowshippe, the same
shalbe ordered Jugded* and determined
accordinge to equitie & conscience agreable which the lawes and Statutes of the
Realm of England one that behalf, yf anie
bee made or provided.

46 The Courtes shalbe always begunne with prayer and
Invocation of the name of God for his

The Courts to begin with prayer.

divine Assistance and gracious direction
in the matters and busynes to be handled,
lykewise they shalbe ended with prayer and thankes-
giuinge.

folio 16.

Concerninge the Brethern of this ffellowshippe within
47 the Cittie of Londone and other partes of the Realm of
England, the Governour or his Deputie

Olde order for ab-
sence and late coming
to Courts: altered as
appeareth by the Act
next followinge.

and Deputees there Respectiuely, shall
and may at all tymes lawfull and convenient warne and call together the Brethren of the said ffellowshippe, wheresoeuer
anie of them are Resydinge to Courtes,
Congregations, Assemblyes and meetinges ffor the busynes or affaires publicke or priuate of the said ffellowshippe
or of the members thereof And whensoeuer anie Court
Congregation Assembly or meetinge shalbe warned as
aforesaid whatsoeuer persone of the ffellowshippe shalbe
absent or beinge warned shall not give attendance at the
tyme, houre and place appointed, yf he bee an Associate
he shall forfeict and pay iij⁸ iiij⁴ sterlinge and yf he bee of

the Generalitie 12^d sterlinge, And yf anie persone shalbe absent three Court dayes together yf he bee an Assistent he shall forfeict and pay ffourtie shillinges sterlinge, and yf he bee of the Generalitie twentie shillinges ster: And whoesoever shall come late to Court warned, that ys after the three strokes giuen with the hammer by the Governour or his Deputie accordinge to auncient,[1] or shall depart and not returne again before the Court breake up and ryse, he shall pay the halfe of the aboue written penalties for absence, lawfull lett or excuse to bee accepted by the Court alwayes excepted. The abouesaid Broakes to bee taken and Collected by the Beadles without favour or pardone, whoe for their paynes shall have twoe pence of each shillinge of the said broakes by them so collected, And whoesoever being demanded by the Beadle shall Refuse to make payment of the abouesaid penalties he shall forfeict and pay the treble of that he ought to pay by this order, lawfull excuse to be allowed by the Court alwayes except as aforesaid, And for the better observinge and executinge of this order, yt ys further ordayned that yf anie brother of this ffellowshippe Incurringe anie of the said penalties and being demanded the same as aforesaid shall denye and will not make payment thereof but obstinately refuseth the performance and fullfillinge of this ordinance then the officer or beadle shall make reporte to the Deputie and giue him Notice thereof in wrytinge to the end that he may aduertise this Court of the same and that the said obstinate persone may bee punished as in case of disobedience ys provided to wytt with the penaltie of ffyve pounds sterlinge to be levyed vpon his persone or goodes

---

[1] Some such word as "custom" or "order" appears to have been omitted by the writer of the manuscript.

here or wheresoeuer they may be found.   And this order
to be obserued by the said Deputie and Beadle, vpon pain
of forfeicture of twentie shillinges sterlinge by the said
Deputie and tenn shillinges by the Beadle ffor euery
tyme that either of them shalbe found ffaultie or Negligent herein.   This order is mended and amplifyed by
Act of the Seventeenth of July Anno domini 1610 as after
ffolloweth next onto this order.

folio 17.   The old penaltie ffor absence and late cominge to
48   Courtes in Londone shalbe ffrom hence-
Niew Order for ab-   foorth ffour shillinges, and twoe shillinges
sence and late com-
ming to ye Courts.   sterlinge, agreable to that which ys here
             taken in Middlebronghe for those kynde
of Broakes, and that yf anie man beinge warned to
Courtes either of Assistents or generall Courtes by the
Beadle by order of the Governour or his Deputie, shalbe
absent or come late without lawfull excuse to bee accepted
by the Court, or by the said Governour or his Deputie,
he shall foorthwith pay the abouesaid penalties, To
Wytt yf he bee of the Generalitie 2ˢ sterlinge and yf of
the Associates 4ˢ sterlinge.   And yf he come late or depart the Court without Return before the Court doe ryse
the halfe, And yf he shall refuse to pay and will not pay
the same or anie other penaltie of the lyke nature provided by former order without lawfull excuse as aforesaid, he shalbe debarred of the Benefyte of the ffree
lycence till he haue paid the broakes he oweth for the
abouesaid cause to the Treasurer or Beadle appointed for
Collection of the same, or otherwise haue giuen satisfaction to the Court or to the sayd Governour or his
Deputie, the Beadle to haue the third of the said Brokes.

49   The ffollowing[1] is a continuation from William Alder-

[1] The remaining sections of this chapter, that is, paragraphs 49,

seys Booke The ould Orders for appearance at Courts att
Middleburg being read and Considered It is enacted for
This Place att Hamburg That the Penalty for non appearance or absence from Court of an assistant shall be
iij^s and of the Generality ij^s and for the late coming of an
assistant xviij^s and of One of the Generalitie vij^d Hamburg
money Thus to be understood only off Ordinary Courtes
and not such as are warned upon pain off [d]isobedience
and The Penaltys to be diu[i]ded One halfe to the Poors
Box and the other halfe to the Beadles.

Whereas the Brethren at Middlebourgh by late letters 50
signify their desire to haue the old act prouided against
such Brethren of the ffellowship as within the consent or
Commission of the same ffellowship shall attempt to gett
or procure any Licence Grant or Priuilledge Touching
the Trade of the Company to their own Priueledge use
Further Explained soe that the Penalty of Two hundred
Pounds in that act prouided may be imposed on all and
euery such Brother or Brothers as shall take upon him or
them or shall enter into any suite of what soeuer kinde
procese matter or buisness For or in the Name of the
Same Fellowship or for or Concerninge the Same or
touching the Trade priuiledges or liberties thereof on this folio 18.
side the Seas or Elsewhere without the knowledge and
special consent Leave and Commission from the said
Fellowship first had and obtained This Explanation of
the said Order If by this Court well liked and Ordeyned
to be taken for the true sense of the same And because
the said Penalty of £200—if not thought sufficient for
such offence in some Casses Therefore It is now Ordained

50, 51 and 52 are in a different hand, being transcriptions made by
the Secretary at London in 1770, cf. fol. 19.

that if any such offence happen to be Commited it shall
be at the choice of the Court either to take the said
Penalty of £200 or Else utterly to disfranchise the partie
or parties offending Enacted the 22 November Anno 1612
In Hamburgh.

51   Whereas there hath been of late certain Arrests made
off Diuers parrcels of Interlopers Goods of which some
are Commodities of England Others warres of Forreing
Countries.   It was now considered whether it were fitting
utterly to restrain all Trade of Unfreemen unto this Place
or only their trade in Commodities growing or made in
England It was afte due debating resolued that it shall
be Tollerated that any Unfreeman may trade in this place
in any fforreingn Commoditie Payinge Unfreemens Toll
for them and submiting himself in such trade unto the
Orde[r]s of the Company and to that end consigning his
goods to a Brother off the same Enacted in Hamburgh the
20 March 1612.

52   Whereas it is found that the Fellowshippe is uery
much preiudiced through the negligent collection of
Broakes Hanses & Fines as likewise through the dilatory
Auditing of Treasurers accounts It is now Ordained and
Enacted That euery Treasurer after the expiration of the
time for which he was chosen to officiate that place (an
other Treasurer being chosen) shall be obliged and
holden within four weeks to deliuer an Account of his
Reciepts and payments unto the Husband for the use of
the Fellowshippe unless he shew cause for the ommting
of the same to the satisfaction of the Court upon the
Penalty of Ten Pounds sterling which said account the
Husband shall within fourteen days after the receipt
thereof draw up and digest into the usual method and
make ready to be audited [unless there be just cause to

the contrary which he shall be obliged to signifie unto the folio 19. Court within the said time] upon the Penalty of fforty shillings sterling and to be further punished att the Discretion off the Court.

And because of the gread prejduce & trouble which redound to the Company by the long standinge out and carryinge over of Debts which by the orders [in former times exactly practised] ought to be cleared by that Treasurer in whose time the same became due It is ordered and enacted that for the futur for Hanses Fines and Broakes att Admissions and all Broakes condemned in Court for any kind of transgressions against the orders of the fellowshipp and all other moneys whatsoever for which there are securitys put in to satisfye the Treasurer the same shall be cleared by each respectiue Treasurer in whose time the said Debts did arise.

And that att the Auditing of his account no such kind of Debts shall be allowed of to stand out in Ballance but shall be reckoned unto him as ready money in Cash.

And lastly that the Treasurer may be ffully informed what moneys doe arrise due to the Fellowshipp in his time and consequently are to be collected by him according as the orders doe sufficiently direct and empower him. It is ordained that the Husband shall within eight days after each Court whether Generall Court or Court of Assistants give up in writinge unto the Treasurer a particular of all such moneys as by order of the said Court shall be found due unto the Fellowshipp to be collected by the Treasurer, upon the Penalty of One Rix dollar soe often as he shall offend therein.

Actum in Hamburgh the 31 January 165⅞. These last Four Articles were transcribed at London the 13th February 1770 by Nehemiah Nisbett Secretary.

Caput Secundum.

ADMISSIONS INTO THE FFELLOWSHIPPE OF MERCHANTES ADVENTURERS OF ENGLAND THE ORDERS THEREOF AND OTHER ORDERS CONCERNINGE ASWELL FFREEMEN AS APPRENTYCES.

folio 23. Euerie persone Admitted into the ffreedome of the ffellowshippe of Merchants Adventurers of the Realm of England, shall pay at suche his admission yf he come in one the old Hanse as yt ys termed, 6ˢ 8ᵈ sterlinge, And yf he come in one the new Hanse tenn markes sterlinge, accordinge to the Rate of the Exchannge, and besydes shall satisfye and pay suche other debtes, duties fines and Assessementes as he himself that ys to be admitted his father or maister by whome he Claymeth the ffreedome shalbe found to stand Indebted to the house or otherwise that he shalbe justly charged withall by the ffellowshippe, or shalbe Imposed vpon him by the same, And to this end when anie brother of the ffellowshippe shall send over sonne or servannt to bee admitted into the ffreedome of the same, he shalbe bound to make the Governour or in his absence his Deputie or the Treasurer of the said ffellowshippe in Londone or the Governour or his Deputie in the Cittye or Towne where he dwelleth acquainted therewith, and from them or either of them bringe and present an orderly letter or Certificate, that he ys not Indebted to the ffellowshippe for Impositions of Clothe or of other Englyshe Comoditye whatsoever shipped out of the Realm of England to the Towne of Calice, synce the fourth day of December Anno Domini 1599, or to the

34

Towne of Embden or to anie other place in Germanie or the Lowe Countryes synce the 28th day of Januarie Anno domini 1597, or for anie other Cause for the which he shall stand either presented or condempned, and after knowledg thereof had, hathe satisfyed paid or giuen Contentment to the Court one that behalf for ought the said Governour or his Deputie or Treasurer doe know or haue knowledg of, And yf he bee Indebted as abouesaid he shall bringe or send or present dew notice thereof from the persons abouesaid or one of them, or make payment to the Treasurer of the ffellowshippe for the tyme beinge one this syde the Seas at the Chief Court, or otherwise giue Contentment and satisfaction to the Court for the same, at or before the admission of suchè sonne or servant, vpon pain for not sendinge or bringinge and presentinge suche letter Certificate or dew notice, or not otherwise observinge the true meaninge and Contentes of this order, not to haue suche sonne or servant admitted, before he haue sent or brought and presented the said letter Certificate or dew notice, and haue performed directly without fraude or guile the true meaninge and Contentes of this order.

No man shalbe admitted but at a Generall Courte one folio 24. this syde the Seas except by order of a Generall Court there for the good and servyce of the ffellowshippe the same bee consented and appointed to bee donne at a Generall Court within the Cittie of Londone.

An Apprentyce to be ffree of this ffellowshippe, shalbe sixteen yeares of age before he be bound to his maister after the manner of Apprentyces and shall serve eight yeares at the least with a ffree and sworn merchant Adventurer which woordes Merchant Adventurer shalbe expressely sett downe in his Indenture of Apprentyce-

hood that so yt may appear that he serveth for the ffreedome of the ffellowshippe, otherwise for default in the
premisses or in anie of them, he shall not bee admitted
into the ffreedome of this ffellowshippe by means or
virtue of suche his seruyce.

Seruice with a merchant Adventurer by Indenture of
Apprentycehood for eight yeares post dated six monthes
or aboue shall not bee of validitie, for the obtayninge of
the ffreedome of this ffellowshippe, but yf the Indenture
bee for longer tyme then eight yeares albeyt that yt bee
post dated six monthes the apprentyce shalbe admitted
the maister first payinge for a fyne to the ffellowshippe
twentie poundes sterlinge, which fyne shalbe taken ffor
euerie Indenture of eight yeares post dated.

No person of what degree or state whatsoever shalbe
admitted into the ffreedome of this ffellowshippe of merchantes Adventurers of England, except he bee rightly
Intituled therevnto either by Patrimonie from his father
an absolute ffree and sworn brother of the said ffellowshippe, before the birth of the said partie Intituled, or
else by seruyce with a ffree brother of the same ffellowshippe by Indenture, orderly made, after the said maister
was ffree himself or except that (not hauinge anie suche
tittle to the ffreedome) he will and doe foorthwith pay for
a fyne or redemption to the vse of the ffellowshippe twoe
hundred pounds sterlinge at least Provided alwaies that
no persone whatsoever not beinge a true subiect of his
kynges Maiestie none Artificer, Husbandman or Handy-
craftesman havinge no iust tyttle by Patrimonie or Apprentyceshippe, no persone of vnhonest behauiour, no
Bondman, Bastard, nor persone not borne of father and
mother bothe Englishe, no Coosener or other infamous
persone for felonie, periurie, or other griuous or Capitall

Cryme Comitted, No Bankrupt that hathe not satisfyed
the Court one that behalf, shall by anie Tittle Claym
wyse or manner whatsoever bee receiued admitted or
accepted into the ffreedome of the ffellowshippe nor bee folio 25.
reputed or held a member of the same: Provided that the
Children of ffreemen born of fforeign born wemen, after
their fathers Readmission within the Realm of England
before midsomer   [1] and synce shall and may bee admitted and enioye the ffreedome of this ffellowshippe by
Patrimonie, Lykewise the sonnes of ffreemen borne as
aforesaid one this syde the Seas out of the Realm of England, may and shall enioye the ffreedome of the ffellowshippe by apprentycehood the clause in this Act one this
behalf notwithstanding.

Redemptioners by the fyne of twoe hundred pounds
sterlinge as afore ys mentioned, shall pay doble Impositions to the house for the space of seaven yeares next
after their Admissions, their apprentyces also at their
Admissions shall each of them pay the fourth parte of the
fyne abouesaid which their maisters paid, But the sonnes
of such Redemptioners borne after the fathers were admitted and the Apprentyces of them and their successors
together with the Apprentyces and successors of the Redemptioners, Apprentyces, taken and bound after that
their maisters were Admitted, shalbe admitted and receiued to the ffreedome of the ffellowshippe for the payment of tenn markes sterlinge besydes suche duties as
may bee Cominge to the house, and as other the sonnes
and Apprentyces of ffreemen ought and are bound to doe.

No ffreehoste or Conseirge not tradinge or bearinge
Charge to the house, no ffree brother or other persone of

---

[1] The date is not given in the manuscript.

the ffellowshippe not tradinge either by Retayle or wholesale shall take anie Apprentyce or Apprentyces to bee
ffree of the said ffellowshippe, vpon pain of twentie
poundes sterlinge ffor euerie apprentyce so taken, And yf
anie suche persone as aforesaid duringe the tyme of his
aboue said vocation, not tradinge or not bearinge Charge
to the house shall take apprentyce or Apprentyces Contrarie to this Order, suche apprentyce or apprentyces
shall not bee admitted into the ffreedome of this ffellowshippe, Prouided alwayes that the Secretarie or sworn
Clerk of the ffellowshippe and the husband may with
licence of Court, take and make ffree apprentyce or
apprentyces as other Brethern may doe by the orders of
the ffellowshippe, Neither shall the sonne or Apprentyce
or anie Bankrupt borne or taken into servyce after his
Bankruptinge (except accordinge to the orders the Court
bee satisfyed one that behalf) bee receiued to the ffreedome of this ffellowshippe of Merchantes Adventurers.

folio 26.   Yf anie persone ys or hereafter shalbe Admitted or
made ffree of the ffellowshippe of Merchantes Adventurers
Gratis, the said Admission and ffreedome ys and shalbe
only for his owne persone, no sonne or Apprentyce of his
shall take anie ffreedome thereby in this ffellowshippe,
And no persone Admitted gratis shall shipp or vse trade
in this ffellowshippe for anie greater proportion or quantitie either in Stints of Clothes or otherwise then other
Brethren of his Continuance or standinge doe or ought to
doe by the orders.

Yf anie man shalbe found not to have borne personall
or Reall Charge in the ffellowshippe in the house in ffour
and twentye yeares, or to haue been disfranchised without Readmission afterwardes, for some offence against the
Ordinances or lawes of this ffellowshippe, no sonne or

apprentyce of suche a one shall have anie ffreedome in
the said ffellowshippe.   Prouided that the sonnes of
Brethren of the ffellowshippe whoe were verie yonge
vnder age at the decease of their fathers, or whose fathers
withdrawinge themselues into the Countrie and givinge
over all trade one this syde the Seas, had dwelt in the
Countrie tenn or twelue yeares before their decease,
shalbe admitted into the ffreedome of this ffellowshippe
for their hanses and other debtes and duties to the house,
anie thinge in this Act to the Contrarie Conteyned notwithstandinge.   And by personall Charge ys only meant,
suche as haue borne standinge Office in ffee of the ffellowshippe, namely Governour, Deputie, Secretarie, Husband,
Clerk or suche lyke Officers, or ministers entertayned in
the Government of the ffellowshippe, And by reall Charge
borne ys only meant, Impositions Prest monie, Polemonie,
Assessmentes, or suche lyke taxes and Charges, Imposed
and sett by the ffellowshippe generally and orderly paid,
and not anie Broakes fines forfeictures or amerciaments
levyed or paid ffor offence or breache of the orders.

   Yf anie persone clayminge the ffreedome of this ffellowshippe by servyce shall come out of tearmes his yeares of
apprentycehood beinge expired and that his maister
shalbe found not to haue borne Charge to the house att
all in four yeares next before his said Clayme, he shall
not bee admitted into the ffreedome of this ffellowshippe
before he have paid a fyne of xxvj^{li} xiij^s iiij^d sterlinge, to
the vse of the ffellowshippe, except his maister haue obtayned lycence of the Court one this syde the Seas, that
he may Come out of tearmes, and that yt bee prooued
throughe the said maisters fault or negligence that
Charge was not paid, but yf he Claym · his ffreedome
within tearmes though his maister haue not borne Charge folio 27.

at all in four yeares next before, or not to the somme of
fourtie and eight shillinges ster: he shalbe admitted payinge 48ˢ sterlinge for suche not bearinge Charge or none
payment, and suche other duties besydes for hanse or
other matter of debt, fine or Impositions dew to the
house.

Euerie Apprentyce taken and bound for the ffreedome
of this ffellowshippe shalbe Enrowled with one of the
Secretaryes or sworn Clerkes of the said ffellowshippe, yf
taken at Londone within six monthes, yf out of London
within a year after the takinge of suche apprentyce to bee
reconed ffrom the date that his yeares beginne one, vpon
pain of fourtie shillinges sterlinge to the vse of the
ffellowshippe: And everie Secretarie or sworn Clerk of
this ffellowshippe shall keep a perfect Register of all En-
rowllements, expressinge the day and the year of the
entry of euerie Enrowlement, which he shall Authenticquely Endorse vpon each Indenture of Apprentyceshippe to him brought and Enrowled, which order the
Brethern of this ffellowshippe within the Cittye of Yorke
shall also observe, vpon pain of ffourtie shillinges sterlinge: for not doeinge accordinge to the same, or for
euerie Indenture found otherwise then by this order ys
sett down and provided.

Yf anie Apprentyce bound for the ffreedome of this
ffellowshippe of Merchants adventurers shall not serve
his maister well & truly in euerie respect and point
accordinge to the tenure of his Indenture agreable with
the good orders of the said ffellowshippe, And namely
shall marrye within the tyme of his apprentyceshippe, or
shall without licence of Court at his maisters request
obtayned, before he haue served ffull seaven yeares,
(althoughe with his maisters particular leaue) shall doe

feat of merchandise to his owne vse or benefyte (except yt bee in the trade of the Staple, his maister or himself beinge free of the said Staple or of Spain or of other places where the ffellowshippe ys not priuileged, and that also with Consent of his maister, or shall absent himself willinglie or of purpose by the space of one monthe out of the seruyce of his maister without his Consent so to doe, suche apprentyce shall not haue, or yf he bee admitted within termes shall not enioye anie ffreedome in the said ffellowshippe.

Euerie brother of this ffellowshippe shall send his apprentyce or apprentyces yf he haue anie bound for the ffreedome to bee admitted and sworn before the expiration of his or their termes of yeres of apprentyceshippe vpon pain of ffyue poundes tenn shillinges ster: for each apprentyce which without lycence of Court shall not be admitted & sworn accordinge to this order.

No sonne of anie brother of this ffellowshippe, shalbe folio 28. admitted by Patrimonie into the ffreedome of the said ffellowshippe whereto he ys Intituled by Right of his father, before he bee full twentie yeares of age, And no apprentyce shalbe admitted before he bee one and twentie yeares of age, & haue served his maister twoe yeares together by Indenture, except suche apprentyce were four and twentie yeares olde before his byndinge, and had served ffyve yeares before with some other occupyer beinge none Artificer, In which Case he may bee admitted after one yeares Servyce with a ffree brother of the ffellowshippe.

No sonne of anie brother of this ffellowshippe either alredie begotten by an Alien woman and borne synce midsomer 1556 or hereafter so to bee begotten and borne out of the Realm of England and dominions thereof,

shall haue anie ffreedome in this ffellowshippe in righte
or Tittle of his father, but beinge naturalised and servinge for the said ffreedome as others the subiectes of
England shalbe admitted by virtue of suche service and
not otherwise.

When anie sonne or apprentyce of a brother of this
ffellowshippe, shall come to the place of the Companyes
Residence one this syde the Seas, to bee admitted into
the ffreedome of the said ffellowshippe, he shall in dew
tyme repair to the Secretarie or sworn Clerke and husband of the house, with suche wrytinges, letters and
Certificates, as he hathe for the Clayminge of the foresaid
ffreedome, and no persone shalbe admitted before he
haue performed this order and procured his Charges from
the said husband.

Yf anie persone shall claym the ffreedome of this
ffellowshippe by Patrimonie, he shall not bee admitted
into the same before yt appear by good Certificate or
other sufficient proofe to the satisfaction of the Court,
that he ys the true and legitimate sonne of him in whose
Right or Tittle he Claymeth the said ffreedome, and was
borne after his father was made ffree, and that he ought
not to bee debarred of the libertyes of the ffellowshippe,
for anie Cause or matter Conteyned in the ordinances of
the said ffellowshippe, or for offence donne against the
same or any of them.

Euerie Apprentyce beinge to bee admitted into the
ffreedome of this ffellowshippe either within termes or
without, shall in open Generall Court shew or produce
his Indenture of Apprentyceshippe in dew forme made
accordinge to the Custome of England one that behalf,
with a letter from his maister or persone whome he serveth
withall signed by the Wardens of the Companye whereof

folio 29.

he ys ffree yf he bee of Londone, and beinge of some
other Cittye Towne or place of the Realm, signed by the
Governour or his Deputie there, or by the Mayor Baillife
or other head Officer of the said place or the next adioyninge, together with his maisters subscription (except the
maister of suche apprentyce bee at that tyme present in
Court and requyre that his apprentyce may bee admitted)
yet always servinge his Indenture as abouesaid, else for
default in the premisses not to bee admitted.

No sonne or apprentyce of anie brother of this ffellowshippe shall doe feat of merchandise one this syde the
Seas where the ffellowshippe is Priuileged, for himself or
for his father or maister or anie other persone before he
bee Admitted and sworne into the said ffellowshippe
vpon the forfeicture of tenn poundes sterlinge vpon euerie
hundred pound bought, solde bartered or otherwise
handled, halfe to the vse of the ffellowshippe the other
half to the presenter. And yet by leaue of Court yt
shalbe lawfull for anie yongeman beinge the sonne or
apprentyce of a ffree brother of the ffellowshippe, to receiue and pay and bee in pack house vnder a ffreeman or
other that hathe taken oath to the ffellowshippe till his
admission, so that he in other matters demean himself
accordinge to this Ordinance.

No Brother of this ffellowshippe duringe the space of
seaven yeares next after the expiration of his yeares and
dew Certificate of his service, whereby he shalbe ffully
ffree and may trade for himself, or duringe the space of
seaven yeares next after his admission by Patrimonie,
shall take retayn or haue bound vnto him at one Instant
or tyme aboue one apprentyce to be ffree of this ffellowshippe. Neither after seaven yeares till twentie yeares
anie more then twoe apprentyces at once, neither at

anie tyme after twentie yeares anie more then three
apprentyces to bee ffree of this ffellowshippe. And if
anie Brother of this ffellowshippe shall doe the Contrarie hereof or take retayne and haue bound vnto him
more apprentyces at once then ys above prescribed, he
shall forfeict and pay to the vse of the ffellowshippe ffor
euerie apprentyce so taken retayned and bound the
somme of twentie poundes sterlinge, and Nevertheles
suche exceeded apprentyce shall not haue anie ffreedome
in this ffellowshippe, but for an amendes the maister
shall pay vnto hym (so he bee Ignorant of this Stint and
Order) for euerie year which he hathe serued before the
Claym and denyall of the ffreedome vpon the same,
within six monthes after suche Claym and denyall after
the rate of twentie poundes sterlinge by the year, to be
recouered before Court of this ffellowshippe by plaint or
folio 30. Action, And yf the maister shall not make the said payment of 20^{li} a year, or otherwise shall not giue his servant
Contentment one that behalf he shall not make ffree
sonne or servant or haue anie other benefyte of the ffreedome of this ffellowshippe before he have made satisfaction as aforesaid. And yf such apprentyce have served
the ffull terme of eight yeares or more, duely and truly
accordinge to his Indenture and that he bee Ignorant of
the aboue said Order or Stint and that his maister doe
not or will not make amendes as ys abouesaid, suche
maister (yf the Court bee so moved or for or see yt Convenient) shalbe first disfranchised, and then the exceeded
apprentyce shalbe admitted vpon the same hanse the
maister was ffree of, payinge suche debtes and duties as
are owinge to the house by the said maister, And so for
one maister first disfranchised makinge ffree one apprentyce and no more, Prouided that yt shalbe lawfull for

anie ffree brother of this ffellowshippe while he ys a
trader to haue at anie one tyme besydes the number or
stint above limited one apprentyce which by Patrimonie
may enioye the ffreedome, whoe notwithstandinge duringe the tyme of his apprentyceshippe shall not occupye
or trade in other manner then as to other apprentyces ys
permitted, or the Apprentyce of some other man orderly
bound for the ffreedome of this ffellowshippe whose
maister ys deceased, hathe giuen over trade, or ys de-
cayed or become Insolvent, or otherwise so alwayes that
he exceed not the aforesaid stint at anie tyme, aboue
suche one apprentyce, and that the dutyes of the house
bee paid, which the father of the one, or the first maister
of the other, shalbe found to owe or bee Indebted to the
ffellowshippe.

An apprentyce which for reasonable Cause agreable
with the orders of this ffellowshippe cannot serue his
maister the full term of yeares which he ys bound for,
may and shall with Consent of his said maister (yf he bee
livinge, or may bee asked Consent) or of his executors
foorthwith procure to bee sett over to some other brother
of the ffellowshippe ffree of the same hanse, that his
maister was ffree of, and so serve well and truly first and
last eight yeares Compleat or else suche apprentyce shall
not haue or enioye anie ffreedome in this ffellowshippe.

And the settinge over of euerie apprentyce shalbe before a Court of Assistents or Associates one this syde the
Seas or in England, which shalbe authenticquely noted
signifyed of over, yf yt bee donne at Londone within six
monthes after, vpon pain of fourtie shillinges ster: but yf
the settinge over bee in some other place in England, yt
shalbe signifyed over within one year after vnder the
seale of the place where the same is donne, or vnder the

seale of the next Cittye or Towne to that place, vpon
pain of 40ˢ sterlinge.

When the Apprentyce of anie brother of this ffellowshippe whether bound or sett over, shall decease or
depart out of his maisters servyce, suche brother shall
sufficiently advertyse and giue knowledg thereof to or at
a Generall Court one this syde the Seas, within six
monthes after suche decease or departure out of servyce
vpon payn of ffourtie shillinges sterlinge.

None Apprentyce or other persone of this ffellowshippe
whatsoever shall take his Pack-house or Chamber in a
suspected house or place of yll rule, or shall haunt or
lodge in anie suche house or place, vpon pain of ffyve
poundes sterlinge.

Euerie Apprentyce within fourteen dayes after his
Cominge to the Marte Towne shall wryte the place of his
lodginge in one of the beadles bookes and shall not without good and reasonable Cause bee out of the said lodginge after tenn a Clocke at nighte in the Pasche and
Sinxon Martes, nor after nyne a Clock at nighte in the
Balms and Cold Martes, vpon pain of Correction or punishment at the discretion of a Court of Assistentes or
Associates.

None apprentyce or other shall haue his lodginge or
pack house in anie Inns, Taverne or Victuaillinge house,
vpon pain of ffyve poundes sterlinge to bee forfeicted to
the vse of the ffellowshippe for euerie monthe that he
shall so haue his lodginge or pack house.

None apprentyce shall boord or keep his Carfe out of
the Conserrges or ffreehosts housen, vpon pain of 40ᵈ
fflemishe for euerie meale eaten elsewhere, except he be
guested abroad, or that yt shall please the ffellowshippe
vpon his or his maisters request to give leave, that he

may for learninge of language boord in a strangers house for a year after his first Cominge over or shorter tyme, 28^d of the broake to the poor 6^d to the presenter and 6^d to the hoste.

None apprentyce shall make anie sett Bankett dinner or supper either at his lodginge or in anie other place saue at the Conserrge or freehosts house neither shall he there or elswhere make bankett, dinner or supper, but for the furtherance and Advancement of his maisters busynes vpon pain to bee punished therefore at the discretion of a Court of Assistents or Associates.

Yf anie apprentyce shall vse anie excessiue quaffinge or drinkinge himself, or provoke others thereunto in his drinke, or shall playe openly or secretely at Cardes tables dyce or anie other game for above 4^d in a game, or shall by vauntinge, vyinge, bettinge, pacting or by anie other way exceed the said valew he shalbe punished at the discretion of a Court of Assistents or Associates.

Yf anie Apprentyce shall in the Judgment of the Governour or his Deputie & the Court, weare anie apparaile not fytt for his estate or qualitie, but rather beseeminge some Courtier servinge man or some other lyke persone, golde or silver Buttons, lace or twist Juivells of golde pearles or precious stones, he shall for the first tyme have the same taken from him, and sent to his maister, and offendinge the second tyme shall either bee shipped away or otherwise dealt withall and punished at the discretion of the Governour or his Deputie and Assistents or Associates. folio 32.

Yf anie apprentyce comonly or inordinately shall vse dauncinge, mumminge or walkinge abroad in the night seasone at vndue houres, or knock or ringe at mens doores, beat at windowes or miscary himself, in anie

other the lyke vnrulye or vnciuile manner, to the dis-
quietinge, trouble or hurt of others in their beddes or
lodginges, he shall for the first bee warned by the Governour or his Deputie thereof, and yf after suche warninge
he doe not surcease his disorder or yf anie apprentyce
shall keep anie whoor or yll disposed woman or abuse
himself with anie suche, or by gaminge excesse or other
misrule shalbe prooued or knowne to consume his maisters goodes, he shall for the same either haue his maisters
busynes and other Charge taken from hym, bee shipped
home to his maister and banished the Companie one this
syde the Seas ffor twoe yeares, and then also not to
return but at the Request of his maister and surties sett
for his good and honest Caryage euer after, or else shalbe
dealt withall and punished otherwise at the discretion of
the Governour or his Deputie and the Assistents or
Associates.

Yf anie apprentyce vpon malice or euill purpose shall
Intercept or break vp the letters of anie other of his
ffellowshippe, or of anie strannger or foreign, he shalbe
shipped home into England not to return again to doe
anie busynes in these partes in three yeares after.

Yf anie apprentyce or Covenant servant of a brother of
this ffellowshippe shalbe found and iustly prooued to
quarrell or fighte or to giue anie iust occasion of quarrellinge or fightinge to or with anie strannger of what
estate, Nation or Countrie soever, in these partes where
the ffellowshippe ys Resident, except yt bee in his owne
defence, he shalbe foorthwith sent away into England
and shall not in three yeares after return into these partes
vpon pain of one hundred poundes sterlinge to bee forfeicted and paid to the vse of the ffellowshippe by the
maister or other persone employinge or settinge suche
offender one worke.

No apprentyce or other persone ffree of this ffellow- folio 33. shippe shall Cary vnder his arme or otherwise bear throughe the streetes, anie thinge that cannot decently and vnseen bee borne or Caryed vnder his Cloake or garment, vpon pain of 3^s 4^d sterlinge.

None Apprentyce except he bee his maisters factor and Atturney shall sett out of the formes or place appointed for apprentyces at Generall Courtes vpon pain of 6^d fflemishe, neither shall he holde vp his hande vnto anie thinge to bee passed, or speake in anie matter propounded otherwise then ys by the Orders for keepinge of Courtes provided, vpon the same penaltie of 6^d fflemishe.

An apprentyce hauinge well and truly served seaven yeares by Indenture, yt shalbe lawfull for him with Consent of the Court at the Request of his maister obtayned one that behalf, to Trade for himself and shippe out one hundred Clothes a year in all sortes of woollen Comoditie, duringe the Remayner of his yeares vnserued. But no maister shall giue leaue to his apprentyce to trade for himself or to his owne vse, before he haue fully serued seauen yeares, upon pain of ffourtie poundes sterlinge to the vse of the ffellowshippe, Neuertheles yt shalbe lawfull for anie maister to vse and Employ his apprentyces stock in ffeat of merchandise, to the benefyte of his said apprentyce, and to licence his servannt to vse the Trade of the Staple or other remote and straunge Trades, yf he bee free thereof without Incurringe anie penaltie for that Cause.

An Apprentyce havinge donne his service duely and truly the maister of suche apprentyce shall not of yll will, Stomack, or malice, deneye to giue him sufficient Certificate thereof, vpon pain of twentie poundes sterlinge.

An apprentyce havinge served his ffull tearme of Ap-

prentyceshippe shall at a Generall Court one this syde
the Seas where the ffellowshippe ys Resydent, present
sufficient Certificate of his dew seruyce within one year
after the expiration of his tearmes, vpon pain of tenn
poundes sterlinge which Certificate shalbe of this manner,
yf the apprentyce bee of the Cittye of Londone, the
Wardens of the Companie whereof the maister ys ffree
shalbe procured, by their letters by them subsigned to
Certifye the Servyce of suche apprentyce donne dewly
and truly, to which letters also the maister shall subscribe.

folio 34.   Yf the apprentyce bee of some other place of England,
then the Certificate shalbe from, the Governour or Deputie or by the Mayor Baillife, or other head Officer or
other Credible persons of that place, together with the
subscription of the maister. But yf the maister himself
doe at a Generall Court by woord of mouthe openly
signifye the due seruyce of his apprentyce, yt shalbe
accepted for a sufficient Certificate, and the apprentice
shall not bee bound to procure anie other, but from
thence-foorth the Certificate beinge true, bee taken and
Enregistered a ffree brother of the ffellowshippe.

Yf anie brother of this ffellowshippe shall Certifye or
or Cause to bee Certifyed that his servannt or apprentice
hathe well and truly served him accordinge to his Indenture, and that suche Certificate shalbe proofed false, the
maister Certifyinge falsely shalbe disfranchised and pay
for a fyne tenn poundes ster: and the apprentyce and servannt so Certifyed shall not enioye anie ffreedome in this
ffellowshippe but bee depriued and expelled out of the
same.

The Indentures of apprentyces bound for the ffreedome
of this ffellowshippe, shall hereafter bee signed and

sealed in the presence of the Governour or his Deputie or
Deputees or one of the Secretaries of the said ffellowshippe, whoe shall plainly sett downe with their handes
vpon each Indenture the daye & yeare of suche signinge
and sealinge, And where there ys no Governour Deputie
or Secretarie, the same shalbe donne in the presence of
some head Officer of the Towne or place where the Indenture ys to be signed and sealed, with annotation of
the year and day as aforesaid, And this order to bee observed by each brother takinge and byndinge an apprentyce to bee ffree of this ffellowshippe vpon pain of tenn
poundes sterlinge, to bee paid before his said apprentice
shalbe admitted into the ffreedome of this ffellowshippe,
yf yt bee found that he haue neglected or not performed
the same.

No apprentyce or other persone Clayminge the ffreedome of this ffellowshippe shalbe admitted at Embden or
elsewhere out of the place of the Chief Court one this
syde the Seas, before advertisement be procured and
thither giuen or sent orderly from the said Highe Court,
whether suche apprentyce or persone ought to bee admitted, with note of the duties by him to bee paid or
answeared to the house, which he shall pay or answear
before his admission, Neither shall anie Certificate of dew
seruice bee accepted in the lower Court, but Referred to
the Highe Court, there to bee accepted and Enregistred,
or otherwise to bee dealt with or determined and ordered
as to the same Court shall seem good.

The Wardens of the poores boxe shall receiue of an folio 35.
apprentyce for his welcome or Enhansement (as yt ys
aunciently termed) 2^s 6^d fflemishe, and of euerie persone
else not beinge an apprentyce, but beinge or Intendinge
to bee a brother of the ffellowshippe, suche reasonable

peece of monie as shalbe Judged by the table or Companye by whome he ys Enhansed, And yf anie shalbe
found so froward that he will not bee Conformable to this
order in euerie Marte Towne where the ffellowshippe ys
or shalbe Priuileged, then shall yt bee lawfull for the
Wardens or anie other persone or persons there present
to disburse so muche as the partie ought or was awarded
to pay, and vpon knowledg thereof giuen to the Governour or his Deputie and the Assistents or Associates, the
partie refusinge shalbe compelled to pay vnto the dis-
burser of the said monie the doble of the monie disbursed,
and makinge further refusall shalbe holden for a disobedient persone and accordinglye bee Corrected.

SHIPPING, SHEWINGE, SELLINGE AND OTHER ORDERS IN FFEAT OF MERCHANDISE.

No persone of this ffellowshippe shall Carye or Trans- folio 41. porte or Cause to bee Caryed or transported out of the Realm of England anie merchandise whatsoeuer to or for anie other porte Towne or place within the Lowe Countries, East friesland, Germanie or the places neare adioyninge between the Somme in fraunce, and the Schage in Dutchland, then only to suche Porte Towne or place where the ffellowshippe or some parte thereof ys by order resident Nation wyse and keepeth the ordinarie martes, Neither shall anie brother of this ffellowshippe by himself or by anie other directly or Indirectly, buy or sell or Offer to buy or sell or shew or view with Intent to buy or sell, anie wares or Commodityes of the Realm of England or other foreign wares or Commodityes, or in anie wyse vse the Trade of a merchant Adventurer anie where in the Countries aforesaid, or in anie Towne or place of the same, but only in and not foorth of the Marte Towne or place where the ffellowshippe ys Resident as aforesaid, vpon pain of fourtie shillinges sterlinge vpon euerie short clothe and vpon other woollen Commodities of England after the Rate, and vpon all other wares and merchandises caryed transported, shewed or viewed, with Intent to buy or sell bought or sold, Contrarie to the true meaninge of this Order for euerie hundred poundes worthe ffyve and twentye poundes sterlinge for the first Offence and for the second offence the lyke fyne, and for the third

4   53

Offence the persone and persons Offendinge to bee disfranchised, And ffurther, yt shall not bee lawfull for anie
persone of this ffellowshippe to take vp or deliuer anie
monie by exchannge, but for the Marte Towne or Townes
where the ffellowshippe ys Resident or Priuileged, vpon
pain of tenn poundes vpon euerie hundred poundes so
taken or deliuered, Prouided that yt shalbe lawfull for
anie brother of this ffellowshippe to shippe and exercise
merchandise to and in the Townes of Embden and Calais,
so that he giue notice to the Governour or his Deputie or
the Appointers in Londone, of the iust quantitye and
qualitie of the goodes thither shipped and pay the Impositions dew for the same vnto the Treasurer for the
tyme beinge, and that before the shippinge thereof, at
least before the ende of the Marte wherein the said goodes
were shipped and not otherwise vpon pain to bee punished as a misshipper, Provided also that yt shalbe law-
folio 42. full, to vse the frank fortes martes, to make vp monie
thether by Exchannge from anie parte or place, and to
buy all kynde of foreign Commodityes there so that the
said Commodityes or wares bee sent to the marte Towne
there to bee shipped into England. Lykewise in any
place whatsoeuer to buy horse, harnas and all kynde of
munition for the Warres, Bookes, Fuelles, Furres (but
not at Hambroughe) bow staues, Wainscott Clapboord,
Deleboord, millstoanes, sopeashes pitche, Tare, all manner
of Cordage and all other thinges belonginge to the Rig-
ginge and settinge out of shippinge, and these kynde of
Victuailles and none other, To wytt all sorte of graine,
ffishe, ffleshe, butter, Cheese, Oynionseed, Wine, Oyle
and Ryce.

The Caryinge giuinge or sendinge of markes of Clothes,
settinge of pryce or by any meanes else enteringe into

Bergain or Contract for Clothes or other Englishe or
Foreign wares, by a mans owne self or by some other out
of the marte Townes the dealinge or handlinge by a
mans owne selfe or for anie other openly or Covertly one
this syde the Seas or in England with anie traders, vnto
or in anie forbidden partes out of the marte Townes
whether the said traders bee Brethren of this ffellowshippe
or vnffree subiectes, borne within the Dominions of the
Kynges maiestie, the sellinge vnto suche persons or anie
of them anie the Commodityes of England, or bryinge of
them anie foreign wares the Employinge of them or anie
of them as factors or doers for anie manner of trade of
merchandise, or takinge vp of monie by Exchaunge or
Depositum, receiptes or paymentes, ys vnderstood and
shalbe taken for Indirect dealinge, and Contrarie to the
true meaninge of the abouesaid Order.

Yf anie Englishe borne subiect beinge vnffree or no
member of this ffellowshippe of merchantes Adventurers,
shall of his owne wronge Intermedle with or exercise
trade of merchandise in the Low Countries, East friesland, Germanie or in anie Cittye Towne or place of the
said Countries, Contrarie to the Charters and Priuileges
graunted to the said ffellowshippe the wares and merchandise to bee sold or that are bought in the said partes
belonging to suche subiect, shalbe attached and seised
upon, wheresoeuer they may bee found and so remain
Irreplenisable till the penalties or forfeictures herevnder
ensuinge bee fully satisfyed and paid, viz. for euerye
short Clothe shipped into the said Countries or anie of
them ffourtie shillinges sterling and for other woollen
Commoditye after the Rate agreable with that of the
Custome house in Londone, And ffor euerie hundred
poundes worthe of other wares and merchandises handled

folio 43. or dealt in ffyve and twentie poundes of lyke monie, and that for the first and second tyme, but yf suche persone shall be found offendinge the third tyme, he shall forfeict the halfe of suche wares or merchandises as can bee seised vpon, and euer after shall incurre the same penaltie, so often as he shall doe against this Ordinance, And yf no wares or merchandise of suche persone can bee found, his bodie shalbe attached and Committed to prisone, there to remain without bayle or mayn prise vntill he haue satisfyed the foresaid penalties or haue at least ffullfilled suche order as he shalbe Enioyned vnto by the Court, Provided notwithstandinge that yt shalbe lawfull for anie subiect of the Realm of England or Ireland, by himself or by others at all tymes and in all the places aforesaid, to buy and Transporte into the said Realmes, horse, harnas, gunpowder, and all other munition of Warre, Bookes, Corne and graine of all sortes, butter Cheese, fishe, ffleshe, and suche lyke kynde of Victuaill for the Necessarie provision service and defence of the said Realm against the Ennemie and not otherwise, Provided also that this Ordinance shall not extend to the preiudice of the merchantes of the Staple or the East Countrie merchants, but that they may ffreely vse their Trade accordinge to their Priuileges, without empeachement or hinderance as heretofore lawfully they ought to doe, or might doe.

No Act or Ordinance shalbe made Concerninge shippinge without the advyce of the brethern of this ffellowshippe dwellinge in Londone, first Requyred and had therein, Provided that whereas of Late diuerse men Combine themselues in partnershippe in far greater number of partners then heretofore hathe been accustomed, namely three, four, fyve, or six in a Companie which oftentymes turneth to the preiudice of the whole ffellow-

shippe, especially when matter of shippinge for these
partes ys to bee handled and resolued vpon, yt shall not
bee Lawfull for anie twoe persons partners in one Companye to haue voice or hand in anie matter Concerninge
shippinge out of the Realm, but one of them shall depart
the Court.

No Brother of this ffellowshippe shall shippe or transporte or cause to bee shipped or transported anie Clothe
or other Englishe woollen Commoditie ffrom or out of the
porte of Londone into the Lowe Countries, East friesland
or Germanie or into anie Towne or place of the said
Countries or lyinge between the Somme in ffraunce and
the Schage in Dutcheland, (Embden and Calais by pro- folio 44.
vision excepted) but only suche as shalbe appointed to
bee laden by the ordinarie appointers of this ffellowshippe
ffrom tyme to tyme beinge, and in suche shippe or
shippes as by them shalbe appointed to lade, Neither
shall anie Brother of this ffellowshippe of whatsoeuer
place or porte of England, his Scotche or woollen Commoditye beinge once within the Cittye, or surburbes of
the Cittye of Londone or within twoe miles of the said
Cittye, send the said goodes or anie parte thereof ffrom
thence to some other porte or place there to bee shipped
or transported into the Countries aforesaid, or anie Towne
or place lyinge or scituate within the abouesaid destrict
or Compasse, vpon pain of ffourtie shillinges sterlinge fine
for euery short Clothe so transported or misshipped out
of the appointed shippes and twentie shillinges sterlinge
for euerie short Clothe misshipped in the appointed
shippes, to Wytt not appointed by the appointers or putt
into fardell or trusse to the Enlarginge or makinge thereof
greeter or more in sett Clothes, etc. then was appointed
by the said appointers, & for all other Clothe and woollen

Commodityes after the Rate, a third parte to the presenter.

Yt ys by the Deputie and Assistentes with the Assent
of the Generalitie further ordeyned and enacted, that yf
anie brother of this ffellowshippe shall haue or send
downe in the passadge boat of Lee or in anie other boat
shippe or Vessell, great or small anie Englishe woollen
Commoditye, to anie appointed shippe after the Clearinge
thereof from Londone for anie porte one this syde the
Seas, To Wytt middlebroughe Stoad or elswhere to bee
laden in such appointed shippe or shall lade or send
downe by any means whatsoeuer anie Englishe woollen
Commoditie, to bee laden in anie vnappointed shippe
boat, or vessell, great or small whatsoeuer, althoughe
bothe the one and the other Commoditye so laden or sent
downe to bee laden, by or means of the Governour of the
said ffellowshippee or his Deputie in Londone bee taken
out and brought back again out of suche appointed or
vnappointed shippe passage boat of Lee or other boat
shippe or Vessell great or small, the said brother ladinge
or sendinge downe of his goodes to bee laden shalbe
holden and reputed an actuall and reall offender, and
shall forfeict and pay to the vse of the ffellowshippe 6ˢ 8ᵈ
sterlinge for euerie Clothe, sent downe to bee laden or
laden in an appointed shippe, and fourtie shillinges sterlinge for euerie Clothe sent downe to bee laden or laden
in an vnappointed shippe boat or Vessell great or small,
and for all other woollen Commodityes after the Rate, to
follo 45. bee levyed Without favour or pardone, vpon the persone
or goodes of the said Offendor, wheresoever they may be
found either here one this syde the Seas or in England,
and in the mean while the said offender not to haue anie
benefyte of the ffree licence, till he haue paid and Con-

tented to one of the Treasurers of this ffellowshippe
either here or in England the said penalties, And yf the
Deputie or his substitute in Londone shall giue suche an
Offendor anie ffree licence, the said Deputie or his substitute for his Offence or Negligence one this behalf, shall
forfeict and pay to the vse of the ffellowshippe 6ˢ 8ᵈ sterlinge for euerie Clothe that he shall giue the said Offendor of the said ffree licence, Enacted at Middlebroughe
the 17ᵗʰ day of July anno 1610.

Yt shalbe lawfull for anie Brother of this ffellowshippe
or other persone not ffree, yf he so thinke good) att all
tymes to shippe or Cause to bee shipped in anie porte of
the Realm of England, Clothe Kersye, or other Englishe
or foreign Commoditye to the marte Townes thence
directly to bee transported into Italie or some other place
not lyinge within the Compasse or district of the Priuileged Countries, without Incurringe anie penaltie or forfeicture for so doinge, So that he putt in suertyes not to
vent or put to sale the said Clothe, Kersye or other Commoditie or anie parte thereof, in the foresaid Countries,
or in anie Towne or place of the same, lyinge between
the Riuers of the Somme in ffraunce, and the Schage in
Dutchland.

No man shall send or Cause to bee sent from the marte
Towne anie Englishe Commoditye, but he shall first give
knowledg of the qualitie and quantitie thereof and haue
licence of a generall Court so to doe, vpon pain of ffourtie
shillinges sterlinge to bee forfeicted vpon euerie Clothe
otherwise sent away and vpon other Commodityes after
the Rate.

Yt shalbe lawfull for the Brethern of this ffellowshippe
by Provision to shippe Clothe and other woollen Commoditye to the Towne of Calais in fraunce as also to anie

other Towne or place thereaboutes, in the Archdukes
Countries directly out of the Realm of England, Provided
that whoesoever Intendeth so to shippe shall first pay his
Impositions for so muche as he will passe or shippe out,
and then he shall haue from the Deputie or his substitute
in Londone a note or warrant signed and sealed with the
seale of the ffellowshippe to the kynges customers or
ffarmers, signifyinge the number of the Clothes or quantitie of woollen Commoditye with the qualitie and sortes
thereof, whether the same doe passe vpon licence or may
be shipped without licence, payinge the Custome only.

No brother of this ffellowshippe shippinge Clothe or
other woollen Commoditye to the Towne of Embden in
East friesland, shall from thence transporte or Cary the
same to anie other place within the Lowe Countries, East
friesland or Germanie there to bee sold or Vented, save
only to the Marte Townes, vpon pain of fourtie shillings
sterlinge for euerie short Clothe sold or vented elswhere,
and for all other woollen Commoditye after the rate.

For that of late sundrye brethren of this ffellowshippe
contrarie to all order doe as well by colourable as open
means and practyses not only transporte ffrom Embden
and other places one this syde the Seas, & in England
great store of Clothe Kersye and other Englishe Commoditie to the Townes of Hambrough, and Amsterdam,
and other places of Highe and Lowe Germanie, and
there sett and put the same to sale but also doe forestall
and Engrosse diuerse sortes of wares & merchandises
servinge for return, and which otherwise would bee
brought to the marte Townes, yt ys therefore Ordayned
and Enacted, that whoesoeuer of this ffellowshippe or
other subiect of the Realm of England, shalbe found to
have offended or hereafter shall offend in the premisses or

in anie parte thereof, he shall not only encurre the penalties heretofore provided for tradinge out of the Marte
Townes, but also being a freeman shalbe debarred of all
benefyte and ffreedome of the ffree licence, till he have
duely satisfyed and payd the said penalties, or else beinge
presented orderly, shall by oath or other manifest proofe
agreeable with the orders haue cleared or discharged
himself of the said presentment to the Contentment of the
Court, Provided that suche as by tolleration doe transporte Clothe and other Englishe woollen Commoditie to
the Towne of Calais in ffraunce, or into the Archdukes
Countries thereaboutes, directly out of England shall
not Incurre anie penaltie for suche transportation or sale
there made, And yet yt ys not meant that they shall
shippe out anie Clothe for the said places vpon the ffree
licence.

Whensoeuer generall or sett shippinge shalbe ordayned folio 47.
no persone of the ffellowshippe shall lade or shippe, or
doe to be laden or shipped anie manner of goodes wares
or merchandise in anie other Vessell or shippe then only
in the appointed shippes and have them readie aboord to
bee taken in by the day limited and not after, vpon pain
to forfeict for euerie peece, bee yt fardell, trusse Ballett
maund, chest, ffat, butt, pype, barrell great or small,
bound or vnbound, of whatsoeuer merchandise yt bee
(except woollen commoditie) tenn markes sterlinge, and
for euerie block of Tynne, fodder of lead, thowsand waight
of Tallow, starch, alome, or suche lyke ware twentie
shillinges ster: all manner of victuaille excepted, which
yt shall be lawfull att all tymes and euerywhere to shippe
at the pleasure of the owners.

Yf anie persone of this ffellowshippe when there ys a
Generall Restraint of shippinge or abstinence of Trade

into Highe or Lowe Germanie or anie parte or place
thereof, agreed vpon and commaunded, shall shippe or
lade or cause to bee shipped or laden, anie kynde of merchandise whatsoeuer out of the porte of Londone or out
of anie Porte Haven or Creek within the Realm of England, he shall forfeict and pay for euerie short clothe so
laden or shipped, fourtie shillinges sterlinge and for all
other woollen commodityes after the Rate, and for all
other wares and merchandises vpon the peece, as ffardell,
trusse, maund etc. tenn markes sterlinge, And whoesoeuer shalbe found to offend three tymes in a marte against
the true meaninge of this ordinance he shall be dismissed
of and from the ffreedome and Privileges of this ffellowshippe.

A day or tyme of ladinge beinge sett, each brother of the
ffellowshippe havinge clothe or other wollen commoditie
to shippe from the porte of Londone, shall have the same
waterborn and aboord the appointed shippe or shippes for
that purpose, yf the wether serve, before or by the last
day of the tyme limited or of the day sett, vpon pain to
forfeict for everie clothe laden, after the daye or tyme
prefixed 6^s 8^d sterlinge, and for other woollen commodityes after the Rate.

Yf anie man enter clothes etc. with the appointers in
Londone, and havinge them redie packed at the water
syde, or at least in his house redye to pack, he shall forfeict and pay 10^s sterlinge per clothe, for as many clothes
or the quantitie thereof in other wollen wares as by view
of the appointers (whoe thereto are authorised he shall
be found to want of the number entred.

folio 48.   The Appointers in Londone or visiters thereto Authorised shall take view of the Clothe and wollen Commoditie
in the house or possession of euerie brother of the ffellow-

shippe, makinge Entrie with the said appointers, and shall bringe into the Court a true reporte of suche their view, And yf anie persone of this ffellowshippe shall make entrye with the appointers of goodes which vpon view shall not bee found in his house, or at the water syde ready packed, or to make vp his Entryes, shall borrow clothes etc or make anie coulorable bergain, thereby to deceiue or prevent the viewers, he shall forfeict and pay for euerie clothe so wantinge, borrowed or coulorably bought, the somme of tenn shillinges sterlinge, The lyke penaltie shalbe levyed of euerie persone which shall borrow or lend anie turne, except suche brother wantinge clothe in house will and doe take his oath that the Clothes etc wantinge are either abroad at dyinge or dressinge, stamped with his marke or seale, or els are orderly shipped or stand redye at the water syde to bee shipped.

The Governour or his deputie in Londone, vpon presentment or reporte of the appointers or viewers or other Officers notes, taken out of the Custome-house deliuered vnto him of the defects found in mens entryes, Coulourable bergains borrowinge of Clothe to deceiue the said appointers or viewers, misshippinge of anie fardell or trusse or loose Clothes Encreasinge of fardells and trusses, in sett Clothes Kersyes or other woollen Commodityes, or vpon anie other reporte or presentment made for misshippinge, Contrarie to the Orders, shall Cause the same to bee examined at some Court of Associates, there within twoe monthes to bee held after suche report or presentment, and fyndinge the same true shall within one monthe after, Certifye ouer the Offence to the Court one this syde the Seas, to the end that punishment may bee Inflicted vpon the Offendors, vpon pain of twentie poundes sterlinge, And yf the Governour or his Deputie here shall not within one monthe after suche knowledg receiued, cause the said Offences to bee presented and handled before the Court where yt appertayneth and accordinglie proceed against the transgressors, he shall lykewise forfeict twentie poundes sterlinge to the vse of the ffellowshippe, and yet the said transgressors shall not bee discharged or acquyted.

Yt shall not bee lawfull for anie man to shippe Clothe for store in anie other mans name then his owne, vpon pain of fourtie shillinges ster: for each clothe so shipped, And the Deputie in Londone may giue anie brother of the ffellowshippe a bill of store without the appointers bill.

folio 49. No persone of this ffellowshippe shall enter or Cause to be entered in the Custome house, anie goodes wares or merchandise whatsoever in a wronge or surmised name, or sett thereone or wronge or Counterfeit marke or not his owne accustomed marke, nor shall send over or Conveighe suche his goodes wares or merchandise to bee receiued or taken vp by stranngers or others in defraudinge of the orders or dutyes of the ffellowshippe, or for anie sinister respect, vpon pain of forfeictures of the said goodes wares or merchandise.

After the aryuall of anie appointed shippe or shippes at the Marte Towne, No persone of this ffellowshippe shall lade in anie other vessell, bottome or shippe, anie goodes wares or merchandise for the porte of Londone, but in the said shippe or shippes, yf order bee giuen for them or anie of them to staye and lade, vpon pain of fourtie shillinges sterlinge, vpon everie peece or parcell of goodes wares or merchandise shipped or laden in other shippe bottome or vessell, Likewise when anie shippe or shippes whatsoeuer shalbe appointed by the Appointers one this syde the Seas, to lade for the porte of Londneo,

no persone havinge goodes or merchandise to lade for
that porte shall lade the same in anie other shippe or
shippes vpon the penaltie before mentioned, Provided
notwithstandinge that yf anie persone haue in the appointed shippes goodes or wares, to the valew of one
hundred poundes sterlinge, he shalbe ffree to lade where
he listeth, yf he yet haue more goodes to shippe.   Lykewise yt shalbe lawfull to lade in anie shippe or bottome
at all tymes, munition of Warre, fruite, Ruffe and Gruffe
wares.   To Wytt, Pytche, Tarre, Hoppes, blacksope,
Oyle, fethers, Wainscott, browpaper, sparres, mastes,
Wowe for Dyers, or also these kynde of Victuaille namely
Corne, Wyne, ffleshe, ffishe, Cheese, Reysins, figges, and
beer, Nevertheles the Brethern of this ffellowshippe tradinge in Hoppes, shalbe holden to lade the same in Englishe bottoms only, and shall not pay or allowe for the
fraight of a sack of Hoppes into England aboue ten
shillinges ster: poena vt supra.

After the Appointed shippes are laden and haue been
visited by the appointers, no man shall lade anie goodes
in anie of the said shippes without knowlegd & Consent
of twoe of the said appointers, vpon pain of fourtie shillinges ster: to bee forfeicted vpon each peece or parcell of
goodes so laden, to the vse of the ffellowshippe one third
parte to ye presenter.

Within ffour and twentie houres after the ladinge of
anie goodes or wares, the owner or lader thereof shall
Clear the Tolle & other duties therefore to bee paid, vpon
pain of fourtie shillinges sterlinge, to bee forfeicted for
each parcell of goodes vncleared to the vse of the ffellowshippe, one third parte to the presenter.

Yf anie shippe bee stayed for want of Clearinge of the folio 50.
Tolle, or other dutyes in dew tyme, the Treasurer for the

tyme beinge shall Clear the same and the doble thereof shalbe levyed of the partie making Default, besydes the penaltie aforesaid of fourtie shillinges sterlinge.

No persone of this ffellowshippe shall pay vnto the surveyour or other officers of the Custome house in England, more then the old dutyes for Cocquetts sealinge monie etc, vpon pain of fourtie shillinges ster: Soties quoties.

No man willfully runinge into daunger for not clearinge the Tolle and other duties to bee paid, or for breache of lawe, shalbe assisted with the Priuileges Entercourse or Compositione of the ffellowshippe.

No man for his dispatche shall pay vnto the Cramemaisters, Tolleners or Lyke Officers more then is dew to them by Contract, made with the ffellowshippe vpon pain of fyve poundes sterlinge to the vse of the ffellowshippe one third parte to the presenter, And yf he Continue in the said abuse he shalbe punished as a willfull violator of the Privileges of the ffellowshippe an abstract whereof eache persone ys to fetche from the Secretarie, vpon pain of ffyve poundes sterlinge.

No persone or persons of this ffellowshippe shall privately fraight or lade or cause to bee fraighted or laded, anie Vessell or shippe aryvinge out of England at the marte Towne, except suche shippe bee first refused to bee laden by the ffellowshippe or that he or they have Consent of the appointers so to doe, or else that suche shippe were hyred before her aryuall at the said Towne, and therevpon bergain and orderly Charter partie were passed, vpon pain of ffyve poundes sterlinge, and nevertheles the shippe to serve or bee laden for the ffellowshippe.

Euerie persone misenteringe his goodes Contrarie to the Rightes of the Custome house in anie parte of England, shall forfeict and pay to the vse of the ffellowshippe

6^s 5^d sterlinge for euerie Clothe so misentered, and for other Commoditye after the Rate.

No man shall bringe into these partes of beyond Seas, in Highe or Lowe Germanie anie woolle of the growinge of the Ile of Shepey in England, vpon pain of one hundred poundes sterlinge.

STINT OF SHIPPINGE.

folio 51.

Euerie Brother of this ffellowshippe which hathe or might haue traded for himself the space of three yeares, may shippe or cause to bee shipped ffor his proper accompt into the Lowe Countries Germanie and the places neare adioyninge, in one year twentie fodder of lead and not aboue, And he that hathe or might haue traded for himself the space of Seaven yeares, may shippe in one year three skore fodder of lead and not aboue, he that hathe or might haue traded for himself the space of tenn yeares, may shippe four skore fodder of lead and not aboue.

Euerie Alderman of the Cittye of Londone or of other Cittyes or Townes within the Realm of England, that hathe or might haue traded the space of fovrteen yeares, may shippe out one hundred fodder of Lead, and no man else of what standinge or Continuance soever aboue four skore ffodder of lead at the moste in anie one year, And whoesoever shall offend against this Ordinance or doe anie thinge Contrarie to the true meaninge thereof, shall forfeict fourtie shillinges sterlinge for euerie fodder of lead by him shipped or Caused to bee shipped in anie one year aboue the foresaid Stint.

Yt shall not bee lawfull from hencefoorth after the second day of Julie next comminge, for anie brother or other

Anno persone of this ffellowshippe to shippe transporte or carye
1609. out, or cause to bee shipped transported or carryed out,
from out of the Realm of England or anie parte thereof,
into the low Countries, East friesland or germanie or into
anie parte of the said Countries or unto the Towne of
Calais in ffraunce, anie more or anie greater number or
quantitie of clothe to bee vnderstood of all manner of
Englishe woollen Commoditie, accordinge to the Entryes
made in the Kynges Customehouse wrappers, and all,
then by the Stint Quotisation or proportion herevnder expressed sett out ordayned and permitted To Wytt.

An apprentyce havinge licence to trade for himself
within termes may shippe out in one year the number of
one hundred Clothes, or the quantitie of one hundred
Clothes in Englishe woollen Commoditye, in all and no
more, And none of them to bee vpon the ffree licence.

A ffreeman the first second and third year, after he ys
absolutely ffree Certifyed and Enregistered, may shippe
out euerie of the said yeares the number or quantitie of
ffour hundred clothes in all, wrappers & others & no
more, of which number he may shippe one hundred and
twentie clo: vpon the ffree licence, which ys monthly
tenn clothes vpon the said licence.

folio 52.   The fourth year he may shippe 450 Clothes or the quantitie thereof in all sortes of Englishe woollen Commodityes, and thereof one hundred & fyve and thirtie Clothes
yearly vpon the ffree licence, which ys monthlye 11¼
Clothes vpon the said licence.

The fift year he may shippe 500 Clothes to bee reconed
as aforesaid, and thereof 150 Clothes vpon the free licence
yearly, which ys monthlye 12½ Clothes vpon the said
licence.

The sixt yeare he may shippe 550 Clothes, to bee reconed as aforesaid, whereof 165 clothes vpon the ffree licence yerely, which ys monthly 13¾ Clothes vpon the said licence.

The seauenth year he may shippe 600 Clothes to bee reconed as aforesaid, whereof he may shippe 180 clothes vpon the ffree licence yearly, which ys 15 clo. monthly vpon the said licence.

The eight year he may shippe 650 clothes and thereof 195 vpon the ffree licence yearly which ys 16¼ clo: monthly vpon the said licence.

The nynth year he may shippe 700 Clothes and thereof 210 vpon the ffree Licence yearly, which ys 17½ clothes monthly vpon the said licence.

The tenth year he may shippe 750 clothes, and thereof 225 vpon the ffree licence yearly, which ys 18¾ monthly vpon the said licence.

The eleuenth year he may shippe 800 Clothes and thereof 240 Clothes vpon the ffree licence yearly, which ys 20 Clothes monthly vpon the said licence.

The twelft year he may shippe 850 Clothes in all and thereof 255 clothes vpon the ffree licence yearly, which ys 21½ Clo: monthly vpon the said licence.

The thirteenth year he may shippe 900 Clothes in all and thereof 270 Clothes vpon the ffree licence, which ys 22½ Clothes monthly vpon the said licence.

The ffourteenth year he may shippe 950 Clothes in all, and thereof 285 Clothes vpon the ffree licence yearly, which ys monthly 23¾ Clo: vpon the said licence.

The ffyfteenth year he may shippe one thousand Clothes in all and thereof three hundred Clothes vpon the ffree licence yearly, which ys monthly fyve and twentie Clothes vpon the said licence.

And so fourth how longe tyme soeuer anie man of what folio 53.

5

estate or degree soever shalbe ffree of this ffellowshippe,
Yt shall not bee lawfull for hym to Shippe or Cause to
bee shipped out in one yeares space aboue the last mentioned number of one thousand Clothes to bee as aforesaid reconded, wrappers and all, but he and all others of
lesse standinge, Shall Content him and themselues, as
well with the abouesaid Stint Generall, as with the particular yearly and monthly Stint or quotisation of the ffree
licence afore expressed, without exceedinge either in the
one or the other directly or Indirectly, vpon the penaltie
of fourtie shillinges sterlinge per Clothe to bee forfeicted
and paid to the vse of the ffellowshippe without favour or
pardone, for euerie Clothe so exceeded Contrarie to the
true meaninge of this order, and for all other woollen
Commoditie reduced into Clothes after the same rate.

And whereas by former order yt was not lawfull to
anticipate the tyme, that ys to shippe out at the begin-
inge of the year or at some other tyme when a man listeth
within the year, To wytt between the second of Julie and
the second of Julie next followinge, So many Clothes at
once or shortly one after another as are alotted for his
whole yeares shippinge vpon the ffree licence, that order
by provision onely and toleration ys presently left open,
in hope of a due care and discretion to bee had and vsed
in Londone, of the orderly equall and reasonable distribution, devidinge, and givinge out of the said licence, to
which ende the Deputie and his substitute the Secretarie
in the said Cittye, are requyred and hereby Charged, to
haue a Speciall good regard, and to bee verrie Circum-
spect and equall in deliueringe out bills for the said ffree
licence, that nothinge by their fault or oversighte bee
donne or passed in preiudice of this order or anie tradinge
brothers righte.

Yt ys also further Ordayned that no brother of this
ffellowshippe beinge partner with others one or more, shall
in one year shippe out in companie anie more clothes vpon
the ffree licence or otherwise, then accordinge to the part
& portion which he dothe adventure in stock or Credite
with his Companie, with whome he parteth not equally or
halfe and half, Adventure, proffyte and losse vpon pain
to forfeict vpon euerie Clothe shipped out contrarie to the
true meaninge of this Order, or aboue the said parte or
portion fourtie shillinges sterlinge to the vse of the ffellowshippe, to bee tryed by the oath of the partie, As for
example he that hathe but a fourth parte in stocke or
Credite with some other & Consequently participateth but
a fourth parte of the gaynes etc, shall in one year shippe
out but the fourth parte of the Stint alotted and sett out
for him to shippe by the aboue written order accordinge
to his Continuance and standinge in the ffreedome of this folio 54.
ffellowshippe and so of the rest, And yt shalbe lawfull for
the Governour or his Deputie and Assistents and Associates one this Syde the Seas and in Londone, to warne and
call before them yearly before the last day of August, all
the ffree brethern of the ffellowshippe partners and others
and to examine them vpon their Corporall oathes, whether
they have shipped or donne contrarie to the abouesaid
order or anie parte clause or point thereof, and he that
shall not appear by the said last day of August euerie
year, or shall refuse or will not or shall neglect to take
the said oathe and purge himself in dew manner, shall
forfeict and pay to the vse of the ffellowshippe the somme
of twentie pounds sterlinge without favour or pardone,
and further bee deprived of the vse and benefyte of the
ffree licence till he haue taken the said oathe and declared
(yf he haue offended) the number of the Clothes and other

woollen Englishe commoditye shipped, or exceeded contrarie to the true meaninge of this order, and yf the said
partie beinge after warned to appear and take oathe, shall
not appear and take oathe, he shall forfeict and pay for
a fyne the some of twoe hundred poundes sterlinge for
suche his willfull Contempt, and further bee dealt withall and Censured as one whoe hathe offended this order.

Furthermore no brother of this ffellowshippe, shall at
anie tyme directly or Indirectly borrow or lend, buy or
sell, give away, exchaunge or Compound for the ffree
licence, vpon which he may shippe out Clothes or for
anie parte thereof, Neither shall yt bee lawfull for anie
brother of this ffellowshippe to fetch or take out from the
Deputie or his substitute in Londone, anie parte of the
said ffree licence, to anie other end or Intent but onlie to
the proper vse of him or them by whome the lycence ys
so fetched out, But shalbe holden by him or themselues
to shippe the same number and quantitie of Clothes to
the Marte Townes one this syde the Seas, accordinge to
the Ordinances of the ffellowshippe standinge in force,
and agreable with the Charters and graunts of the said
ffree licence, vpon pain that euerie brother which Contrarie to the true meaninge of this ordinance, shall either
borrow or lend, buy or sell, give away, exchaunge or
Compound for, the said ffree licence, or anie parte thereof,
to other end or Intent then as ys abouesaid, shall forfeict
& pay for euerie Cloth borrowed, or lent bought or solde,
given away, exchaunged or Compounded for, the some of
fyve pounds ster: without favour or pardone, to the vse
of ye ffellowshippe.

folio 55.   Accordinge to former Order and vpon the penaltie
heretofore one this behalf Provided in the Act of stint
of shippinge, yt ys ordayned and Enacted that euerie

Brother of this ffellowshippe that shall make entrie of
Clothe to bee shipped out vpon the ffree licence, whether
the entrie bee made in his owne name or in the name of
anie other persone or persons of the said ffellowshippe,
suche Clothes so entred to bee shipped out vpon the ffree
licence, shalbe all bought with the proper Stock and
Credite of him or them in whose name or names they are
so Entred and he or they shall directly and plainly bear
bothe the Adventure of them and the hazard of proffyte
or losse by them whichsoever shall happen, And yf anie
ffree brother of this ffellowshippe shall at anie tyme
directly or Indirectly, borrow or lend, buy or sell, give
away, Compound for or exchaunge the ffree licence, vpon
which he may shippe out Clothes or anie parte thereof
aswell all and euerie suche borrower as lender, suche
buyer as seller, suche giuer away as receiuer, as also all
and euerie suche Compounder for, or exchaunger, of the
ffree licence or anie parte thereof, shall forfeict and pay
vpon euerie woollen Clothe so borrowed or lent, bought
or sould, giuen away or receiued, exchaunged or Compounded for, Contrarie to the true meaninge and Intent
of this present Act, the somme of tenn shillinges sterlinge
monie to be levyed by the Treasurers here one this syde
the Seas, and in Londone, from tyme to tyme the one
halfe to the vse of the presenter makinge dew proofe
thereof, and the other halfe to the vse of the ffellowshippe.

Finally yt ys Ordayned and Enacted that the Deputie
in Londone or his substitute the Secretarie there, shall
keep an orderly plain and perfect Register of all the bills
by him from tyme to tyme deliuered out to anie man for
the abouesaid ffree license, to bee in readines to bee
audited at euerie six monthes ende by those appointed
for the Auditinge of the Treasurers accompts in the said

Cittye, or by some other to bee there appointed by the
Court for that purpose, a Copie whereof shalbe yearly
sent over to the Court here, vpon pain that the said Secretarie herein makinge default, shall forfeict to the vse of
the ffellowshippe and pay out of his stipend or Entertayn-
ment the somme of twentye poundes sterlinge, as often as
he shalbe herein found faultie without all favour or pardone, and in Consideration of his paynes one this behalf
to bee taken, he shalbe allowed over and aboue his yearly
stipend of one hundred pounds ster: which he now enioyeth the some of ten poundes ster: to bee paid him by
the Trer: in Londone at euerie yeares ende, this servinge
for the said Treasurers warrant one that behalf.

SHIPPINGE, ETC.

No persone whatsoeuer whoe synce Easter 1581 hathe
been admitted or hereafter shalbe admitted gratis, into
this ffellowshippe shall shippe out anie Clothe vpon the
ffree licence or vpon anie purchased licence, vpon pain of
fourtie shillinges sterlinge, for euerie Clothe so shipped
out to be levyed one halfe vpon the persone or goodes of
the partie so shippinge, and the other halfe vpon the
Deputie or his substitute that shall have given out bill or
warrant for the passinge out of suche Clothes.

Because that some Brethern of this ffellowshippe havinge of late dayes made entrye with the appointers of
Clothes in trusses and fardells sett, with the wrappers
thereto belonginge, doe vse to fetch their licence bills at
the hands of the Deputie for the whole number of the
Clothes sett, and wrappers in the said Trusses, or fardells,
and yet notwithstandinge in payinge of Custome afterwardes doe only enter their sett Clothes vpon the ffree
licence or bought licence and the wrappers of them Course

thereby Consuminge the said licences Indirectly, in passinge out more Clothes vpon the same then in right Construction they ought, the wrappers beinge supposed to
bee of the same Nature that the sett Clothes are, Therefore yt ys Ordayned that the said practyse shalbe no more
vsed vpon the penaltie of 6ˢ 8ᵈ sterlinge for euerie Clothe
that shalbe found entered or passed out Contrarie to the
true meaninge hereof, Enacted at Stoad the 8ᵗʰ of October
anno 1589.

No Brother or Brethern of this ffellowshippe by him or
themselues or by anie other for them, shall make entry
with the appointers in Londone, in their bookes therefore
provided, of anie Clothe, Kersyes, or anie other Englishe
woollen Commodityes, but only of suche as are his or
their proper goodes, and in his or their housen or possession, in whose names they are to bee entred or are
entered, and suche as he or they purpose to send and
shippe in the appointed shippes vnto the marte Towne or
Townes, for which he or they doe make entrye as aforesaid, Lykewise no brother or brethern of this ffellowshippe, shall at anie tyme borrow, sell, giue, lend, transporte or Chaunge his turn of shippinge, to or with anie
other Brother or brethern of anie Cause or Condition, or
by anie manner of means, whatsoever, but shalbe held to
shippe his or their Clothes and goodes accordinge to the
name qualitie and quantitye sett downe in his or their
Entryes, by hym or them, or by anie other for him or
them made in the appointers bookes, Neither shall yt bee
lawfull for anie man in or for the makinge of such Entrye
to borrow or lend the name or surname of anie other per- folio 57.
sone whoesoever, yet yf happilye anie brother after suche
his entrye made shall dispose of all or anie of the Clothes
etc by him entered, otherwise, suche brother shalbe fur-

ther holden to giue notice of suche his disposinge or
Chaunge of mynde vnto the appointers in Londone for
the tyme beinge or to one of them at suche house or place
and at suche tyme as they shall sitt at to receiue entryes,
within eight dayes after suche disposinge or alteration of
mynde, to the end that the bookes may bee Crossed of the
said Clothes etc as matter void and of none effect, And
whatsoever brother of this ffellowshippe shall not performe and doe accordinge to this order, and the severall
pointes thereof, but shall offend against the same in
whole or parte directly or Indirectly, he shall forfeict and
pay to the vse of this ffellowshippe vpon euerie Clothe
and vpon all other woollen Commodityes after the rate,
the some of twentie shillinges sterlinge without favour
or pardone.

SHIPPINGE FROM EXCESTER.

Yt shall and may bee lawfull for the tradinge brethern
of Excester at four sett tymes and seasons of the year,
To Wytt the 15th of February 15th of Maye 15th of August
and 15th of November to shippe at their pleasure in what
shippe or Vessell that they will, at the Porte of Londone,
their Countrye Commodityes, properly belonginge to
them or anie of them to bee landed and vented one this
syde the Seas, in the Marte Towne or Townes and no
where else, vpon the penaltie of misshippinge, And at
the aryuall of the said goodes at the Marte Towne, the
said brethern shalbe bound to enter the same in the house
with the Secretarie sworn Clerk or husband, and that before the takinge vp thereof, vpon pain of tenn poundes
sterlinge makinge therein default, And this to bee vnderstood of the ffree brethern of this ffellowshippe dwellinge
at Excester only, and of their goodes and Countrye Com-

modities onlye, and none other woollen Commodityes, and those to shippe but four tymes a year one the dayes aforesaid from Londone although that anie of them may have partner or partners in or about Londone.   And to the end that no fraude bee herein vsed, Yt ys further Ordayned that suche brethern of Excester as shall send vp their goodes to Londone from thence to bee shipped accordinge to this order, shalbe bound withall to send an orderlye and true Certificate, vnder oathe taken before the Mayor of the said Cittye of Excester, that the said goodes are properlye belonginge to them or their partner or partners ffreemen of the ffellowshippe of Merchantes Adventurers of England and None other, directly or In-directlye.   And their factors or servants as shall lade the said goodes shall lykewise take oathe at London before the Governour or his Deputie there that the propertie of the said goodes ys not altered, And that they shalbe directly shipped to the Marte Towne or Townes and take out due Certificate thereof to bee sent over with the other passed at Excester, upon the penaltie of misshippinge yf they shall neglect to performe the pointes above written or anie parte thereof.

folio 58.

SHIPPINGE.

No Brother of this ffellowshippe havinge goodes arvyed from anie the out portes of the Realm of England, shall procure the same or anie parte thereof to bee discharged or vnladen before he have brought vnto the husband of the house or some other appointed for that purpose or the Secretarie, a perfect and true note of the said goodes with the qualitie and quantitie thereof, as he will aun-swear therevnto vpon his oathe, vpon pain of ten poundes sterlinge.

SHIPMAISTERS.

The Owners maisters and maryners of shippes and Vessells ladinge for or servinge the ffellowshippe and euerie of them, shalbe bound to observe and keep suche Orders, Conditions and Articles as one their behalf are provided by the Ordinances of the said ffellowshippe, and are agreed vpon and Covenanted betwixt the appointers and them, and euerie of them, and to make payment of suche penalties and forfeictures as are therevnto dew vpon pain to bee debarred and Crossed from the service of the ffellowshippe, vntill suche tyme as he or they shall have submitted him or themselues, and paid doble ffyne or otherwise have given satisfaction to the Court, To the dew and better effectinge whereof, and all other pointes and Articles Concerninge the Owners and maisters of shippes and their maryners, with all other necessarie Covenantes and Agreements as accustomed, together with suche also as lately were agreed vpon and advertysed to Londone, yt ys in lyke manner agreed that the foresaid Appointers for the tyme beinge, shall from tyme to tyme, cause all the same to bee Orderlye inserted in euerie Charter partie, which together with the owners or maisters bondes for the dew performance thereof, and to bee made and signed as ys requisite, and that before the shippe or shippes of suche maister or owner shall beginne to lade, vpon pain that the said Appointers faylinge in anie point abouesaid shall forfeict & pay euerie of them ten pounds ster: without favour or pardone.

The Appointers in London from tyme to tyme shall deliuer vnto euerie maister of Appointed shippe Immediatelye after the appointinge of the same, a iust, true and particuler Content in wrytinge, of all suche goodes as they shall haue appointed in suche shippe, with

Charge vnto the said maister that he take order with his
mate, Purser, Botesman and saylers, that manner of folio 59.
goodes bee by them or anie of them taken into his shippe
then onlye suche as are written and sett downe in his
said Content a Duplicke or Copie whereof firmed and
vnder written by them the appointers shall send vnto the
Governour or his Deputie and ffellowshippe resident in
the Marte Towne, whether suche appointed shippe shalbe
destinate and laden, Accordinge to which Content and
the Cocquets that euerie maister with all Convenience
after his aryuall ys to deliuer vnto the husband, or other
Officer appointed to receiue them, the said maister shalbe
Charged by the fforesaid Governour or his Deputie and
Certain of the Assistentes or Associates and purged by
his Corporall oathe, whether he haue brought over in his
shippe or Vessell more goodes then by the appointers
Content were appointed one this said shippe or Vessell,
And anie difference beinge shall make deliuerie vpon his
said oathe of further notice of anie thinge laden or
brought over, and not Comprehended in his said Content,
with the quantitye and qualitye thereof and for whome,
to the end that the misshippers by this means beinge
found out, may bee dealt with accordinge to the Orders,
and that euerie maister which shall bringe over more
goodes ffor anie man then one his shippe or Vessell were
appointed, may pay vnto the ffellowshippe bee he maister
or owner, a fine of 5ˢ sterlinge per Clothe vnorderlye
taken in, laden and brought over and ffor all other Commoditye after the rate without favour or pardone.

Yf anie Brothers goodes of this ffellowshippe packed
or made vp into ffardells Trusses or Bales, shalbe opened
made loose, vnbound, vntrust, or vnbaled in whatsoever
packinge yt bee, and that yt bee found to bee donne a

shippeboord by the maister owner of the said shippe or
Vessell, or by anie of his Companie or anie other persone
or persons for hym or them or anie of them, the maister
or owner of suche shippe or Vessell where suche thinge
shalbe Committed or donne (without the Consent of the
owner of the goodes first had) shall for euerie peece or
parcell of goodes so opened vnbound vntrust or vnbaled,
forfeict and paye ffyve poundes sterlinge to the vse of the
ffellowshippe without favour or pardone.

The maister or owners of shippes or Vessells appointed
or laden ffrom Londone shall not lade or suffer or Cause
to bee laden in their shippes or Vessells anie goodes
whatsoever either outwardes or homewardes bound vpon
or aboue the hatches, vpon pain of ffourtie shillinges ffor
euerie peece or parcell so laden, And no brother of this
ffellowshippe shall pay fraight for anie goodes so laden
folio 60. vpon the same penaltie but shall bringe the said fraight
into the handes of the Treasurer to bee disposed of as
shall seem good to the Court, And yf by default of anie
brother of this ffellowshippe anie goodes shalbe laden
aboue hatches, he shall forfeict suche penaltie as the
maister or owner as aforesaid ys to vndergoe.

Yf by the frowardnes of anie maister owner, maryner
or maryners, of anie shippe, the Appointers shalbe letted
or withstood in doeinge their Office, visitinge or vnlad-
inge anie shippe pestered accordinge to the Orders suche
maister, owner or procurer of suche lett or Residence,
shall forfeict doble the penaltie provided for ladinge
above hatches, or otherwise vpon knowlegd & proofe of
suche misdemeanour shalbe dealt withall and punished
at the discretion of the Court.

SHIPPINGE.

Yf in Visitation of shippes or Vessells either homewardes or outwardes bound, the Appointers shall fynde
anie shippe or shippes pestered or with goodes laden
aboue the hatches they shall foorthwith discharge and
take out suche pesteringe or goodes at the Charge of the
maister or owner of suche shippe or shippes, or of the
owner of the said pesteringe or goodes where the fault
shalbe found.

No maister or owner of shippe or shippes appointed,
onlye for the service of the ffellowshippe, shall vnder
what Colour or pretence soeuer directly or Indirectly
suffer anie straungers, foreigns Vnffreemen, Interlopers
or suche lyke disorderly persons, to lade anie goodes or
merchandises in their said shippe or shippes from Londone to the partes of Vpper or Lower Germanie, Neither
after the said maister or owner with his shippe ys Cleared
from Londone, shall vpon the waye take in or deliuer out
anie merchandise whatsoever, except vpon necessitie or
vrgent occasion not to bee avoyded by wynde wether or
perrill of Sea and that vpon pain of ffyve poundes sterlinge, to bee forfeicted or paid ffor euerie peece or parcell
of goodes or merchandise so laden, taken in, or deliuered
out, besydes three yeares Banishment ffrom all service of
the ffellowshippe yf the Offence bee found so to deserve
by the Court, which order shalbe also obserued and kept
by the maisters and owners of shippes homewardes bound,
vpon the same penaltie yf the necessitye of the tyme so
requyre, and that they bee warned by the Governour or
his Deputie or the Appointers one the behalf of the
ffellowshippe to observe and keep the same.

Those of the ffellowshippe tradinge in these partes of folio 61.
beyond the Seas and their ffactors, Atturneys and ser-

vants, shall from tyme to tyme bringe into the handes of
the Governour or his Deputie for the tyme beinge, or
some other appointed thereto by the Court, a true and
perfect note vpon his Corporall oathe of all Clothes and
other Englishe woollen Commoditye with the righte
nature, qualitie and quantitye thereof by them had taken
vp or receiued at or between the ordinance appointed
shippinges ffrom tyme to tyme to bee performed, by a
Certain daye to bee sett by the Court, vpon the penaltie
of ffiftie poundes sterlinge and no man to departe the
Marte Towne without bringinge in of the said note and
takinge oathe as aforesaid, vpon the same penaltie, and
yet not to bee discharged of that he shalbe presented or
iustly Charged with for this Cause.

Forasmuche as yt is daylie found that sundry abuses
are Committed by the maisters of Trades, and Pinkes,
ladinge ffor these partes, somme whereof make their
porte at fflushinge and some in other places discharge
their ladinge or parte thereof, verie vnorderlye to the
hurt and trouble of the ffellowshippe, as well in regard
of the multitude of Interlopers thereby maynteyned, as
also of vnorderly brethern whoe by means hereof cannot
bee so well mett withall and restrayned as were to bee
wished, Yt ys therefore Ordayned and Enacted, that no
brother of this ffellowshippe shall lade anie goodes whatsoever, in anie Crayer, Pynke or lyke Vessell either
Englishe or Dutche bound for these partes, which after
Clearinge ffrom Londone or Gravesende shall breake
Bulkk or discharge her ladinge or anie parte thereof by
the waye, or in anie other place then this Towne of
Middelbroughe onelye where the ffellowshippe holdeth
their Staple or Residence, and where the Brethern of the
said ffellowshippe are by the orders to lade their goodes

and merchandise ffor England and no where else, vpon
pain of ffyve poundes sterlinge to bee forfeicted vpon
euerie peece and parcell of goodes or mercandise so laden
or shipped except yt shall otherwise seem good by the
Governour or his Deputie and the Court, and further to
bee dealt withall as a transgressor of the orders, provided
against shippers of goodes at other places then the Marte
Townes.

The maisters and owners of the Appointed shippes
aryvinge from Londone at the Marte Towne or Townes,
shall observe their turnes as well in discharginge as in
ladinge homewardes, accordinge to their severall lottes &
shall not lye longer then the dayes assigned by the
appointers for their reladinge and Clearinge awaye, vpon
pain of fyve markes sterlinge without especiall licence of
the Governour or his Deputie.

MAISTERS OF SHIPPES, ETC.

After the Appointed shippes or anie of them are laden
from hence and visited by the Appointers, no brother of
this ffellowshippe shall lade in the said shippe or shippes
without Consent of twoe of the Appointers at least, vpon
payn to paye ffor euerie peece and parcell of goodes so
laden vnder the worthe of one hundred poundes, ffourtie
shillinges sterlinge, and for euerie hundred that the said
peece or parcell of goodes ys worthe aboue one hundred
pounds, ffourtie shillings sterlinge to the vse of the
ffellowshippe.

Yf in discharginge of anie shippe Commanndment or
warninge shalbe given by the Governour or his Deputie
to discharge No more or to holde vp the maister or owner
of suche shippe shall obey suche Commanndment, vpon
pain of tenn shillings sterlinge vpon euerie packe, fardell,

or trusse or parcell of goodes discharged after suche
Commanndment or warninge given to bee paid by the
said maister or owner yf yt bee his fault, or by the partie
receiuinge suche goodes yf yt bee his fault.

The maisters and Owners of the appointed shippes shall
after their aryuall with all possible speed enter their
shippes where they ought to bee entered, and no shippe
shalbe appointed to lade homewardes till yt bee knowen
that the same ys orderlye Cleared Inwardes.

No man shall lade in anie shippe bound for Londone
the maister or Owner whereof hathe not first licence of
the Govenour or his Deputie to lade, and then bee orderlye appointed by the Appointers, vpon pain of fourtie
shillinges sterlinge for eurie piece or parcell of goodes
laden in suche shippe.

No maister or owner of shippe appointed or laden by
the Brethern of the ffellowshippe, shall exact or take
aboue the rate accordinge to Which yt shalbe thought
meet and agreed by the Appointers, that they ought and
shall receiue fraight by or accordinge to twoe rates agreed
vpon and ordayned by Authoritye of the ffellowshippe
the one for the bigger the other for the lesser shippes of
burthen & Charge and accordinge to which the appointers
in Jugdinge, the maisters and owners of shippes in receiuinge, and the merchants or laders of the ffellowshippe
in payinge fraight shall direct and demean them selves
without exceedinge, vpon pain of ffourtie shillinges ster:
for euerie piece or parcell of goodes for which fraight
shalbe exacted or demannded or paid aboue, the said appointed rate or Contrarie to this present order.

folio 63.   The Brethern of the ffellowshippe shall pay to the
maisters and owners of the appointed shippes for Dover
peer monie outwardes twoe pence sterlinge vpon each

trusse of 9 Clothes sett, ffour pence vpon eache ffardell of 28 Clothes, And Inwardes the said Brethern shall pay a farthinge vpon each shillinge that the fraight he payeth shall amount vnto, and with this allowance the said maisters and Owners shall Content themselues, whether their shippes shalbe full fraighted or noe.

The Brethern of this ffellowshippe shall not paye or allowe anie fraight for the Wrappers of their Trusses, packes or ffardells of clothes, or other woollen Commodityes, havinge no more wrappers to a trusse pack or ffardell of Clothes etc^a then hereafter ys sett downe, vpon pain of tenn Shillinges sterlinge for euerie wrapper so paid or allowed for, Contrarie to the true meaninge hereof.

A pack or trusse of ten Clothes sett and vpwardes to twentie Clothes, havinge But twoe wrappers no fraight shalbe paid for the said twoe wrappers, reconinge other woollen Commoditie or wares ratably and proportionablye.

A pack or ffardell of twentie Clothes sett and vpwardes to thirtie Clothes hauinge but three wrappers no fraight shalbe paid for the said three wrappers.

A pack or ffardell of thirtie Clothes sett and vpwardes, havinge but four wrappers no fraight shalbe paid for the said four wrappers, and of the rest accordinglie, Provided that yf anie man shall putt into a trusse or pack fewer wrappers then ys abouesaid, he shall not therefore abate anie thinge, but pay fraight for all the sett Clothes in the said trusse pack or ffardell.

The shippes ladinge from Antwerp shalbe Enregistred with the Secretarie of the ffellowshippe or his substitute, from whome the maisters or owners of the said shippes shall receiue a bill for the Clearinge of them in the Sealandes Tolle, payinge him for the said bill 2^s 6^d ffes.

6

Yf anie maister or owner of shippe or Vessell shall
promise to serve the Companye and bee appointed to
lade ffrom Londone, and after that vpon other private
Cause or advantage, shall refuse to serve and will not
lade accordinge to promise suche maister or owner shall
forfeict fyve poundes ster: to the ffellowshippe to bee
levyed vpon him or his shippe at his next aryuall in
these partes beyond the Seas where the ffellowshippe ys
Resident.

folio 64   When anie shippe or Vessell servinge the ffellowshippe
shall aryue in these partes where anie Court of the
ffellowshippe ys held or Resident the maister or owner
shall within halfe a daye after his aryuall, deliver over
all the Cocketts or Certificates of ladinge none excepted
to the Treasurer, Secretarie or husband or other persone
appointed for the receipt thereof, at least a iust Content
or note of all his ladinge vpon his oathe to bee taken
thereto before the Governour or his Deputie and Certain
of the Assistentes or Associates, but omittinge to performe this Order he shall forfeict and pay tenn poundes
sterlinge without favour or pardone.

All Debates Controversies and questions arysinge between the Brethern of the ffellowshippe and the maisters
and Owners of shippes servinge the said ffellowshippe,
shalbe decided by the Appointers or by the Court, yf
they cannot decyde them.

None appointed shippe aryvinge in the place of Residence of the ffellowshippe one this syde the Seas, shall
serve anie private persone whomesoever, to be laden or
fraighted for anie porte or Countrie, without especiall
licence of the Governour or his Deputie, vpon pain to bee
debarred from servinge of the said ffellowshippe vntill
the maister or owner of suche shippe shall have paid

ffyve poundes sterlinge fyne to the house, except suche maister or owner were before his settinge foorth out of England bound by Charter partie for such voyage, otherwise he shall attend the Companies pleasure accordinge to his Charter partie for reladinge.

No maister or owner of shippe appointed shall take into his shippe, either goeinge or Comminge at one tyme aboue four passengers, beinge not brethern or bretherns servants of this ffellowshippe vpon pain of.[1]

The maister and owner of anie shippe Intendinge to serve the ffellowshippe shall not by himself or by anie other persone for him, make suite or labour to haue his shippe or other Vessell appointed vnto anie other persone whomesoever but the Governour or his Deputie and the Appointers, nor procure anie letters of Recommendation or means from anie other, to help him to lade then from suche as are ffree of the ffellowshippe, And yf anie maister or owner of shippe or other Vessell shall doe here against, yt shalbe lawfull (yf the appointers see Cause) to appoint him for that tyme, but he shall not bee admitted to serve the ffellowshippe in three yeares after by himself or with suche shippe or anie other.

CARYINGE OUT OF FORBIDDEN WARES. folio 65.

Yf anie persone of this ffellowshippe Carye or Conveye or Cause to bee shipped, Caryed, or Conveighed anie goodes or merchandise, forbidden to bee shipped, caryed or Conveighed or shall through willfullnes or negligence omitte to paye, suche Customes, Tolles or Duties as he ought to paye, so that throughe suche shippinge or willfull dealinge or negligence, the shippe or Vessell wherein

---

[1] The penalty is not given.

suche goodes are laden bee arrested and stayed, to the trouble and hinderance of other laders not offendinge in the lyke, suche persone shall not onlye bear and paye all the Costes and Charges which shall or maye aryse by suche arrest or staye, but over and above shall forfeict and paye one hundred poundes sterlinge to the vse of the ffellowshippe without favour or pardone. But yf yt shall please the Court at the humble suyte of suche persone to affoord vnto hym suche ayd as Convenientlye may bee given, the Charges Notwithstandinge shalbe borne by him, and so shall not at anie tyme after demannd anie amendes or allowans of the ffellowshippe; or of anie lader in the said shippe or Vessell arrested beinge none offender in the premisses, vpon pain of tenn poundes sterlinge.

No persone of this ffellowshippe shall enter anie goodes in the Tolle or Conveye one this syde the Seas, in anie other mans name then in the true owners thereof, vpon pain of ffourtie shillinges sterlinge.

Whatsoeuer persone of this ffellowshippe shall haue pack ffardell, trusse, maund, ffatt, tonne or other Vessell or thinge with merchandise to shippe, he shall within ffour and twentie houres after the bringinge downe thereof to the shippe or Water syde, Clear the Tolle by the right name and greatnes thereof, vpon pain of ffourtie shillinges sterlinge.

The Selandes Tolle shalbe Cleared and paid within ffour and twentie houres after the receipt of anie goodes or merchandise by anie brother of this ffellowshippe vpon pain of ffourtie shillinges sterlinge.

SHEW DAYE.

No Brother of this ffellowshippe by himself Broaker or anie other Persone whomesoever shall make anie shew or

sale of anie Englishe woollen Commoditye, but onlye
vpon three dayes in the weeke, that ys to saye one Mon-
daye, Wedensdaye & frydaye and vpon none other daye
or dayes, vnles for Consideration the Court shall otherwise appoint and ordayne, vpon pain to forfeict after the
Rate of 6ˢ 8ᵈ ster: per Clothe vpon all woollen Commoditie, which otherwise then by this Order is sett downe
shalbe solde ffourtie shillinges sterlinge for the shew follo 66:
onlye and besydes twentie shillinges for the officer or
pardone presentinge the same, whereof shalbe taken without favour or pardone. Provided Notwithstandinge that
yt shalbe lawfull to Conclude anie Bergain by buyinge or
sellinge so as the same bee orderlye shewed vpon the
shew daye, and that vnder Colour of deliuerie thereof
there bee not anie shew or sale made of more than was
before absolutely shewed & sold, and also vpon an unshew
daye to sell anie the aboue said Commodityes, by the
marke vnsight and vnseen, and absolutely, without shewinge the same, and not otherwise vpon the penaltie aboue
mentioned.

SHEW DAYE.

As often and whensoever as to the Court yt shall seem
good to appoint and nominate a sett shew daye either
vpon the aryuall of a Clothe ffleet, from Londone, or vpon
anie other Reasonable occasion, yt shall not bee lawfull
for anie persone of what degree or qualitie soever, to
make shew sale Certain pryce or deliuerie or to make
offer of shew sale Certain pryce or deliuerie, of anie Clothe
kersye or other Englishe woollen Commoditye, before the
said appointed shew daye vpon the penaltie of twentie
shillinges sterlinge for each Clothe so shewed, solde, made
Certain pryce of or deliuerye, Contrarie to the true mean-

inge of this Order, and for all other Englishe woollen
Commoditye after the rate to bee forfeicted and paid to
the vse of the ffellowshippe, And to the end that this
Order may bee the better observed and kept yt ys further
Ordayned and Enacted that no persone of this ffellowshippe of what degree or qualitye soever shall depart the
marte Towne, before he haue orderly purged himself by
oath before the Governour or his Deputie or in their absence before the Treasurer or Secretarie for the tyme
beinge, Concerninge the true observation of this Order,
vpon pain of ffyftie poundes sterlinge. yf either he shall
so depart without orderlye purginge himself by oathe, or
that he shall refuse to take the said oathe to bee forfeicted
and paid to the vse of the ffellowshippe.

No Brother of this ffellowshippe shall shew sell or deliver anie Clothes or other Commoditye whatsoeuer in
tyme of the sermon or divine exercise, or vpon anie
publicke fastinge daye, vpon pain of twentie poundes
sterlinge without favour or pardone, Neither shall anie
persone buy, sell, barter shew Cheapen or take view or
sighte of anie wares or merchandise whatsoever, in tyme
of Court generall or of Assistents or Associates, vpon the
same penaltie of twentie pounds sterlinge.

folio 67.   SHEW, SELLINGE.

The oath ffor shew dayes shalbe taken by euerie one of
this ffellowshippe, before or at the end of euerie three
monthes from three monthes to three monthes vpon the
penaltie of twentie poundes sterlinge.   And the oath for
keepinge the Marte Townes before or one the 23th daye of
Julie next, anno 1605 and so successiuelye ffrom the 23th
of Julie to the 23th of Julie next, euerie year except other
order bee taken vpon the penaltie of twentie poundes

sterlinge, and for euerie monthes not takinge or neglectinge to take the said oathe, after the days aboue sett
downe twentie poundes sterlinge per monthe, and the
offender to bee held suspect of the breache of the Orders,
and not to enioye anie benefyte of the ffree licence till he
have taken the said oathe for keepinge the Marte Townes,
and giuen the Court satisfaction one that behalf, Moreover no man to depart the Marte Towne before he have
purged himself by the said twoe oathes, vpon the foresaid penaltie of twentie poundes sterlinge, to the vse of
the ffellowshippe a third parte to the presenter.

No persone shall stand watchinge at the Corners or
ends of streetes, or at other mens Packhouses or at the
house or place where anie Clothe merchant or draper ys
lodged, nor seeinge anie suche in the Street shall run or
ffollow after hym with Intent to Entyce or lead hym to
his packhouse, vpon pain of fyve pounds ster:

No person shall lett or Interupt another in his Bergain
whether buyinge or sellinge nor by anie signe devyce or
other means by himself. Broaker or other shall attempt
to hinders or breake of another proceedinge, vpon pain
of ffyve poundes sterlinge.

No persone shall sett one worke anie broker not sworn
or allowed of by the Court, vpon pain to forfeict after the
rate of ten shillinges sterlinge: per Clothe ffor all Englishe
woollen Commoditie, and ten shillinges sterlinge vpon
the hundred ffor all other Commoditye sold with anie
suche Broaker, without favour or pardone, Neither shall
anie vnffree broaker receiue anie broakerage for wares
sold for a brother of this ffellowshippe, but the seller
shalbe bound to pay the same vnto the Treasurer to the
vse of the Companye or presenter of the aforesaid Offence.

ORDERS IN TRADE.

No persone of this ffellowshippe shall sett his goodes to
bee solde in the handes of anie yonge man his servant or
other persone, that ys not ffree of the said ffellowshippe
or his Atturney in these partes, but all and euerie persone
folio 68. of this ffellowshippe which shall haue Trade or doeinge
in these partes where the ffellowshippe ys Priuileged,
shall haue ffreemen which have taken oathe and Charge
to the ffellowshippe accordinglye to doe his or their busynes, or to bee their ffactors and Atturneys, vpon pain of
tenn poundes sterlinge, to bee forfeicted to the vse of the
ffellowshippe ffor euerie hundred poundes worthe of wares
goodes or Commoditye, bought or solde by anie persone,
otherwise then by this order ys appointed, An Atturnye
may bee made by a letter of the Constitutor signed by
him and one of the Wardens of his Companie and directed
to the Governour or his Deputie and the Court signifyinge what Authoritie more or lesse ys giuen to the said
Atturnye ffurther then the which the said Constitutor
shall not stand Charged or aunswearable, And when an
Atturnye ys to be dismissed the lyke order ys to be observed one that behalf.

No persone of this ffellowshippe shall buy or sell, for
anie foreign or vnffree persone of the ffellowshippe, nor
shall Colour or ffree the goodes or merchandise of anie
suche, or send or Conveighe the same by water or land
nor haue parte deale or portion with him in anie merchandise (Fuelles horse, harnas, Victuaill, Munition of
Warre thinges for store or household stuffe, not to bee
put to sale again always excepted) nor in his name shall
Conveighe or Transporte their goodes Covertly or ouer-
lye, by sufferinge his name or his marke to bee vsed by
him, Neither shall take vp suche foreign or vnffreemens

goodes for him, Neither shall Cover or Colour the same
by entrie in the Custome house or other place Inwardes
or outwardes, or by anie other means whatsoeuer, vpon
pain of one hundred poundes sterlinge for euerie tyme he
shalbe found or approoued to haue offended in the premisses or anie parte thereof, Notwithstandinge yt shalbe
lawfull to receiue vp and sell for anie vnffree persone the
Commodityes of England, ffraunce, Spain, Portuigall, and
other straunge and foreign Landes, as also to sell in anie
place of the Lowe Countries, or other Countrie where the
ffellowshippe ys Priuileged, anie Kynde of merchandise
brought by Sea directly by the owners thereof out of
ffraunce, Spain, Portuigall Eastland or out of anie other
Countrie saue England, payinge Impositions & dutyes to
the house for the same and not otherwise.

No Brother of the ffellowshippe shall take or deliuer
by exchaunge or rechaunge anie monie for the vse or be-
hoofe of anie persone not ffree of this ffellowshippe, vpon
pain of tenn poundes vpon euerie hundred poundes so
taken or deliuered, Except suche monie to bee Employed
for some far voyage or to bee transported into some other
Countrie then England, or for the Charges of somme
Student, Trauailer or suche lyke persone the Kings true
subiect.

No persone of this ffellowshippe by himself or by anie folio 69.
other whoemsoeuer, shall bergain or sell within the
Realm of England to anie straunger foreign or vnffree
persone of the said ffellowshippe, anie Clothes, Kerseyes,
or other woollen Commodityes of the said Realm with
Condition to bee paid for the same in anie other place
without the said Realm, nor for anie other monie, then
for Current monie of England.   Neither vnder Colour of
deliuerie of the said monie growinge of anie suche sale

by exchaunge or otherwise, shall assure or bear anie
Adventure of the said goodes by him so solde, or of anie
parte or parcell of the same, vpon pain to forfeict and
paye vpon euerie Clothe twentie shillinge sterlinge fyne,
and vpon all other woollen Commodityes after the rate,
solde or disposed of as ys aforesaid.

No person of this ffellowshippe shall suffer anie foreign
or unffree persone or straunger, to stand or bee with hym
or to have anie goodes in his pack house shew house etc,
or shall parte or deale with anie such either in buyinge
or sellinge, vpon pain of fourtie shillinges sterlinge Toties
quoties.

No persone of this ffellowshippe shall make anie retayler or vnffreeman perfectlye privye to his buyinges, or
shew hym his letters of advyce, Invoyces or Accomptes,
or give advyce of the pryce of foreign wares to anie suche;
neither shall sell his wares to anie vnffreeman for Current
monie of England, after anie manner rate or reconninge
of the exchaunge expresselye; but simply and plainlye
without anie manner of Colour of deceipt, vpon pain of
twentie poundes Sterlinge as often as he shalbe herein or
in anie parte hereof found faultie.

No persone of this ffellowshippe of what Estate or Condition soever, shall suffer anie manner of straunger born
or straungers servant, to keep his shewhouse or pack
house or to bee privye to his sales or buyinges of his
goodes, by Consigninge the same to bee sold or bartered
or disposed by straunger or straungers servant, or shall
stand in packhouse or shewhouse with anie suche, vpon
pain of three skore poundes sterlinge for euerye tyme he
shalbe found to offend herein or in anie parte hereof. And
yf anie persone of this ffellowshippe shall sett anie suche
stranger or straungers servant one worke, or emploYe

anie suche in the sale of Englishe woollen Commoditye,
he shall forfeict and pay to the vse of the ffellowshippe
over and aboue the aforesaid penaltie of three skore
pounds sterlinge, a fyne of twentie shillinges sterlinge
vpon euerie Clothe by suche straunger, sold bartered or
disposed of, Contrarie to the true meaninge of this Order,
and upon all other woollen Commodityes after the rate.

TRADE. INDIRECT DEALINGE. folio 70.

Yf anie persone of this ffellowshippe by himself or by
anie other, openly or Covertly directly or Indirectlye one
this syde the Seas, or in England, shall deale or handle
with anie trader or Traders, vnto or into anie forbidden
partes out of the Marte Towne or Townes, in anie place
one this syde the Seas, where the ffellowshippe ys or
shalbe hereafter Privileged, whether yt bee in the Lowe
Countries or in Germanie, or in anie other Countrie
Towne or place lyinge between the Riuers of Somme in
ffraunce, and the Schage in Dutchland, or whether the
said Traders bee ffree of the ffellowshippe of Merchauntes
Adventurers of the Realm of England, or bee not ffree,
or subiectes borne within his Maiesties Dominions, or
shall sell or barter vnto them or anie of them directly or
Indirectlye, anie the Commodityes of the foresaid Realm,
or shall buy or sell or retayne or handle for them or anie
of them, whether yt bee in or out of the marte Townes
anie wares or Commodityes whatsoever either Englishe
or foreign, or shall employe them or anie of them or anie
foreigne or straunger borne, as factors or doers for anie
manner or Trade trafficque or ffeat of merchandise,
whether yt bee in sale of Englishe wares or other or for
the providinge or return or furnishinge of foreign wares,
deliveringe or takinge vp of monie by Exchaunge, In-

tres, or deposits, receiptes or payments, or by anie other
means shall Countenance, Credite abett, or maynteyn or
sett them or anie of them aworke, to the preiudice of the
orderlye trade of the abouesaid ffellowshippe or to the
furtheringe, vpholdinge or Cherishinge of Indirect dis-
orderlye, Intrusiue, Coulorable or fraudulent dealinge,
and doeinge Contrarie to the laudable and good orders of
the said ffellowshippe, and the true meaninge thereof
heretofore made & provided or Contrarie to this present
Act or Ordinance, Likewise yf anie persone of this ffellowshippe shall giue cary or send, or Cause to bee given
caryed or sent the markes of Clothes, Kerseys, or other
Englishe woollen Commodityes, sett pryce, or by anie
means Covertlye or Ouertlye directly or Indirectlye shall
enter into anie Bergain or Contract for Clothes, Kersyes
or other Englishe woollen Commodityes, or for other
wares of the Realm of England bee yt either by himself
or by some other in anie place prohibited by this present
Act or Ordinance, or by anie other Act or Ordinance in
force, he and they as abouesaid in anie point or Clause
aforesaid specifyed or mentioned offendinge, shall encurre
the paynes and penalties made and provided by anie
former Acts or Ordinance or orders against Indirect or
Coulorable dealinge, trading out of the marte Townes or
against the Infringers Transgressors, offendors Violators
folio 71. or Impugners of the said Actes, orders, or Ordinances, or
of anie of them presentlye in force or vnrepealed and accordinge to the pourport tenure and true meaninge of the
same, to bee levyed and paid without favour or pardone
to the vse of the ffellowshippe, Provided that yt shall and
maye bee lawfull for anie ffree brother of this ffellowshippe by provision and till other order bee taken by
Court in anie parte or place lyinge within the Lowe

Countryes one this syde the Seas, to buy or sell foreign
Commodityes or Wares to Chaunge and rechaunge to receiue and paye take up and deliver monie at Intrest, or
Deposits to his owne vse, or the vse of somme ffree
brother of this ffellowshippe or of other persons permitted
by former order.

INDIRECT TRADE.

No persone of this ffellowshippe shall take or receiue
over into his handes in Bergains or otherwise, the bill or
obligation of anie other brother of the said ffellowshippe
due in these partes, except he make the said brother or
his factor or servant privye to suche takinge or receivinge
over, and have the Consent of him or one of them in his
absence so to doe, vpon pain of twentie poundes sterlinge
vpon euerie hundred poundes of suche or lyke monie as
the bill or obligation taken and receiued over ys fflemishe
or sterlinge, to the vse of the ffellowshippe.

Yf anie manner of persone of whatsoever place or Countrie he bee shalbe indebted or owe anie somme of monie
Little or much, to anie brother of this ffellowshippe, or
by Contract or bergain made hathe promised to deliuer
wares or goodes, whether yt bee for his owne proper debt,
or for anie other persone. And when he shalbe demaunded payment or to performe Covenants, denyeth or
refuseth to doe, as a good and iust merchaunt ought to
doe, or in defraudinge of his Creditors taketh advantage
of the ffreedome of the marte or martes in the partes
where the ffellowshippe ys abydinge, after suche personne
shalbe found prooved or knowen to have donne anie of
the premisses no brother of this ffellowshippe shall buy
or take in barter anie goodes or wares to hym (yf suche
brother knowe yt) belonginge in what place or whose

handes soever the same bee sett, nor willinglye shall sell anie Clothe or other merchandise vnto him or vnto anie other for him or in his name for dayes of respyte or tearme of payment in anie manner directlye or Indirectlye, but shall receiue his redie monie before he deliuer his Clothes or other merchandise out of his packhouse or Custodie, vpon pain of twentie poundes sterlinge to bee forfeicted & paid, the one half to the vse of the ffellowshippe and the other half to the presenter.

DELAYNINGE OF DEBT ETC.

And yf anie persone whatsoever straunger or other, shall vnivstly stoppe or withold anie parte of his dutie or debt, ffrom anie brother of this ffellowshippe vpon surmise pretence or Caville whatsoever, vpon knowledg thereof, The Governour or his Deputie or in his absence the Treasurer for the tyme beinge shall by a beadle give warninge vnto suche persone, yf he bee in Towne foorthwith to make satisfaction or payment to suche Brother or else that at the next mealtyde the Brethern of the ffellowshippe shalbe forbidden to deale with him in trade of merchandise, till he have agreed with the partie grieved or have given him satisfaction, and that the same appear and bee knowen, And yf vpon suche warninge he refuse to make satisfaction or payment as aforesaid The Governour or Deputie or in their absence the Treasurer shall foorthwith at the next mealetyde, whether yt bee dinner or supper give Commaundment over the tables generallye, that no man of the ffellowshippe vpon pain of ffyve poundes ster: doe directly or Indirectlye, buy, or sell, barter shew or take view of anie wares or otherwise deale with suche persone or anie for him willinglye, wittinglye or to his knowledg, till he have made payment or satis-

faction as aforesaid, and that the same bee publickely
made knowen and signifyed over the tables, wherein
Ignorance pretended by beinge absent at the warninge or
Commaundment givinge, shall not bee accepted, And
suche brother beinge therevpon or afterwardes satisfyed,
shall foorthwith Intimate the same to the Governour or
his Deputie or in his absence the Treasurer, to the end
that yt may bee signifyed over the tables at the next
mealtyde, and that men again may bee at libertie to deale
with such merchant as aforetymes; The lyke order shalbe
observed for suche as havinge bought Clothe Kersye or
other Englishe or foreign wares or Commodityes whatsoever of a brother of this ffellowshippe, for dayes of payment shall Refuse or not give his bill or obligation for the
same, made in dew fforme accordinge to Contract or bergain passed, before he departe out of the marte Towne,
And yf anie Merchant depart the marte Towne without
Consent of the merchant seller, before he haue given
Contentment for anie wares as abouesaid by him bought,
whether yt bee by bill or obligation or other Contentment
the Brethern of the ffellowshippe, vpon Complaint of the
partie grieved, shalbe foorthwith publickely warned by a
Beadle by order of the Governour or his Deputie or in his
absence by the Treasurer for the tyme beinge, not to
deale in ffeat or trade of merchandise, in anie sorte with
suche persone till he haue satisfyed and Contented the
partie grieued, vpon pain of twentie poundes sterlinge,
And yf anie persone of this ffellowshippe shalbe found to
Complain without iust Cause, or havinge receiued his
Contentment after suche warninge shall not foorthwith
give knowledg thereof to the said Governour or his
Deputie or in his absence the Treasurer for the tyme
beinge, to the end that it may bee publickelye signi-

folio 73.

fyed, he shall forfeict a fyne of tenn poundes sterlinge twoe third partes to the vse of the ffellowshippe the other third parte to the presenter.

ORDERS IN TRADE.

The Cottons solde within the Towne of Bergen op Zoom, shalbe there measured vpon pain of ffourtie shillinges sterlinge, to bee paid by the seller not causinge the same to bee measvred as aforesaid, or sufferinge them to bee measured elswhere.

No persone of this ffellowshippe shall buy anie Clothe or other Englishe woollen Commoditye within the Towne of Middelbroughe, and sell the same again in Antwerp, vpon pain of ffourtie Shillinges sterlinge per Clothe and vpon all other woollen Commodityes after the rate.

No Brother of this ffellowshippe whatsoever for himselt or for anie others directly or Indirectly, shall handle or deale openlye or Covertly one this syde the Seas or in England, with anie traders into Norenberch or other the Townes or partes of Highe and of Lowe Dutchland, whether such Traders bee brethern of the said ffellowshippe or bee other subiectes of England, not ffree of the said ffellowshippe, Neither in sellinge vnto them or anie of them anie the Commodityes of England, nor in buyinge of them or anie of them anie foreign Commodityes or wares vpon pain of fourtie shillings sterlinge, for euerie Clothe and other Englishe woollen Commodityes after the rate so sold, and twentie poundes sterlinge, vpon euerie hundred woorth of foreign wares so bought, handled or dealt in with the said Traders or anie of them, Contrarie to the true meaninge hereof, to bee levyed vpon the offenders or their goodes without favour or pardone.

No Brother of this ffellowshippe shall lycence his apprentyce to vse the Trade of a merchant Adventurer for himself or to his owne vse, before suche apprentyce haue served the ffull terme of seauen yeares by Indenture, & have leave of the Court, so to doe vpon pain of ffourtie poundes sterlinge, Provided that yt shalbe lawfull for anie maister to vse & Employe his servants stock in feat of merchandise for his said servants benefyte, & to licence him to vse the Trade of the Staple or other straunge trades, without Incurringe anie penaltie therefore.

TRADINGE WITH APPRENTYCES.

folio 74.

None Apprentyce or sonne of anie man of this ffellowshippe, that might Clayme the ffreedome of this ffellowshippe by Patrimonie beinge an Apprentyce or Covenant Servant, whether bound to serve for ·wages or without shall at anie tyme duringe his apprenticeshippe or tyme of Covenants by way of merchandisinge, buy sell occupie or Trade for himself, nor for nor with anie other mans apprentice or Covenant servant, nor ffor nor with anie ffreeman of this ffellowshippe, nor anie other persone whomesoever without the privitie or Consent of his maister agreable, with the orders of the ffellowshippe in this behalf first had in writinge, vpon pain that suche Apprentyce or Covenant servant shalbe ipso facto, exempted and depryved of all Claym of ffreedome and libertie in the said ffellowshippe, And yf anie ffree Brother of this ffellowshippe beinge a Covenant Servant (whereby he ys in state and qualidie of an apprentice) whether he serve for wages or without, shall att anie tyme by way of merchandisinge, buy or sell, occupie or trade, either for himself or for or with anie other persone or persons ffree or vnffree, without speciall licence of his maister

7

first had in wrytinge, he shalbe ipso facto Disfranchised
vtterlye dismissed and exempted of and from all the libertyes & ffreedome of this ffellowshippe.   Moreover yf
anie apprentyce or the sonne of anie ffreeman of this ffellowshippe, beinge an apprentice or Couenant Servant for
tyme, or yf that anie ffree brother that ys a Couenant servant, whether he serve for wages or without, or whether
he hathe orderlye licence of his maister to trade and
occupie for himself, or not, doe at anie tyme lend out his
maisters monie, or morgage, pawne sell or alienate his
maisters bills of debt, or his debtes or Actions, or take vp
anie monie by exchaunge or pay anie monie by exchaunge, or accept or subscribe anie bill of exchaunge,
or anie bill of debt, for anie man then onlye for and to
the vse and behoof of his maister or otherwise shall become bound or suertie for anie man, except yt bee with
the speciall Consent and licence of his maister first had
in wrytinge, he shalbe ipso facto deprived exempted and
expelled, of and from all the liberties and ffreedome of
this ffellowshippe.   And furthermore yf anie ffree Brother
of this ffellowshippe shall at anie time, have anie manner
of dealinge by way of merchandisinge, with or for anie
apprentice, without the privitie and Consent of his maister
agreable with the Orders of the said ffellowshippe first
had in wrytinge, or shall enter partnershippe with anie
suche apprentice or shall have anie manner of dealinge
folio 75. by way of merchandisinge with or for anie Covenant servant (vnless by some Clause in his Covenant he may
trade for or with other men besydes his maister to his
owne vse and thereto bee also qualifyed by the Orders of
the ffellowshippe, whether suche apprentice or Covenant
Servant doe serve for wages or without, or yf the said
ffree brother shall accept or subscribe anie bitt of ex-

change or take vp anie monie by exchaunge, or pay anie
monie by exchaunge, for or to the vse of such apprentyce
or Covenant seruant, in qualitie as aforesaid, without the
privitie and Consent of his maister first had in wrytinge,
or shall receive, retayne buy or sell or cause to bee receiued retayned bought or sold, anie wares merchandise
goodes or things for or to the vse or behoof or by the
direction of suche apprentyce or Couenant Servant as
aforesaid, without the privitie and Consent of his maister
first had in wrytinge, or yf anie ffree brother of this ffellowshippe doe cause anie apprentyce or Covenant Servant in qualitye as aforesaid, by way of merchandisinge
to buy or sell anie manner of goodes wares or merchandise for suche ffree brother, or doe Cause him to subscribe
or accept his bill or to giue out anie bill to his vse or
become bonnd or suertie for hym or to lend sell chaunge
transporte, morgage pawne or alienate anie of his maisters
billes monie debtes goodes or merchandise, vnles yt bee
by and with the privitie Consent and licence of his maister ffirst had in wrytinge, the said ffree brother so Enteringe into partnershippe or that shall have anie manner of
doinges or dealinges with or for anie suche apprentice or
Couenant Servaunt as aforesaid, shall forfeict a fyne of
one hundred pounds sterlinge for the first offence, to the
vse of the ffellowshippe without favour or pardone, and
offendinge the second tyme in the premisses or in anie
point thereof shalbe ipso facto disfranchised vtterlye exempted and dismissed of and ffrom all libertie and ffreedome of this ffellowshippe, Provided that by this Act the
libertie heretofore giuen to apprentyces for tradinge in the
Staple or into Spain, or other partes out of the lowe Countries and Germanie or elswhere, where the ffellowshippe
ys not privileged with licence of their maisters, or ffor

tradinge with licence of the Court and their maisters
after he or they have served seaven yeares duely, shall
not bee abridged. Neither one the other syde ys yt
meant that hereby the former whereby men are restrayned
ffrom givinge leave to their apprentyces to trade for themselues and their owne use, before they have duelye served
seaven yeares, shalbe repealed. But the said order to
stand in as full fforce and Virtue as yf this Act or ordi-
folio 76. nance had never been made, And further yt ys Ordayned
that none apprentyce or Covenant servant shall presume
to doe or doe the busyness of anie other persone whomesoever besydes his maisters and his partners Joint Companie before his maister have by his letter sufficiently
Certifyed this Court and that yt bee enregistred that the
said maister hathe given leave to his said apprentyce or
Covenant Servant, to doe the busynes of the said persone
and nominate hym, vpon pain of disfranchisement for
suche apprentyce or Covenant servant, and of ffyftie
poundes sterlinge fyne for the maister for not Certifyinge
as aforesaid, Provided also that yf anie man shall Enter-
tayne a ffree brother of this ffellowshippe to bee his Covenant Servant and shall not thereof orderlye advertyse
this Court, before he employe his said Covenant Servant
one this syde the Seas, and that anie ffreeman of this
ffellowshippe shall for want of suche publicke advertisement Ignorantlye and vnwittinglye Committ anie thinge
in dealinge with the said Couenant servant Contrarie to
anie Clause or point in this Ordinance specefyed, he shall
not therefore Incurre the daunger of disfranchisement,
but bee Censured by the Court for his doeinges or fact as
they in reasone & equitie shall fynde to bee meet and apperteyn, And yt ys ffinally Ordayned that the old Act
formerly made and appointed to bee read at the Admission

of men to their ffreedomes and at other tymes Covenient, shall from the 29th day of September next anno 1608 bee repeled and held voyd and of none effect, and that then this Present Ordinance shall Comme in place and bee of validitic, and shalbe read at the Admissions of apprentyces, within termes one this syde the Seas, and at Generall Courtes in England four tymes everie yeare at least at the begyninge of the Martes or once a quarter vpon pain of ffourtie shillinges sterlinge to bee by the Governour or his Deputie and by the Secretarie and either of them, forfeicted to the vse of the poor, yf through their negligence or forgettfullnes the said Ordinance shall not bee read in manner as aboue said, Made at Middelbrough the 19th day of the monthe of May Anno 1608.

No Brother of this ffellowshippe shall fetche anie wagon or wagons, or make anie Composition or Contract with wagoners for the Caryage of his goodes, or take the Wagone horses by the head, vpon pain of tenn shillinges sterlinge.

ORDERS IN FEAT OF MERCHANDISE.

No persone at the Comminge or aryuall of the poste from anye place shall enter into the Porters lodge, but shall receiue his letters at the windowe without the lodge vpon pain of 40^d fflemishe toties quoties.

No persone of this ffellowshippe shall Carie throughe the streetes anie strawe, mattes, ropes, Sarplers or suche lyke baggage or anie goodes wares or merchandise, except he maye Conveighe the same closely vnder his arme or in his sleeve, vpon pain of 40^d sterlinge for euerie tyme.

No persone of this ffellowshippe residinge in the marte Towne or Townes, shall lodge, or keep his pack house in anie Inne, Taverne, Victuaillinge house, or suche lyke place, vpon pain of ffyve poundes sterlinge for euerie monthe that he shall Lodge or haue this pack house.

No manner of persone Englishe or straunger, vsinge the ffeat of a Broaker vnder the ffellowshippe, shall or may tell to hyre by direct or Indirect means, anie Chamber, Packhouse or Warehouse to anie persone of the said ffellowshippe, or other, neither shall he receiue to table as guest or boord anie manner of persone whomeso-ever otherwise then Gratis, without especiall licence of the Governour or his Deputie and the Court first had, vpon pain of dissmission for one whole year, In the which tyme none shall speake ffor his readmission or tolleration, vpon pain of tenn poundes Sterlinge, Yf yt bee an Assist-ent or Associate, and ffyve poundes sterlinge Yf yt bee one of the Generalitie that shall speake one his behalf, And for that yt ys not alone found preiudiciall that anie Broakers of this ffellowshippe shonld either lodge table or boord anie persone of the said ffellowshippe or other as abouesaid, But withall that anie Brother should hyre or take and house, and let out parte thereof again to Broak-ers or to giue anie Broaker lodginge or habitation in his said house or dwelling, as some haue donne and practysed thereby Indirectlye Endevouringe and goeing about to frustrate and make void the aboue written order, Yt ys therefore further Ordayned and Enacted that no Broaker of the ffellowshippe shall lodge or haue his dwellinge or habitation either ffreelye or for or without rent or Con-sideration therefore to bee giuen or paid, within anie house or dwellinge taken or to bee taken by anie brother of the ffellowshippe, vpon pain of suspensation ffrom his Vocation of ffree broaker for one whole year, And no Brother of the ffellowshippe shall hyre or lett out for rent or Consideration, or giue vnto anie free Broker house

room lodginge or habitation in anie house or dwellinge
by him hyred, vpon the penaltie of fyve pounds ster: for
euery monthe that anie suche Broaker shall abyde lodge
or haue habitation in his house or in any parte thereof
directly or Indirectlye.   folio 78.

No Brother or this ffellowshippe shall take or hyre out
of the handes of anie other brother his Chamber, Pack
house or Warehouse so longe as he will keep the same or
hathe not given yt ouer vpon pain of twentie poundes
sterlinge, and yet not to enioye anie suche Chamber,
Pack house or Warehouse, neither shall anie man take
or hyre anie more pack houses, warehouses or shew
houses, then he presentlye shall himself occupie or need,
and so lett them out to others at higher pryces then he
hyred them for, vpon pain of tenn poundes sterlinge.

No persone of this ffellowshippe shall departe the marte
Townes without payinge his duties, to the Tolleners Convoy maisters, meaters ployers, or suche lyke, vpon pain
of payinge doble to him that will laye out the monie and
pay suche duties for the said persons.

No man buyinge wares in the marte Townes or in these
partes to bee sent into England, shall vtter or sell or
Cause the same to bee vttered or solde (Victuaill or
Munition of Warre excepted,) but where the Buyer or
proper owner of the said Wares ys dwellinge or resident,
or in the porte or place where they shall aryue from these
partes in England, without sendinge or Convoyinge of
them or anie parte of them to anie other place to bee
solde or vttered, vpon pain of tenn pounds sterlinge.

No person of this ffellowshippe shall buy anie Gantish
Linnen Clothe, except the same haue lyen open and vn-
packed the space of one monthe and a daye before, vpon
pain of ffourtie shillinges sterlinge, Neither shall buy or

Cause to bee bought anie Gantishe or other Linnen Clothe made in fflanders, without the same bee folded and ployed halfe a fflemishe ell in lengthe or thereaboutes, beinge also vnbennden, vpon pain to forfeict for euerie, Maund, Pack, or other lyke thinge so bought, tenn poundes sterlinge.

No Brother of this ffellowshippe by himself or other directly or Indirectley, shall buy or Cause to bee bought anie kynde of silke wares accustomed to bee measured by what name soever the same may bee Called, or Clothe of Golde or Silver with anie kynde of measure but as ffolloweth To wytt whoesoever shall buy anie Velvitts, shall reduce the palmes of euerie peece of Velvitt severally into flemishe ells, by addinge four palmes and no more to euerie hundred palmes, and so Consequently to lesse number of palmes after the same rate, and then devide the same by three as hathe been accustomed, And shall reserve the Choice vnto himself either to aceept of

folio 79. suche measure as aforesaid without other measuringe or to haue the same measured by the Bridges ell, as the manner and Custome ys in the Cittye of Antwerpe to measure, Bologna Silkes, florence, and all manner of other lyke silke wares, And yf anie man shall offend Contrarie to the true meaninge hereof he shall forfeict ffyve poundes sterlinge, vpon each peece of silke by him bought, and otherwise measured or receiued, to the vse of the ffellowshippe without favour or pardone.

Euerye Brother of this ffellowshippe buyinge anie wyne, Oyl, Soap, or such lyke wares, at Bergen op Zoom shall alwayes reserue and Condition in the bergain makinge, that the seller shall pay the accyse dew for the same, vpon pain to forfeict the valew of the goodes.

Euerie persone buyinge woad shall diduct for Tare of

a bale six poundes, and of a Ballett four poundes vpon pain of 5^s sterlinge vpon euerie bale or Ballett, ffor which he shall deduct lesse Tarre.

No persone of this ffellowshippe shall send anie wares or merchandise to fayres or marketts in England, agreable with an Act made in Snixon marte 1500 and Confirmed by the Kynges Maiestie, vpon pain of ffourtie poundes sterlinge.

No Brother of this ffellowshippe shall by himself or others to his knowledge falsefye or fraudvlentlye, mingle, handle, vse or pack pepper, hoppes or anie wares or Commoditye whatsoever, Neither shall buy anie suche ware or Commoditye which he knoweth before hand to bee falsefyed, fraudulently vsed, mingled, handled, or packed, vpon pain of ffourtie poundes sterlinge.

No persone of this ffellowshippe shall pay or allowe for anie monie by exchaunge taken or deliuered within the Cittye of Londone, vnder Colour or pretext of reward, Courtosie or other Consideration, aboue 2^s 1^d vpon the hundred poundes, and so after the rate for lesse sommes or bigger, vpon pain of ffourtie shillinges sterlinge.

No Brother of this ffellowshippe shall pay or receiue anie monie dew by exchaunge either for himself or anie other in anie other place, but whereas the bill of exchaunge maketh mention, And no man takinge or deliveringe monie by exchaunge within the Realm of England, for the Lowe Countries, Germanie or these partes neere adioyninge, shall make or Cause to bee made his billes payable in anie other place or Towne then where the ffellowshippe holdeth marte or Residence, vpon pain of fyve poundes ster: vpon euerie hundred poundes.

No persone of this ffellowshippe shall sett one worke folio 80. anie Meater or employe anie other in that feat or facultie,

except he bee orderlye admitted and established therein
vpon pain of ffyve poundes sterlinge to bee forfeicted to
the vse of the ffellowshippe, as often as he shall offend
against this Order, Neither shall anie man sett one worke
anie ployer or Ployers of Linnen Clothe or Canvas
bleached or vnbleached, but onlye suche as are Admitted
by the ffellowshippe vpon pain of fourtie shillinges sterlinge, And no man shall cause or suffer anie Linnen
Clothe whatsoever or Canvas, which he hathe bought to
bee measured folded or ployed in the house, lodginge or
pack house of the seller, vpon pain of ffourtie shillinges
sterlinge.

No ffardells packes, fattes buttes, chestes, maundes,
pypes, or anie other lyke luggage or goodes, shalbe
brought into the Englishe house by anie man of the
ffellowshippe beinge none Officer of the same vpon pain
of fourtie shillinges sterlinge.

No persone vsinge the ffeat of trade of merchandise into
these partes beyond the Seas where the ffellowshippe ys
Privileged, shall by himself or by anie other persone or
persons for him, or to his vse Indrape, worke or make or
Cause to bee Indraped wrought or made anie Clothe,
Kersye, Worsted or anie other woollen Commoditye, nor
shall parte deale or make Companie by anie manner of
means with anie suche persone or persons as shall En-
drape worke or make of woollen Commoditye or that
keepeth anie open shewhouse shop or·retayle others, then
ys lawfull by the orders of the ffellowshippe, vpon pain
of three skore poundes sterlinge.

No Retayler shall parte or deale with an occupyer in
Grosse nor no dealer in Grosse with a retayler, vpon payn
of three skore poundes sterlinge.

No Brother of this ffellowshippe or other for hym or to

his vse shall Cutt out Sell or retayle anie Englishe
Clothe Kersye or other woollen Commoditye by the ell or
halfe Clothe half or kersye etc. or suche lyke or lesse
quantitye in the Towne of Middelbroughe or elswhere one
this syde the Seas, vpon pain of three skore poundes
sterlinge. And nevertheles to bee obnoxious to the
mulctes and penalties of the Lawes of the Towne or place
where suche Cuttinge out retaylinge or Sale shall happen.
Yf by the Retaylinge drapers of the said Towne and
specially of the Towne of Middelbroughe aforesaid, he
shalbe sued or troubled for doinge Contrarie to the Privileges of the said retaylinge drapers or shopkeepers, except in Case in the order Concerninge retaylinge permitted.

No persone of this ffellowshippe dwellinge within the folio 81.
Cittye of Londone, and vsing or exercysinge by himself
or by or with anie other in Companie the ffeat and Trade
of a Merchant Adventurer into the Lowe Countries or
Germanie, or other Privileged place one this syde the
Seas, shall by anie means Sell or Cause to bee sold for
him by retayle or Cuttinge out anie Kynde of merchandise, nor shall keepe open shoppe or shewhouse, vpon
pain of three skore poundes sterlinge, And ffor better explanation of this order all sale, in or by the lesse quantitie
then hereafter ys sett downe, ys vnderstood to bee retaylinge or Cuttinge out viz:

Mercerie and all other silke wares by the peece.
Draper and damaske by the peece.
Gantishe Clothe by six peeces at least.
Holland Oversysell and suche lyke Linnen Clothe by
the peece.
Normandie Canvas whited and vnwhited by the peece.
Camerick or lawne by the halfe peece.

Workinge or Coshion Canvas by the peece.

Canvas broad or Narrow by the hundred aulnes or elles.

Napkin Canvas by the peece or dosen.

ffustians, milamis, Jene, and bombasine by the tenn peeces.

ffustians of other Sortes by the Bale.

Buckrams of Bridges by the half Chest.

Buckrams of other makinges by the doosen or half doosen.

Sack Clothe by the three peeces.

ffustians Naples by the six peeces.

Chamletts by the tenn peeces.

Sayes, Moccadoes and others of lyke bredth by the tenn peeces.

Stitchinge and sowinge silke by the twoe poundes at least.

Silke lace and all kynde of silke Ryband by the tenn doosen.

Gold and silver thred by the pound.

Frisado by the Case at least.

Peper by the hundred poundes.

Suger, Almondes, Ryce lycorys by the hundred.

Annysseed, Comminseed, Brasile graynes, gawles, Bayes by the hundred.

Corents Prunes Dates by the twoe hundred.

Synemon and all fyne specerie by the 24lb at least.

Ginn and Coperos by the twoe hundred.

All other drogerye and Grocerye as they are bought here.

Onionseed by the hundred.

folio 82. Oyle Civile by the pype.

Rape Oyle and honye by the barrell.

Pytche Tarre and Sope ashes by the half last.

Madder by the Bale.
Wood by the Bale.
Soape by the barrell.
Spanishe Soap by the fflaskett.
Flaxe and Hemp by the Hundred.
Alam by the Bagge.
Waxe, Rosen, Cottone Woole by the hundred.
Hoppes by the sacke or pockett.
Brown paper by the twentie Bundells.
White paper by the twelve Realmes.
Fethers by the Bagge.
Bottles by the doosen.
Nitral by the two hundred.
Glasses by the Case or Chest.
Woollen Commodityes of all Sortes by the peece.
Pinnes by the twelve doosen.
Wool Cardes by the tenn doosen.
Playinge Cardes by the twelve doosen.
Parrys thred by the ffytie boltes at least.
Pack thrid by the hundred doosen.
Knyves by the six doosen.
Boulter Clothe by the Bale or twelve peeces.
All other small wares by the Grosse.
Buffe Hydes by the peece.
Spanishe Roamishe, Flaunders, Skinnes by the half
doosen.
Baste or Strawe Hattes by the Maund.
Brushes of Heath and Hayre by the Grosse.
Blades by the thousand.
Needles by the doosen thousand.
Inckle by the doosen peeces.
Peecinge thred by the doosen pound.
Barres of Irron ffor Windowes by the Hundred.

All other Iron by the Tonne.

Dryppinge and fryinge pans & all other Iron Worke by the hundred.

Wyre by the twoe ringes of three hundred poundes.

Batterye by the hundred.

Lockes and Hindges and suche lyke by the doosen or as they are bought here.

Tapistrye ffrom aboue 2ˢ 8ᵈ th' elles & vpwards by the peece.

Tapistrye ffrom 2ˢ 8ᵈ to 12ᵈ the ell of all sortes not lesse then 25 doosen.

Carpettes Linsye and suche lyke by the six doosen.

Turnhout Tykes by the Maund.

Brussells and Counterfeyt Tykes by the tenn peeces.

Cushion Clothes fyne by the three doosen.

Cushion Clothes Course by the six doosen.

Verdure and Middlebankes by the twelve peeces.

Budge Black by the doosen.

ffrenche dornicx by the peece.

Castridge Wool by the sack or half sack.

Quiltes by the doosen or half doosen.

Yt shalbe lawfull for anie persone of this ffellowshippe not dwellinge within the Cittye of Londone, to sell anie his ware or merchandise at the porte where he shall aryve or within his owne house as well to Inhabitants of the place where he dwelleth as to others or to keep open shop or shewhouse, so that he haunt not nor ffollowe ffayres, or retayle not by lesse measure then yard or ell, nor by lesse waight then a pound, Lykewise yt shalbe lawffull to sell by retayle & in Grosse in open shop or shewhouse or otherwise elswhere within the Realm of England, All manner of Victuaill Iuelles of Golde, or silver, precious stoones, or pearle, brought or Transported out of anie for-

eign Countrie, and also in Grosse to sell all manner of
Commoditye growinge or wrought within the Kynges
Dominions, Lykewyse yt shalbe lawfull for anie brother
of this ffellowshippe dwellinge in Londone to sell by retayle or otherwise so as he keep no open shoppe anie
kynde of Munition of Warre to anie persone whatsoever,
And also to sell by the best means he can anie goodes or
merchandise which beinge Spoyled or Empared by anie
mischaunce at Sea, or otherwise are not vendible to the
Retaylers at the same Cittye without all fraude or Couen,
And also to Cutt out by the yards and otherwise to serve
himself and his ffreendes and acquaintance one or two
peeces of kersyes, or a Clothe or twoe, which he shall
within one year dye for himself, or his store, and also
suche Remnant of dyaper damaske or other stuffe (so yt
bee not silke) within one year after he shall have Cut out
for his owne vse wearinge or occupyinge somme parte
thereof. Further yt shalbe lawfull ffor suche Brethern of folio 84.
the ffellowshippe as have trade into and out of ffraunce,
or anie the dominions thereof, to sell suche Canvas or
Linnen Clothe as they bringe from thence in suche Cittyes
Townes and other places as they haue accustomed in
wholesale, Also yt shalbe lawfull to buy for anie of the
Lordes and others of the Counseill or to sell in England
to anie of them, anie manner of Commoditye whatsoever
or howsoever, and moreover to buy for anie ffreend anie
provision of howshold or other thinge, not exceeding
therein the value of tenn poundes sterlinge, in a Marte,
And yf anie Brother of this ffellowshippe shall by anie
means worke, devise or procure the breakinge or makinge
voyd of this Order or anie parte thereof, he shall forfeict
ffourtie poundes sterlinge.

Yf anie persone of this ffellowshippe being a retayler or

shopkeeper within the Cittye of Londone or elswhere, in
other sorte then ys prescribed by the aboue written order,
shall Intend to leave of his retaylynge and becomme a
merchant in Grosse, he shall one whole year before he
attempt to doe anie ffeat of merchandise in these partes,
signifye or declare by woord or wrytinge in open Court
one this syde the Seas, suche his intent vpon pain of
three skore poundes sterling, And so leavinge to retayle
keep shop, shall not return vnto the same again in ffyve
years after ffollowinge, vpon pain lykewise of three skore
poundes sterlinge.

Yf anie brother of this ffellowshippe shall by uniust or
fraudulent dealinge, or by discontinuinge of his Trade or
Comminge over one this syde the Seas, as accustomed
deferre or protract the payment of his debt, aboue the
space or tyme of six monthes, havinge no sufficient or
reasonable Cause to alledge for the Justifyinge of suche
his doeinge, suche persone shall not in anie wyse bee
Chosen Assistent or Associate, but shalbe holden and
Esteemed as in State of Bankrupt one that behalf, And
yf anie man vsinge or exercysinge the ffeat of merchandise or seekinge his lyvinge by Trade of buyinge or sellinge, shall forsake the place of his aboad or dwellinge for
debt and without payinge his Creditors, or shall embesell
or Conveighe away privilye his goodes, to the defraudinge of those to whome he ys iustley Indebted, or aband-
oning his house or goodes, flyeth or take the sainctuarie
or keepeth himself hyd or Close within his house or without in somme other place, Or yf anie persone shall volun-
folio 85.
tarilye suffer himself to bee arrested or outlawed or shall
Bank-
ruptes.
willinglye yield himself to prisone for dutie or debt growinge of wares solde or monie delivered, or other iust or
lawfull Causes, he shalbe reputed deemed and taken for

a Bankrupt, And yf anie persone of this ffellowshippe
shall becomme bankrupt or Insolvent in manner as aforesaid, and that within one year after the same ys openlye
knowen he doe not plainly and snfficiently declare and
prooue before a Court of Assistents, or to suche as shalbe
appointed by the said Court to take knowledg of his Case,
that suche his Bankruptinge and Insolvencie proceedeth
of pure necessitie or of suche accydents or occasions as no
merchant or trader can well eschew, he shalbe from
thencefoorth dismissed of and from the libertyes of this
ffellowshippe, Never to Enioye or recover the same
again, Neither shall anie sonne or servant of his borne or
bound after that tyme receiue anie ffreedome of the said
ffellowshippe by his Tittle, but performinge the aboue
written order and bringinge a true accompt vpon oathe in
dew tyme or Shewinge by other good proofe to the Contentment of the Court that his faylinge proceeded not of
fraude or sett purpose but of meere necessity etc, as aforesaid, he shalbe Continued in his former ffreedome, saue
that he shall never bee taken or Chosen to bee Assistent
or Associate in the ffellowshippe, And further yf anie
man shall not pay or satisfye his Creditor or Creditors for
suche monie as he shall take vp by exchaunge, within six
weekes after the day that yt falleth dew, (except there
bee reasonable Cause therefore and so bee found by the
Court) he shalbe forever disfranchised of and from the
liberties of this ffellowshippe and never bee admitted to
the same again as a Bankrupt, Lykewise yf anie persone
which may Claym or ys Intituled to the ffreedome of this
ffellowshippe by Patrimonie or otherwise vsinge trade of
merchandise or retaylinge in England or elswhere shall
becomme bankrupt or Insolvent before he make Claym or
bee admitted to the same ffreedome he shalbe holden to

8

present an Accompt and give satisfaction to the Court, ffor suche his Insolvencie or Bankruptinge, within the tyme of twelve monthes after the same, in default whereof he shall never bee admitted into the ffreedome of this ffellowshippe, but for ever bee debarred, ffrom the libertyes thereof, his Clayme or Tittle, notwithstandinge, Lastlye yf anie man Clayminge the ffreedome of this ffellowshippe whether the same bee by Patrimonie or by service before suche his Claym, shalbe found a Coosener or felon and of suche lyke heynous Crymes Convict, he shall not in anie wise bee receiued into the ffreedome or libertyes of the said ffellowshippe, And yf yt fall out (which God forbidd) that anie havinge taken oath to this ffellowshippe shall after his admission bee found to bee anie Coosener or ffelon and thereof or of suche lyke

folio 86. heynous Crymes, Convict as aforesaid suche persone shall
Tare.[1] ipso facto bee Clean debarred cast out and Cut of ffrom that his said Required ffreedome, and never after bee Readmitted, And everie Snixon marte there shalbe four persons Chosen & deputed by the Assistents to enquyre who haue been Bankruptes or Insolvents or have behaued themselves Contrarie to the order abouewritten or anie parte or branche thereof the year goinge before, and a table of their names shalbe hunge vp in the Secretaries Office or Court house to the end that they may bee publickly knowen.

No persone of this ffellowshippe shall doe good anie Certificate or Shortnes in Clothe measured at Cullen or elswhere by the yard as of late hathe been practysed, vpon pain of ffyve poundes sterlinge and the Secretarie

[1] The orders concerning the "tare" begin with the second half of the folio.

shall not make him attestation of the said abatement vpon the same penaltie.

From the first day of Maye anno *1605* yt shall not bee lawfull for anie of the ffellowshippe to sell or Barter anie Clothe vpon anie other (but better Conditions in Construction of the Court) then these herevnder sett downe, and agreed vpon the twentith of February in the abouesaid year, between the merchantes or Traders in Englishe Clothe dwellinge in the Vnited Provinces one the one partie, and those of this ffellowshippe one the other partie, approved and allowed by the Lordes, States Generall of the said Provinces by an Act of theirs bearinge date the 16th day of the said monthe of February, vpon the penaltie of ffourtie shlllinges sterlinges per Clothe for each Clothe sold or bartered otherwise to the vse of the ffellowshippe without favour or pardone.   All Clothes wherein anie faultes are or may bee found shalbe visited and tared in the place of the first sale thereof either by good men Chosen by the parties buyer and seller, or by sworn Visiters alredie Ordayned or to bee ordayned by the magistrate Indifferently, either before the Clothes bee Caryed from thence or after at the Choyce of the buyer.   Provided that all shortness and narrownesse the same appearinge by orderlye Certificate of sworn men or meaters of the Townes where the buyers are dwellinge Conformable to the old manner of meatinge, with a right or yust Brabantes ell, and none other shalbe donne good without anie difficultie or question, The said sworn men or meaters for the preventinge of all fraude shalbe bound to measure all Clothe pretended to bee short or narrow, the same beinge first made wett in suche manners as by mutuall agreement shalbe found to bee most meet and Convenient, Yt ys also vnderstood that no Clothe hold-

inge wett two Brabantes ells bredth, shalbe accompted
narrow, neither shall their bee anie abatement made to
the seller for a quarter of a Brabantes ell shortnes in anie
Clothe. The Charges of the Clothes returned shalbe
borne by the sellers, but the Adventure by the buyers,
And to avoyd all needles sendinge back, and adventure
yf so bee that anie faultes of linnen or Cotton threddes
appear in the dyinge or that anie faultes bee pronounced
doubtfull after visitation in the place of the first sale, the
finall visitation and estimation of the said faultes shalbe
made in the Townes where the buyers dwell, Conditionn-
allye that the sellers shalbe advertised thereof, that so
they may either take back their Clothes or doe good the
Tare.

And the Seller shall alwayes haue his Choice after that
Tare ys made either to take back his Clothe or to doe
good the Tare yf the Tare amount vnto three powndes
flemishe or aboue, The tyme of eleven monthes after the
sale of anie Clothe being expired no man shall pretend to
haue anie Tare, or gett anie amendes for anie faultes
whatsoever.

For as muche as this ffellowshippe of merchantes Adventurers throughe the large Privileges vnto them
graunted by this Towne of Embden are ffree here of all
Tolles or Customes, as well in bringinge in as in Caryinge out of their goodes and merchandises yet notwithstandinge throughe the late sinister practyse of some
merchantes straungers & especially Netherlanders (for
their own lukers sake) have offred vnto Certaine Brethern
of the said ffellowshippe to sell them wares here, but to
make deliverie thereof at Breame and other places out of
this Towne yea also at the verie gates of Bome without
the Towne, And so to bee hether brought and Conveighed

in vpon suche Bretherns adventure and Charge, not onlye
to the defraudinge of the dew Tolles, which for suche
wares by the said Straungers ought here to bee paid, And
thereby bringe the said ffellowshippe in great Contempte,
but also to hazard the losse of the said Privileges or at
least to bee abridged, And so muche the narrowlier
looked vnto and Exacted vpon like as at Antwerp Hambroughe (throughe such Indirect dealinges) hathe been
to muche apparant, And vpon suspition alredie here
partly begonne, yf in dew tyme the same & lyke practyses bee not by strictnes of order provided for and pre-
vented, Where vpon at a Generall Assembly holden in
Embden the 19th of June anno 1579 after all which well
wayed, Considered & throughlie debated vpon, yt ys of
the Generallitye in the said Assemblie by Erection of
handes Ordayned and Enacted, That no brother of this
ffellowshippe shall from and after this Assemblye by himself or anie other for him in his name, to his vse or by
his Consent & procurement directly or indirectlye in
manner as aforesaid so deale in buyinge and sellinge
within or without this Towne of Embden anie wares or
merchandise whatsoever as the Towles for the same shalbe
Coloured and not here by the merchaunt straunger aunsweared and payed vpon pain that euerie suche brother
so Colourablye vsinge dealinge or doeinge Contrarie to
the true meaninge of this Act shall forfeict and pay
twentie powndes vpon euery hundred powndes of all **folio 88.**
suche wares and merchandises whatsoever so brought in
or Caryed out, to be exerted vpon the offenders without
favour or pardone, Provided alwaies that all suche Brethern which shalbe found offenders in the premisses before
the makinge of this Act to Incurre suche penalties as
hathe been heretofore in lyke Case made & agreed vpon

Provided further that this Acte nor anie Article or Clause therein Conteyned shall extend to the dirogatinge or frustratinge of the Act made at Londone the 7th of May last & Confirmed at Antwerp restrayninge, buyinge & sellinge out of;the Marte Towne.

ORDERS CONCERNING THE BRETHEN OF NEWCASTLE.

None of the Brethern of this ffellowshippe dwellinge at Newcastle vpon Tyne bringinge into these partes where the said ffellowshippe ys Privileged woole Commonly Called black woole, shall sell or vtter the same vnder eleven markes the sack Neither white woole vnder eighteen markes the sack, vpon pain of tenn pouudes sterlinge Toties Quoties.

None of the said Brethern shall sett one worke for buyinge or sellinge or doeinge anie ffeat of merchandise anie persone not ffree of the ffellowshippe, vpon pain to forfeict vpon euerie sack of woole ten pounds and upon euerie hundred ffelles ffourtie shillinges sterlinge, and vpon other Commodityes accordinge to the ffynes provided in lyke Case by the Ordinance of the said ffellowshippe.

None of the said Brethern shall give to anie persone or persones anie ffleece or ffleeces of woolle, vpon pain of twentie shillinges sterlinge Neither shall they or anie of them allowe for Tare of a Sack of woolle aboue four stoane, upon pain of twentie shillinges ster: for euerie sack, neither give or promise anie other gift or Consideration one that behalf vpon the same penaltie.

None of the said Brethern vpon bergain of Wooll shall giue or promise anie Bankett, present or gyft, vpon pain of ffyve powndes sterlinge Toties Quoties, Neither shall anie of them give for Brokerage of Woolles aboue 2s 6d vpon a sack or peke, vpon pain of ffourtie shillinges sterlinge.

None of the said ffellowshippe shall sett one worke anie other Broker, then suche as ys admitted and sworn by the ffellowshippe, Neither shall play Brokerage to anie suche vpon pain of the penalties heretofore Provided by the Orders.

The Brethern of Newcastle shall not shippe or Cause _{folio 89.} to bee shipped woolle felles or other their Commodityes to anie other place within the Lowe Countries or Germanie but to the marte Towne or Townes only, and there only vent sell and vtter the same, vpon the penalties provided by the orders against Traders out of that Marte Towne, except ffor good Consideration the Court shall dispence with this order & give them licence to shippe vnto somme other Towne or place ffor vent of their felles, Lead, Coales, and stones onlye, and no other Commoditye of England, in sale whereof they shall continually ffollow the Orders one that behalf made and provided.

The said Brethern shall not vse or exercyse feat of merchandise elswhere but in and not foorth of the Marte Towne or Townes, lyke as other Brethern of the ffellowshippe are bound to doe by the Ordinances, vpon the penalties therefore provided, except they bee permitted by Court to buy out of the said Marte Townes where they best may provide the same Sope, Hoppes, and Madder as of late hathe been tolerated, or to shippe for somme other place as aforesaid.

None of the Brethern of Newcastle shall take anie more apprentyces to bee ffree of this ffellowshippe then ys permitted to other brethern elswhere vpon the penalties therefore ordayned, Neither shall anie apprentyce to bee bound for lesse tyme then tenn yeares service by Indenture orderly made except suche apprentyce may otherwise bee ffree of the ffellowshippe by Patrimonie, vpon pain of twentie poundes sterlinge.

The Brethern of Newcastle shall Cause their Apprentyces to bee orderlye Enrowled, and suche Enrollment to bee Endorsed with the daye monthe & year of the date thereof vpon the Indenture, vpon pain of fourtie shillinges And yf anie apprentyce shalbe Enrowled at Newcastle the Governour there shall keep Register thereof and yearly send over note of those which shalbe there so Enrowled.

The Brethern of Newcastle shall yearly in the Pasche Marte pay or Cause to bee payd vnto one of the Treasurers of the ffellowshippe or other lyke officer appointed by Court one this syde the Seas, the somme of eight powndes sterlinge by waye of Impositions in the name and for the dew of all those of the ffellowshippe Residinge and dwellinge in the said Towne, vpon pain of the doble omittinge or Neglectinge the same.

folio 90. ORDERS IN FEAT OF MERCHANDISE: DAYES OF
PAYMENT.

Till this Court shall take other order one this behalf, yt ys by Authoritye of this ffellowshippe Ordayned and Enacted that yt shall not bee lawfull for anie persone of the said ffellowshippe for or by himself or for or by anie other whomesoever at anie tyme or tymes in bergain sale barteringe distraction or Creditinge out of anie Clothe, Kersye, or other Englishe woollen Commoditye, to give anie longer daye of payment for or vpon the said Commoditye then onlye six Monthes and no more, either right out or for twoe or more termes of payment at his pleasure, Not exceedinge the said six monthes day of payment directly or Indirectlye by way of abatinge With the buyer of the said Commoditye for redie money or vnder anie Colour pretext or means, or for anie Considerations Contrarie to the true meaninge of this Ordinance, nor allowinge nor givinge in aboue one monthes tyme, nor aboue nyne per Cent for Intrest in rebatinge for the said monie with the said buyer, And to the end that this Ordinance may duely and strictly be observed and Con-sequently doe that good which ys expected thereby, Yt ys further Ordayned and Enacted, that euerie persone ot this ffellowshippe either absolutely ffree or admitted within termes as also suche as are vnder others which presently are here Resident or abydinge, or that hereafter shall repair hether to Trade abyde or bee Resident, shalbe bound to the observation of the said Ordinance vpon an oathe therefore devised or to bee devised to bee taken, by all those here presently Resident or abydinge, between this present daye and a thursday at night next, and by all those that shall hereafter repair or comme hether to trade abydinge and bee Resident here, within four and twentie houres after he or they shalbe warned by one of the Beadles to take his or their oathe Concerninge the observation of the abouesaid Ordinance before the Deputie, Treasurer, and Secretarie or before anie twoe of them & twoe of the Assistentes, vpon the forfeicture of ffyftie poundes ster: to the vse of the ffellowshippe with-out favour or pardone, and Nevertheles to bee Compelled by the Deputie and Assistentes to obey this Ordinance and to take his oathe as appertayneth.

No persone ffree of this ffellowshippe nor anie other for him shall shippe or Transporte or Cause to be shipped or transported anie Clothe or other Englishe woollen Com-moditye, either from Londone or from anie other porte or place of the Realm of England, or from the Towne of Middelbrough directly or Indirectly, to Stade, Hamborow, or to anie other Towne or place Scituate within or near

the River of Elb, vntill suche tyme as by the Court either
here or at Londone a shippinge shalbe agreed vpon and
folio 91. appointed, vpon the penaltie of ffourtie shillinges ster:
per Clothe, for eache Clothe that shalbe Caryed or transported Contrarie to the true meaninge of this Ordinance
directly or Indirectly, to bee levyed vpon the persons and
goodes of the Offenders without all favour or pardone, a
third parte to the presenter.

ORDERS IN FEAT OF MERCHANDISE: PAWNINGE OF BILLES.

No persone of this ffellowshippe of what degree or
qualitie soever, ffrom the day of the makinge of this present Ordinance, shall take vp or prolonge anie monie at
Intrest or in deposito, of or with anie straunger whatsoever in these partes of beyond the Seas, where the
ffellowshippe now ys or hereafter shalbe Privileged, and
besydes his own bill or obligation for the repayment of
the said monie, shall giue deliuer or lay in pawn or
pledge or Cause to bee given, deliuered, layd in pawn, or
pledge, the bill or obligation or the billes or obligations
of anie Clothe buyer, or of anie other merchaunt straunger
his debtor, or the debtor of his maister or of anie other
that Employeth him, or anie Clothe Kersye or other
Commoditye or ware whatsoever either Englishe or foreign, for the assurance of the Repayment of the said
monie at the daye or dayes appointed, Contrarie to the
true meaninge of this present ordinance, directly or Indirectly vpon the penaltie that yf he bee a ffreeman that
shall offend or Transgresse against this Ordinance, and
bee duely Convicted thereof, he shalbe suspended from
all trade and ffreedome in this ffellowshippe or enioyinge
anie benefyte or libertye in the same, the ffull Space of

three yeares next after suche offence Committed and Convicted. And yf he bee a Servant or apprentyce or a factor
in qualitie of a Servant or apprentyce, he shalbe vtterly
disfranchised and Cut of from all ffreedome in the said
ffellowshippe for ever, except he shall shew and make
due proofe to the Court that the bill or billes, or Clothes
or other ware or Commoditye Pawned, pledged or deliuered, ffor Assurance to anie straunger or straungers as
aforesaid, Contrarie to this Ordinance were pawned
pledged or delivered by the expresse order in wrytinge or
by Command or order by woord of mouthe of his maister
or other that employeth him, In which Case the said
maister or other that Employeth the said Servant Apprentice or factor, and Commandeth or giveth him order to
the willfull breach or Violation of this Ordinance, shalbe
suspended from his ffreedome for the term of three yeares
as aforesaid, and the servant apprentyce or factor in
qualitie of a servant or Apprentice shalbe dealt withall,
as the Court in their discretion shall finde meet and Convenient one this behalf. Enacted at Middelbroughe The
29ᵗʰ of Marche anno 1611.

Yf anie persone of this ffellowshippe shall hereafter sell folio 92.
anie Clother or Englishe Commoditie either for dayes of
payment or for other Contentment to anie persone or his
factor whatsoever, he shall before or at the deliuerie of
the said Clothe or other Englishe commoditie, or at or
before the departure out of the Marte Towne of the said
persone or his factor, be bound to demaund and receiue
his Contentment, either by bill of debt in dew forme
made, or by redie monie, or by assignation vnder the
hand-writtinge of the buyer or his factor, for him, upon
the penaltie of 20ˡˡ sterlinge, except presently after the
departure of suche merchant or his factor without givinge

Contentment, the partie grieved doe comme and Complain to Mr Deputie or in his absence to the Treasurer of the Companie for ye tyme beinge, And yt shall not be lawfull for anie persone of this ffellowshippe to sell vnto broakers anie Clother or other Englishe Woollen Commoditie for absent merchants or Clothe buyers by Commission or letters to the said broakers vpon the penaltie of XL sh. sterlinge, to be forfeicted for eache Clothe so sold Contrarie to the true meaninge of this order & the lyke heretofore provided one this behalf, Enacted at Middelbroughe the last day of December anno 1611.

Whereas[1] the Clothiers of our Countrey haue of late yeares taken liberty to them selves to make fase and deceiptefull Cloth in great and intollerable measure, not only to the greate losse of the bretheren of our Company tradinge in the same, but alsoe to the vtter discredit of the draperie of our land and the aduancement of the trade of Clothmaking in other Countreys, and this because the due execucion of the statute prouided by Parliament for the true making of our English Cloth, hath been greately neglected, as well by the bretheren of our ffellowshipp, that are buyers of the sayd Cloth, as by the ouerseers and searchers to whose care and power the sayd execucion of the Statute is lefte and comytted, ffor reformacion of ye sayd neglect on the parte of such buyers as are brethern of this ffellowship. It is by the Deputy and Assistants

---

[1] A change in the handwriting occurs at the beginning of this ordinance, the new hand continuing the manuscript to the bottom of folio 94 where another hand adds two London ordinances of 1617, dated April and August respectively. Then follow January and March ordinances of the same year, and several for 1618 in still another hand. There is also a corresponding change in the spelling.

of this ffellowship with the Consent of the Generallity
of the same in ample nomber assembled, at a generall
Court holden in Hambrough the 27th daye of ffebruary
anno 1612 ordayned enacted and established. That.

Euery brother of this ffellowship that shall at any
tyme buy any vndrest Clothes to be shipped for any the
ports of Germany or the Low Countreys, shall reserue in
his hande Tenne shillings sterling vpon the price of euery
such Clothe for the doing good of all such forfeitures and
penalties as are by the statute of our land allowed to the
buyer of such Cloth, as vpon due search falleth out to be
faultie. And shall by himself or some other for him
within Tenn dayes next after the buying of such Clothes,
waigh open view and measure all & euery of them,
whether sealed as formerly searched or not, and make all
such due search as can be made of them being drye.
And yf by such search there shalbe found, any want or
desert either of length breadth or waight, then he shall
make abatement for the same with the Clothier or seller
as followeth viz ffyve shillings starling for euery pound
waight that shalbe found wanting of 59^{li} in Narrow liste
Pack cloth of 62^{li} in broade list pack cloth of 70^{li} in ffyne
Castell combes, and of 76^{li} in Worcester Clothes and stop-
lists. Also for the breadth wanting of Sixe quarters and
an half, after the rate of Tenn shillings for the whole
Cloth, ffyve shillings for the half Cloth, and twoe Shillings Sixe pence for the quarter. Lastly for such length,
as shalbe wanting of that which is specefied on the seale,
after the rate of three shillings ffoure pence a yarde besides the true value of such want or at least the true value folio 93.
thereof. And for that the Clothiers or Searchers take
advantage by a generall practise of setting on the letters
N. and ff vpon the Seales of their Clothes to signify

narrownes & faults thereby to avoide the giving satisfac-
cion for the sayd faults: it is further enacted & ordained
that euery brother of this ffellowship, that shall buy
any of the Clothes soe marked, shall not withstanding
search the sayd Clothes, and make rebatement for the defects found in them.   All which want of length breadth
and waight soe found as aforesayd, shalbe respectiuely
adiusted and certified ouer to the factor or Seruant, to
whome the sale of such Clothes is comytted, together
with the Invoyce of the same, vpon payne of ffourty
shillings starling per Cloth, for default in any of the
premisses.

And for the finding out of the offendors against this
order, It is further ordayned that euery brother of this
ffellowship, dwelling or residing in London, and trading
in vndrest Cloth, shall once euery quarter, vpon a sett
daye to be appointed by the Court there, come and
appeare before the Governour or his Deputy, and the
former order being distinctly read vnto him, shalbe
purged by his Corporall oath, whether he hath truly performed the same in euery parte and pointe, or not.   And
not coming or refusing to take such oath, shall not be
allowed any Deputie's bill for passing of any goods at the
Custome House, vntill he haue conformed himself in this
behalf.

Forasmuch as by the Lawes of the land, we are
abridged from hauing any allowance of such moneye's as
are abated vs by Merchants Strangers, for defects of our
Clothes, after they are sent beyond the seas, And forasmuch alsoe as in these late yeares, we haue been greately
wronged by the Merchants in those partes and their
Cloth Worker's that buy our Clothes, who make intollerable and insupportable Tares, as well vpon the true as

vpon the faulty Clothes, and in regarde thereof doe keepe
back and deteyne Yearely, greate somes of money very
wrongfully againste all reason or Conscience, to the exceeding greate losse and hindrance of the Bretheren of
this Company, many tymes most vniustly keeping from
vs more then we haue gotten by our Clothes, after our
greate aduentures and large forbearance of our moneys.
And for the sweetenes of the gaine they haue found
thereby doe still Continue their excessive Taring and
extorting vpon. vs ffor reformacion whereof, It is by the
Gouernour Assistants and ffellowship, and by the authority of this Court ordained & enacted as ffolloweth.

That no brother of this Company of Merchants Adventurers of England trading in Cloth or other wollen
Comodities, within the Lymitts of the Empire, whether
he be a dealer therein for himself, or by his ffactor, partner, Covenant seruant or apprentice, shall neither for
him self his Master principally make sale of any such
Clothes or other woollen Comodities by himself or any
other by his or their order or appointment, directly or indirectly, but shall at the bargaine making Couenant and
Condicion with the Merchant or other that buyeth them,
that he or they will allow of no Tare or abatement vpon
any Cloth or Clothes by them soald, vnles the Merchant
or other that buyeth the Clothes will take a view of them,
and measure them dry in the packhouse or some other folio 94.
Convenient place before they be wett or carried out of the
towne, and that the sight and presence of the merchant
that selleth them, which being done it may be lawfull for
him to make tare thereof according to such defects, faults
or Wants, as shalbe then found in the sayd Clothes and
not otherwise. And yf yt shalbe proved that any brother
of this Company of what quallity soeuer he be, shall

make any allowance of any Tare but according to such
lymitacion as is before expressed, whether yt be done
directly or indirectly, by himself or by any other man or
meanes by any ffreeman or other not ffree of the Company, shall forfeit and paye for euery Cloth soe soald as
ffolloweth, viz. Yf he be a ffactor that shall sell otherwise then before is mencyoned, he shall paye vpon euery
Cloth soe soald Twenty shillings starling, and the owner
of the Cloth soe soald Twenty shillings more, and yf the
ffactor being called in question to know who was the true
owner of the Cloth or Clothes soe soald, and will not dis-
close the true proprietor of them: the sayd ffactor shall
paye twenty shillings more for euery Cloth soe soald:
But yf the owners of the said Clothes shalbe found to be
consenting vnto the sale of them, then he shall forfeyt
and pay twenty shillings more. ffurthermore yf any
sonne not ffree, apprentice or Couenant seruant, shall
Contrary to the true meaninge of this Acte, make any
sale of any Clothes, otherwise then in manner as before
is recited, the sayd sonne apprentice or Couenant seruant
shall ipso facto be disfranchised, and made vncapable of
any ffreedome by the Company, and the father, master or
owner of the sayd Cloth, or Clothe's, shall forfeyt and
pay for euery Cloth soe soald Twenty shillings. But yf
afterwards it shalbe proued that the sayd Cloth or Clothes
were soe soald with the privity knowledg or Consent of
the sayd father, master or owner of them, then the sayd
father master or owner shall pay for his offence vpon
euery Cloth twenty shillings more and the sayd sonne
apprentice or Couenant seruant shalbe restored to the
former state of ffreedome.

Lastly yf any persone shall present any offendor or
offendors in this kinde, making due proofe of his pre-

sentement he shalbe requited for his good seruice therein
with the one moyety of that penalty, that shalbe leuied
and taken of the offendor or offendors that shalbe evicted
and condempned by his proof. And the presentor of any
such offence done Contrary to the meaninge of this Acte,
shalbe accompted a true and honest brother, and yf his
meanes be small, vpon his suite vnto the Court, he shall
haue a promise of the next reuercion of anie inferior office
in the Companies guift, and be preferred thereunto before
any other whatsoeuer. Even soe concluded at a generall
Court holden in London the 28ᵗʰ daye of September anno
1610.

Att[1] a generall Court in London the xiiij^th of Aprill
Anno *1617* It was ordeyned that for the giving of worke
vnto the Cloth workers the Breathren of this ffellowship shall cause all their white Clothes before they be
shipped to be by the said Cloth workers weighed opened
pervsed searched and made vpp againe and for this worke folio 95.
beinge done in the day cloth to pay the Cloth worker iij^d
vppon euery Cloth. Likewise that the Tenth cloth at
least of all such whites shalbe wett by the said Cloth-
worker and soe searched, for his paines wherein and in
making the same vpp againe he shalbe paid xij^d for every
Cloth. And yf any brother of this ffellowshipp shalbe
found to faile in the observacion of this order he shall forfeit v^s for every cloth wherein he soe faileth the one halfe
to the presenter of the disorder, and the other halfe to
the house.

Att a generall Court in London the vj^th of August Anno
1617 It was ordered that the breathren of this ffellowshipp shall make such abatement with the Clothier for

---

[1] Change of handwriting.

9

the faults found in the clothes that be searched in the wett as is formerly ordeyned for faults found by dry search, and vppon the like penalties as for default of the said former order is provided.

Vntill[1] the Company set further order herein, it is agreed that it shalbe free and lawfull for euery brother of this Company to transport kersies bayes Perpetuanes and other new draperies and generally all Comodities (except broad Cloth) to any parte whatsoeuer of Germany or the Lowe Countries payinge impositions for the same only after the rate of xij[d] for a short Cloth, and noe Imprest money. London the 21th January anno 1617.

Yf any person of this ffellowshipp by himself or any other shall at any time enterlyne or alter his sealed entries or bill after the same shalbe sealed with the Companies vsuall Seale, or shall practize any other waies whatsoeuer to defraud the howse of ymposicions or imprest moneyes, he shalbe disfranchised and banished from the liberties of the said ffellowshipp for ever. And if any sonne not free, apprentice or Covenant servant vnto any brother of this ffellowshipp, shall committ the abuses aforesaid or any of them, such sonne, apprentice or Covenant servant shalbe made vncapable of the freedom of this ffellowship and be vtterly excluded from all benefitt thereof for ever. Provided that if any apprentice or Covenant servant shalbe constrained by the order and Comaund of his master to doe any thing Contrary to the true meaninge of this Act, such apprentice or Covenant servant shalbe cleared, and his master holden Culpable of the breach of this order, and liable to the punishment of the same. London the 23th March anno *1617*.

[1] Change of handwriting.

Culloured Clothes drest, Baies, Kersies, stockings, Perpetuanes and all new draperies are to be free to be bought and shipped without Stint, and henceforth the stint to be reconed and observed only in white Clothes.

London 7th June anno *1618*.

Noe brother of this ffellowshipp shall send or Cause to be transported any Clothes from one marte towne beyond the Seas to another without first taking oath before the deputy of the Company in the place whence he transporteth such Clothes, that the same haue beene and remayned in the mart towne where they first arrived at the least the space of vj monthes vpon paine of XL^s a Cloth for infringing this order. London the 7th of October & 16th January anno *1620*.

At a generall Court in Londone the 23th of ffebruary anno 1619. Vpon Complaint made by the yong men, that some great traders, doe buy vp such quantities of Clothes weekly, that the yong men cannot get Cloth for their money. It was ordered that whosoever shall hereafter shipp more then his respective Stint, he shall pay doble imposicions and doble imprest for all that he shall soe Shipp.

ORDERS TOUCHING THE DISPOSINGE OF CERTAIN BE-
QUEST MONIE LEFT BY SUNDRY PERSONS TO THE
FFELLOWSHIPPE WITH COPIES OF ARTICLES OUT
OF THE LAST WILLES OF THE SAYD PERSONS CON-
CERNINGE GUIFT OF THE SAYD BEQUEST MONIE.

Whereas thorow the Godlye zeal and good Inclination
of diverse Charitable disposed and well affected persons,
and late Brethern of this ffellowshippe of merchants
Adventurers of England, there hathe been left and be-
1 queathed by the last willes and Testamentes of the said
persons sundrie sommes of money to bee at tymes and
with Conditions ffreelye bestowed, at the discretion of the
worshipfull the Governour or his deputie and ffellowshippe aforesaid, vpon yongemen new beginners and men
of small means. Therefore to the end that the Orderly
Employement and disposinge of the said monie may bee
accomplished to good purpose and accordinge to the Testators myndes and last willes, and that the same may bee
more manifest and knowen both to the Court where the
graunt remayneth (beinge the Chief Court one this syde
the Seas) as also to those that shall becomme sewters.
Yt ys at a Generall Court holden in Middlebroughe the
ffyve and twentith day of Julye anno 1583, by Authoritye
of the deputie Assistents and ffellowshippe of Merchantes
Adventurers of England, Ordayned and Enacted as ffolloweth.

2   Inprimis that all suche monie alredie bequeathed shalbe
payd and repayd in England in sterlinge monie, after

sewt past, at the tymes and in order herevnder sett downe.

Item at the first or second Court to bee kept one this syde the Seas, where the Authoritye of the Companie may bee Resident, euerie Pasche Marte suche as seek to 3 Enioye the vse and benefyte of the monie by the late deceased Mr Jones Mr Carre Mr Roger Knotte Mr Berbeck Mr Rogers and Mr Clerk bequeathed, shall make their suyte by themselues or their ffreendes by woord or wrytinge, which shalbe graunted or denyed at the Courtes discretion and pleasure.

Item Euerie persone that hathe vpon his sewt as aforesaid obtayned graunt of anie parte of the forementioned 4 bequest monie, shall the second day after the begyninge of the Sinxon Marte then Imediatelye next followinge, have delivered vnto him by the Treasurer in Londone for the tyme beinge, the said somme of monie by him graunted and shall Enioye the same Gratis.

Item the said persons whose bequest ys graunted, shall within that marte at a Court of Assistentes in place where the said graunt ys passed, now make and present twoe suerties, whoe after orderly tryall by ballatinge, and so allowed, shall Joinctly with him enter dew boundes for 5 the Repayment of the said monie at the tyme and in order thereby to bee Enioyned, And yt ys to bee vnderstood that after the graunt past euerie suche persone as shall neglect to present & putt in suertyes enter into bondes, or ffor anie other Cause proceedinge by his default, protracteth the Callinge for and receipt of the said monie 5 after the foresaid day limited, shall beare the losse of the tyme and forbearance, and notwithstandinge make Restitution at the verye day in the next Article ffollowinge prefixed.

Item the said monie shalbe repaid vnto the said Treas-urers the ffyve and twentith day of June Immediately after the expiration of the said tyme, for the enioyinge thereof accorded, And the said tyme ffor the Reinbourse-
6 ment limited being delayed and deferred by him that possesseth yt, the monie graunted in the said Pasche Marte to bee alwayes notwithstandinge disbursed and given by the said Treasurers at the verie day appointed by the second Article of this Ordinance, And yf the Court thinke so Convenient the forfeict of the bond to bee foorthwith put in sewt and recouered against that per-sones suertyes that Enioyeth the monie, and neglecteth to make orderlye Restitution.

Item yf anie of the suertyes put in, chaunce to decay or dye then within one monthe after at the furthest an-other to bee presented and accepted of orderlye, at and by
7 the Court of Assistentes as afore ys appointed, And yf the partie to whome suche monie ys graunted, chaunce to de-part lyfe, before the expiration of the tyme for which the said bequest monie was graunted him, then the monie shall by the suertyes bee brought in vnto the Treasurer for the tyme servinge, within one monthe at the furthest after suche decease, within the compasse of which monthe, the Companie in whose hande the disposinge of the monie resteth, shall passe their graunt to some other sewter,
7 whoe within one day after receipt of suche monie by the Treasurer, shall at his hands havinge before sett suertyes, and entered into bond receiue the same. And yt ys to bee vnderstood that after suche partie deceaseth the monie brought in, new graunt passed & accordinglye all thinges accomplished, suche persone as shall haue the

said graunt shall enioye the same onelye for the tyme un-
expired, to the deceased first graunted, with this addition
that he shalbe at libertie against the expiration of the
said terme to becomme sewter with other observinge the
order thereto appointed in manner and forme aboue
written.

Item, ffor that M[r] John Quarles his bequest monie folio 107.
falleth dew in the Pasche Marte, the sewters for the Enioyinge and use thereof shall make their sewtes in the
Cold Marte before, and after the graunt past suertyes to
bee sett boundes deliuered, and the said monie receiued 8
and payd by the Treasurer in Londone for the tyme beinge in the said Cold and Pasche Martes, in order and in
manner as aboue for the other bequest monie in the other
martes ys Ordayned.

Item, after the suertyes bee putt in and allowed ad-
uertisement to bee sent to Londone to the end that the
bondes may bee there, yf not here made; signed sealed 9
and deliuered to the Treasurer for the tyme beinge,
within the tyme before appointed.

Lastly to the end yt may appear to all men how the
said monie and upon whome yt hathe been ffrom tyme to
tyme bestowed, whoe the suertyes and when tyme of ex- 10
piration or graunt falleth, the names of the persones and
their suertyes shalbe sett in a table from tyme to tyme as
the same shalbe graunted, And lyke Table of the Articles
of the Testators willes to bee written foorth, sent to
Londone and Embden, and hanged up in the places where
the Companie here vsually keep Courtes or Assemblyes.

Whereas the late deceased M[r] Jones hathe given ffyftie
poundes sterlinge to bee vpon twoe Jongmen bestowed 11
per moitie, And the late M[r] John Carre also deceased one
and fourtie poundes sterling in lyke sorte, vnto three to

bee distributed, yt ys agreed that the twoe Jongmen to whome the said Mr Jones his monie shalbe graunted shall have the twoe thirde partes of Mr Carres bequest monie and the Remayninge third parte to bee given to another persone with Condition that in respect of the smallnes of that portion yt shalbe lawfull for him to becomme sueter for anie of the ffyftye poundes given by Mr Quarles or M^s Knotte; without that the Enioyinge of the said one third parte shalbe unto his sewt anie lett or Impediment.

In the Last Will of Walter Jones, Late of Whitney in the Countie of Oxford Clothier deceased, Remayninge in 12 the prorogatiue Court of Caunterburye and from thence—

Extracted amonge other thinges, ys Conteyned as followeth.

Item, I give and bequeath to the Governour Deputie 13 and Assistentes of the ffellowshippe of Merchantes Adventurers of the Englishe House and Nation in Flaunders, Holland, Brabant, and Zeland, in parties of beyond the Seas and to their Successors Governour, Deputie and Assistentes of the said ffellowshippe for the tyme beinge folio 108. ffor ever the somme of ffyftie poundes of lawfull monie of England to bee Employed and occupyed in a stocke in the handes of two yong men beinge Englishe men, lyke to prosper and go forward in their Trade of Merchandise for and during the space of twoe yeares together ffreely, without anie Intrest or other reward by them to bee payd for the vse and occupyinge thereof; vpon sufficient bond and suertye to bee had and taken of the said twoe yong men, to bee bound to the said Governour, Deputie and Assistentes, for the tyme beinge for the true Repayment of the same, ffyftie poundes, at the end of the said terme of twoe yeares next after the receipt thereof. Whereof euerie of the seid twoe Englishemen to haue in occupy-

inge to himself ffyve and twentie poundes and after the
same twoe yeares finished, then I will the same 50 li
shalbe lykewise delivered vpon the aforesaid bound and
Assurance vnto twoe other apt and meet Englishmen
most lykest to thryve & goe forward ffreely for the lyke
space of twoe years, and so from twoe yeares to twoe
yeares the same to bee occupyed in a stocke in the handes
of twoe Englishemen lyke to thryve by the discretion of
the Governour Deputie and Assistents there for the tyme
beinge for ever, vpon bond and Assurance in forme as ys
afore declared, without anie fraude particularitye or affection in anie wyse, And that Mr Geoffreye Walkeyeen shall
have the Nomination of the twoe Yongemen for the twoe
first yeares.

COPIE OF AN ARTICLE OF OUR LATE BROTHER ROGER
KNOTTE HIS TESTAMENT CONCERNINGE A LEGUA-
CIE BEQUEATHED TO THE FFELLOWSHIPPE.

Also I give and bequeathe to the Companie and ffellowshippe of Merchants Adventurers of England Resident
now in Antwerp, twoe hundred poundes Currant monie 14
of England to bee paid to the Treasurer of the Companie
beyond Seas, within one year after my decease, for this
end and purpose and so to remain for ever and for none
other, that ys I will and ordayne these sayd twoe hundred poundes aforesaid to bee made over by Exchaunge
and Converted into fflemishe monie, which shalbe devided
into four equall partes and to bee delivered to four honest
poor Jongmen ffree of the same Companie, to have in
occupyinge for twoe yeares space a peece without payinge
anie penye Intrest ffor yt, by any manner of means or
wayes, puttinge in twoe sufficient suertyes a peece, for
euerie of their somme or sommes to the Treasurer of the

14 same Companie beyond Sea for the tyme beinge ffor and
to the vse of the same Companie ffor the good and sure
Repayment of the said somme or sommes of monie again
at the end and terme of twoe yeares aforesaid which
folio 109. eight suerties shalbe tryed by Ballatinge at a Court of
Assistentes to bee good and sufficient or not good and
sufficient, And those good and sufficient suerties shalbe
bound with the Jongman that hathe the monie Joinctly
and severallye for the whole somme, which the said Jongman hathe in occupyinge, And the four poor Yongmen
that shalbe appointed to have the monie in occupyinge
ffrom tyme to tyme, shall at a Generall Court by Erect-
inge of handes bee Chosen that have most handes, which
I requyre to bee suche as ys knowen to have most need,
and the four so Chosen to have yt for twoe yeares as
aforesaid, and at the end of the said terme to repay yt to
other ffower new Chosen to succeed them, and this order
to remayn vnto the worldes end, I will and ordayn
Instantly desyringe the Companie to Choose so many of
my Country men borne in the Countie of Sussex ffrom
tyme to tyme, as have need and shalbe able to repay yt
back again as afore written. Provided further also that
yf there bee wantinge but one hundred poundes Current
monie of England aforesaid to supply my bequests and
leguacies before given, then I will and Ordayn that yt
bee rebated and taken out of the twoe hundred poundes
giuen to the Merchantes Adventurers of England.

IN THE TESTAMENT OF MR. JOHN CARRE WAS NEXT
BEFORE THIS ARTICLE A BEQUEST GIUEN TO MR.
MARSHE THEN GOVERNOUR TO THE FFELLOW-
SHIPPE OF MERCHANTS ADVENTURERS OF ENG-
LAND ETC THEN FFOLLOWED AS HERE VNDER-
WRITTEN.

Item I give and bequeath to the said Governour Assistentes and Commonaltye of the said ffellowshippe of 15
Merchantes Adventurers of England, and to their successors ffourtie and one poundes of lawfull monie of this
Realm, the same Mr Governour Assistentes and Commonaltye of the said ffellowshippe and their successors, beinge
bound to my Executors and ouerseers by their deed obli-
gatorie Sealed with the Common Seale of the said ffellowshippe, that the said somme of 41^{li} shalbe with the consent of thirteen of the Assistents from twoe yeares to twoe
yeares next following my decease vpon sufficient suerties
bee lent & deliuered to somme suche three yonge beginners to trade with the said ffellowshippe free of the same,
as the said Mr Governour and thirteen of the Assistents
for the tyme beinge shall Iudge meet and worthy to be
relieved by the occupyinge of the said somme of one and
fourtie poundes for twoe yeares, as by former good order
taken for vse of monie to the said ffellowshippe given by
one Jones Clothier deceased for lyke purpose hathe been
& ys provided and vsed.

COPIE OF MR JOHN QUARTES DRAPER DECEASED AR- folio 110.
TICLE OF HIS LAST WILL CONCERNINGE HIS BE-
QUEST GIVEN TO THE COMPANIE OF MERCHANTS
ADVENTURERS OF ENGLAND.

Item I give and bequeath vnto the Governour Assistents & ffellowshippe of Merchants Adventurers of England one hundred poundes of lawfull monie of England, 16

to the Intent that they shall ffreely, lend and deliuer the same monie vnto twoe poor Yongmen ffree of the same Companie, that ys to say to either of them ffyftie poundes, that they may have the occupyinge thereof for twoe yeares, they and either of them puttinge in sufficient suertyes to the same Companie for the Repayment of the said monie at the end of the said twoe yeares, And at the end of the said twoe yeares I will that the said monie shalbe lykewise deliuered to twoe other Jongmen of the same Companie for other twoe yeares, puttinge in suerties as aforesaid, And so I will that the said monie shalbe from twoe yeares ffor ever delivered vnto twoe Yongemen ffree of the Companie in manner and forme aforesaid.

EXTRACT OUT OF THE LAST WILL AND TESTAMENT OF GEORGE BERBECKE LATE OF LONDONE MERCER DECEASED.

Item: And freely giue & bequeath to the Companie of merchantes Adventurers the somme of ffyftie poundes Current Englishe monie, which sayd somme of ffyftie 17 poundes my will and desyre ys may bee lent Gratis ffor three yeares vnto one poor Yongman of the Companie, puttinge in twoe sufficient suerties for the repayinge of the monie again, and yf one of the suerties dye the Companie to take another, So I give to the Companie of merchants Adventurers to this vse 50 £.

EXTRACT OUT OF THE LAST WILL AND TESTAMENT OF ROBERT ROGERS LATE OF LONDONE LETHER SELLER DECEASED.

Inprimis. I give to my Cosine William Eyres three hundred poundes and that the Companie of Merchantes 18 Adventurers have one their bond at 6 £ 13s. 4d. per Cento till the said William Eyres comme to the age of one and twentie yeares, and then the three hundred pounds to bee payd him, Note that this William Eyres ys 21 yeares old.

Item. I give and bequeath to the merchantes Adventurers of England twoe hundred poundes in monie, Provided that they shall give out their bond for the payment of twentie poundes a year to Richard ffoxe lether seller or his assynes during his naturall Lyfe, by ffyve poundes a quarter, and after his decease my will ys that the said Companie lend out one hundred poundes vnto Jongmen Gratis ffor three yeares vpon twoe suertyes, so to Continew ffrom three yeares to three yeares ffor ever, the other hundred powndes I give to the said Companie towardes their Charge.

Item I will and bequeath to the Companie of Merchantes Adventurers twoe hundred poundes, Provided that they doe allowe vnto Cicile Parris my Cosin tenn pounds yearly by ffyftie shillinges a quarter, towardes the maintenance of her twoe sonnes Alexander and John Parris, but yf yt shall happen the said Cicile to survive her husband then I will the said 200 £ to bee paid to the said Cicile for her advancement. But yf yt happen the said Cicile to decease before her husband then I will the said tenn poundes yearly to bee paid by them vnto the said Alexander and John Parris duringe their minoritye, and when they shall Comme to one and twentie yeares, I will that the said 200 £ shalbe equally devided between them, or the whole to the surviver of them. But yf yt shall happen that the said Cicile, Alexander and John doe decease before anie of them bee capable of the said 200 £ then I will that the said Companie shall lend the said monie to four Yongemen ffree of the said Companie and traders beyond the Seas by ffyftie poundes a peece for three yeares Gratis, puttinge in twoe good suerties and so from three yeares to three yeares for ever.

EXTRACT OUT OF THE LAST WILL AND TESTAMENT OF ROBERT PERCK LATE OF LONDONE HABER-DASHER DECEASED.

Item to the Companie of merchantes Adventurers with Condition the same shalbe lent gratis to some poor Yongemen ffree of the same Companie for the terme of three yeares, and so successively ffrom three yeares to three yeares, to be Continued to the Worldes end to the relief of other Yongmen Gratis, No one man enioyinge yt longer then three yeares, And the disposinge thereof I deferre to the discretion of the Governour Assistents and Generalitie of the said Companie where the Authoritye shall then bee, I say to this vse I give & bequeath the somme of ffyftie poundes.

PRESENTMENTES AND THE MANNER OF PROCEED-
INGE IN THE CONDEMNINGE AND LEVYINGE OF
BROAKES.

Iff anie presentment or Information of anie delict 1
breache or Offence against anie the Lawes Statutes,
Actes or Ordinances of the ffellowshippe Committed or
donne, shalbe brought by anie persone whatsoeuer to the
Governour or his deputie or to the Treasurer or to suche
lyke Officer (as yt ys lawfull for euerie one that will soe
doe) notice thereof shalbe taken and entred by the Treasurer or lyke Officer for the tyme beinge in a booke for
that purpose, And such entrye beinge made withall
necessarie and Convenient Circumstances of tyme and
place for the better manifestation & proofe of the presentment or Information the Treasurer or other suche
lyke Officer shall within twoe Court dayes of Assistentes
or Associates next after publishe the same before the
Court vpon pain of ffyve poundes sterlinge, neither shall
he Conceale or holde from the knowledg of the Court
anie presentment or Information given in as aforesaid,
vpon pain of ffyve poundes sterlinge.

The Treasurer or lyke Officer shall not discover or 2
make knowen to anie persone presented or other the
matter or Offence for which presentment ys entered, or
the name of anie presenter or enformer thereof; except
yt bee to the Governour or his deputie, yt shalbe notwithstandinge lawfull to declare to anie persone presented
requyringe the same, for what valew or somme he ys to

put in suertie pawn or Caution yet without manifestinge
for what Cause or by whome he ys presented.

3 Yf anie persone shalbe presented for doinge or vehe-
ment suspicion of doeinge anie offence or trespasse or
delict against anie the lawes, Actes, or Ordinances of the
ffellowshippe the Treasurer or lyke Officer shall by one
of the Beadles warne or Command suche persone, yf he
bee present his factor or servaunt, to put in suerties or
pawne for the aunswearinge of the Court, And yf the
partie presented his factor or servant shall refuse or doe
not in dew tyme performe suche order, he or they so refusinge or not doinge one this syde the Seas, shall forfeict
fyve pounds ster: and yf in England tenn poundes sterlinge. But yf the partie presented bee not able or will
not putt in suertie pawne or Caution, beinge warned or
Commanded as aforesaid, he shalbe subiect besydes the
payment of the abouesaid forfeictures or penalties to
abyde suche order as shalbe found meeet or expedient
folio 118. by the Governour or his deputie and the Court one that
behalf.

FORME HOW SUERTYES SHALL SUBSCRIBE TO A PRE-
SENTMENTE.

4 Wee whose names are herevnder written doe hereby
Constitute and put owrselues suerties and doe vndertake
Joinctly and severally for A B to aunswear suche matter
as he standeth Charged with, by the presentment here
against written, and to make payment of suche mulctes
fines and penalties as he shalbe Condemned in accordinge
to the orders.

5 But yf the persone presented bee absent and have
neither servaunt factor or goodes for the answearinge of
the Court, then yf the presentment bee not vnder twentie

poundes sterlinge valew, he shalbe warned by a letter
from the Court to make his appearance by himself or by
some other brother of the ffellowshippe thereto fully
Authorised, before a Court of Assistents or Associates
within three monthes after the receipt of suche letter at
Londone, and within six monthes elswhere, and yf without reasonable or allowable Causes or excuse the said
persone shall not appear or have his Atturnye at the
place where he ought to appear at the tyme appointed,
he shalbe Condemned in the penalties provided by anie
the lawes Actes or Ordinances of the ffellowshippe against
which he standeth presented to have Offended, And
wheresoever his bodie or goodes shalbe found in these
partes beyond the Seas or in England, the same shalbe
arrested and seised vpon and so deteyned till the Court
bee satisfyed, But yf the penaltie to bee Inflicted bee
vnder twentie poundes sterlinge valew, and the persone
presented bee absent, and haue neither factor for vant nor
goodes here the matter shalbe sent over into England to
be examined by the Governour or his deputie and the
Court there by the best means they can, without passinge
anie Judgement or sentence therein, and beinge examined
shalbe returned with advyce what hathe been found to 5
the end that yt may bee here proceeded in accordinge to
the Orders, And yf for anie other Cause yt shalbe found
or appear that anie matter or offence presented to bee
Committed or donne Cannot bee so well tryed out and
examined here as in England, yt shalbe lawfull to remitt
the said matter into England to bee there examined by
the Governour or his deputie and the Associates, whoe
without proceedinge to sentence shall with all Convenient
speed signifye to the Court here, what they fynde to the
end that the said matter may bee ffinally proceeded in folio 119.
10

accordinge to the orders, And yf anie persone of this ffellowshippe in England shall be warned to appear before the Governour or his deputie & the Associates and to put in suerties, shall not appear at the tyme and place appointed and put in suerties, he shall forfeict and pay to the vse of the ffellowshippe tenn poundes sterlinge, and yet not bee discharged of the matter against hym.

6   The suerties pawne or Caution put into the Court shall stand bound and bee Chargeable as well for the foorth Comminge of the partie presented from tyme to tyme, as also for the ffull satisfaction of suche ffynes, mulctes, penaltyes order, awarde or sentence of Court, somme and sommes of Monie, as he shalbe Condempned in and not bee discharged or released, before suche satisfaction made, but stand executable as Principall.

7   Excuse or allegation of Ignorance negligence or oversighte in the breach of anie the lawes Actes or Ordinances of the ffellowshippe shall not bee avaylable or accepted as sufficient to acquyte or Clear the partie presented or offending of the penalties dew for his Offence.

8   No persone shalbe Condempned in Broake or forfeicture for anie trespasse or Offence Committed or donne twoe yeares before the same was presented, but he shalbe wholye acquyted and discharged thereof, except the offence be suche as may bee found out and tryed without presentment, and namely by the Husbands bookes or otherwise, as Stint of shippinge and of Apprentyces, none Enrollements, and suche lyke broakes and forfeictures.

9   No persone Condempned for doeinge against the Statutes and Ordinances of the ffellowshippe, shall make suite for anie grace or Remission in plain or Generall Court or in anie other Court of Justice here or elsewhere, but only in or at a Court of Assistentes or Assocyates,

and that within twentie dayes after the said Condempnation (yf there bee anie Court within that tyme) vpon
pain of fforfeicture of the doble of that he was Condempned in, and this Order not to bee dispenced with.

Yf anie persone Condempned by Sentence of Court, or 10
fined for doeinge against anie the Lawes, Actes, or Ordi- folio 120.
nances of the ffellowshippe after grace or remission hathe
been obtayned and shewed and the determination of the
Court one that behalf to him hathe been signifyed shall
notwithstandinge by himself or some other for him sue
labour moue or solicite for further grace or Remission, or
trouble the Court for that Cause, he shall forfeict the
doble of that he was Condempned in at the first and he
that shall sue labour move or sollicite one the behalf of
suche persone, shall Incurre and pay lyke forfeicture.

No Remission or restitution of Broake or forfeicture 11
shalbe made, but yt shalbe first by ballatinge tryed
whether anie Restitution or Remission shalbe made, and
then yf by the greater number of the Balletts yt appear
yea, yt shall again by ballatinge bee tryed how muche
shalbe restored or remitted and this order in that behalf
to bee Inviolablye observed and none other, yt ys also
vnderstood that no grace shalbe shewed or Broak qualifyed or Remitted in whole or in parte before the Treasurer bee satisfyed for the said Broake, and that he declare
so muche before the Court, to the end that in his Accompt
yt may bee brought as monie and not bee left a debt to
the ffellowshippe, as of late to the losse and hurte of the
said ffellowshippe hathe been verie yll and preiuditially
practysed.

Yf anie Brother of this ffellowshippe shalbe by order 12
of Court examined vpon his oathe Concerninge anie trespasse or offence Committed or donne against anie the

Lawes, Actes or Ordinances of the said ffellowshippe, for
the which he ys orderly presented or Convented, yf suche
persone refuse or will not depose he shalbe holden Guiltie
and accordinglie Condempned in suche penaltie Broake
or sommes of monie as ys provided and sett downe in the
Lawe Act or Ordinance ffor Offenders against the same,
and vpon which he refuseth and will not bee examined
or deposed, And yf anie persone shalbe found and prooved
to have taken a false oathe, or not to have declared a
truthe being deposed or examined vpon his oathe, he
shalbe dismissed and disfranchised out and ffrom all the
liberties and ffreedome of this ffellowshippe.

13   No persone standinge presented against whome lawfull
wyttnesse ys produced ffor the verification of the presentment shall bee admitted to Clear himself by oath except
folio 121. he bringe lyke wytnesse for his Justification ffor the doeinge whereof he shall have reasonable tyme assigned him,
and faylinge at the day to produce his wyttnes, he shalbe
Condempned as guiltie and Convict of the Said presentment.

14   Iff the Court shall pardone anie parte of Broake or forfeicture, or Chaunge the same to some other punishment
or fyne the partie Condempned not accomplishinge and
duely performinge the order of Court, shall Incurre the
penaltie of the first or principall Broake or forfeicture.

15   The presenter shall haue the third parte of the penalties or sommes of monie retayned or reserved to the House,
of Broakes by him presented and Levyed vpon brethern
of the ffellowshippe and the halfe of that which shalbe
taken of Interlopers or onffree persones.   Provided that
no persone shall take advantage or have anie parte of
those brokes which he himself his maister servaunt or
partner hathe rnn into and been Condempned ffor,

Neither shall the Governour or his deputie or anie Assistent or Associate present at the handlinge examininge and Condempninge of anie Broake or forfeicture receive or have to his proper vse anie parte or portion of suche Broake or forfeicture vpon pain of payinge to the partie Condempned the doble of that which he receiued or had, to be recovered by way of plaint or Action before a Court of Assistentes or Associates, ffor the better tryall whereof the partie Complayned one shalbe examined vpon his oathe and yf he refuse to bee examined he shall pay the doble of that he shalbe Charged with or otherwise prooued to have had or receiued Contrarie to the true meaninge of this Order, Provided also that the Beadles shall have 40^d vpon the pound of those Broakes which proceed of presentmentes made by other persons not beinge Beadles, to bee payd them by the Treasurer out of the presenters parte.

Complyces, Consortes, Partners and Companions in 16 Euill or transgression of good Orders, Abetters, Ayders, Consorters and Maynteyners of Euill doers and transgressors of the orders, as also Counsiellors, procurers Causers or Commaunders of euill or transgression in or by others, shalbe held and punished as the principall folio 122. Transgressors or doers of Euill, or otherwise shalbe dealt withall at the discretion of the Governour or his deputie and the Court.

Orders[1] that in such cases where the Members and by 17 Oath obliged to present themselves where the Officers shall haue nothing of the Broakes that shall at anie time arise vpon such presentment. Butt in suche Cases where the members are not obliged by Oath and yett shall pre-

[1] Change of handwriting.

sent themselves and thereby prevent the Beadle of presenting off them there the Beadles shall have there share in the Broakes according as is provided and established in the foregoing order.

Actum 30 April 1660.

This Last Article was transcribed from Alderseys Book of the Fellowships Ordinances, fo. 140, the 15th February 1770 by Nehemiah Nisbett, Secretary.

ARRESTES OF PERSONS AND GOODES PROCESSE AND PURSUITE OF CAUSES BEFORE THE COURT.

No persone of this ffellowshippe shall vexe sue or trouble or Cause to bee vexed sued or troubled anie Brother supposte or Officer of the said ffellowshippe or Cause them or anie of them to bee arrested or Cited to appear before anie other magistrate, or before anie other Court of Justice one this syde the Seas, but before the Courtes of Assistentes or Associates in suche place as the ffellowshippe ys Resident at Nationwyse, there to aunswear anie Civile Cause Action suite quarrell offence misdemeanour Complaint question variance trespasse hurt misprision Exces or Iniurie, vpon pain to forfeict to the ffellowshippe the valew of his Action or demaund.

And ffor avoydinge of vniust molestation and friuolous suites, yt ys ordayned that no brother or persone of the ffellowshippe shalbe by anie other brother or persone of the said ffellowshippe molested arrested or attached in his persone or goodes ffor anie Action or Cause Civile without knowledg and licence of the Governour or his deputie whoe fyndinge the Cause (vpon the openinge of the same) not to proceed of malice or sett purpose without iust or good ground to vexe or molest shall give leave to enter & make the said Action or Attachement.

The plaintiffe havinge obtayned licence as aforesaid shall enter his Action or Attachement with the Secretarie or sworn Clerk in plain termes & woordes expressinge therein the ground or occasion somme or substance of his

demaund Action or plaint and whence yt groweth and
then havinge sett twoe suerties brethern of the ffellowshippe or Caution for the doeinge good of his said Action
or demaund shall prosecute the same with effect otherwise suche Entrye to bee voyd.

The debitor or partie against whome Action ys Entred,
shalbe warned by a Beadle to put in Caution or twoe
sufficient suertyes brethern of the ffellowshippe to vndertake for him and aunswear to the Creditor or plaintiffe
from tyme to tyme and to fulfill the sentence of Court,
And yf the debitor or defendant refuse and will not or
bee not able to put in suerties or Caution or bee in Acttn
Jugæ that ys vpon point of runninge away or absentinge
himself, he shall foorthwith by Order of the Governour
or his deputie bee apprehended and putt in saufe keepinge, there to remayn till he haue putt in pawne Caution
or suertie to suche purpose as aforesaid, or otherwise
haue Contented the Creditor or plaintiffe or that by the
Consent of the Creditor or plaintiffe he shalbe released.

The Beadle for warninge anie man to put in suertye to
Action or to appear before a Court or Commission shall
have paid him by the plaintiffe or requyre of suche warninge 6^d fflemishe and for the Intimation of an attachement
as muche. And the Beadle for apprehension of anie man
shall haue six stuyuers fflemishe and for saufe Keepinge
of him twelue stuyuers a day wherein the night ys to bee
reconed, and the defendant or partie apprehended shall
bear his owne Charges of meat and drinke yf he bee
iustly apprehended, yf oniustly the plaintiffe or Causer
of suche apprehension or arrest shall bear all the Charges
of the defendant at the discretion and Taxation of the
Court.

The debitor or defendant beinge absent reasonable tyme

folio 128. appears in margin.

shalbe Assigned him to make appearance by himself or
by his lawfull Atturnye a brother of the ffellowshippe
ffully and sufficiently Authorized, And yf he make default beinge warned by wrytinge from the Court and doe
not appear at the day as aforesaid, the Court may and
shall proceed to sentence, except the debitor or defendant
doe shew or make some reasonable or lawfull excuse requyringe a longer day or tyme for his appearance or
Sendinge of his Atturnye, in which Case further reasonable tyme shalbe given him at the discretion of the Court.

Yf anie persone of this ffellowshippe or other subiect to
the Jurisdiction thereof ffor anie Action suite question or
presentment or for anie other Cause whatsoever whereof
the Court may or ought to take knowledg shalbe warned
by a day peremptorily or a Court appointed and sett per-
sonally to appear and aunswear to the partie grieved or
plaintiffe, or to the Court and shall willfully obstinately
or Contemptiously make default or absent himself without reasonable lett or excuse to bee accepted by the Court
or appearinge shall not aunswear as apperteyneth or shall
depart or goe away again without Consent or leave of the
Court, he shalbe proceeded against as yf he were present
and Confessed the matter against him brought and Con- folio 129
sequently shalbe Condempned as a Contemner of Justice
and good order, accordinge to equitie reasone and Conscience, and as by the Court one this behalf shalbe found
meet and to appertayn.

Yf yt so fall out that the plaintiffe himself appear not
at the day sett, and that the defendant appear, the said
defendant shalbe discharged of the Court and absolued of
the Instance or suite And the plaintiffe shall not bee
suffered to beginne a new Instance or suite before he have
paid all the Charges of the former and besydes a penaltie
of 40^d ster: to the use of the ffellowshippe.

Yf the debitor or partie defendant bee suspected to bee fugitiue or Bankrupt or bee ffugitiue bankrupt Insolvent dead or Cannot bee present whether he bee a brother of the ffellowshippe or otherwise bee the Kinges subiect, yt shalbe lawfull for the Creditor or plaintiffe by licence of the Governour or his deputie to attache with a beadle in his owne handes or in the handes of anie other of the ffellowshippe the monie goodes debtes or other thinge belonginge to the debitor or defendant Enteringe his Attachement and the tyme the same was made with the Secretarie or Sworn Clerk wherein yf he Can he shall particularly in plain termes and woordes sett downe and expresse the thinge and thinges attached, but yf he Cannot and that the Attachement bee made in generall woordes vpon monie goods debtes etc^a in Packhouse Chamber or Countinghouse of the debitor or partie defendant, suspected to bee fugitiue or Bankrupt or that ys in deed fugitiue Bankrupt Insolvent dead or that otherwise Cannot bee present, then the Treasurer or lyke Officer takinge with him the Secretarie or sworn Clerk and a Beadle shall Enter suche Chamber Packhouse or Countinghouse and there Inventarise wryte seale and shut vp and Committ to saufe keepinge or sequester all suche monie wares goodes billes of debt etc^a as he shall there fynde or bee belonginge to the said debitor or partie defendant. And yf anie persone shall Breake or pull of the lockes or seales sett vpon Coffers Chestes Countinghouses Packhouses or suche lyke thinges or places by the said Treasurer Secretarie etc^a or shall Conveighe anie thinge in breach or Contempt of the said arrest he shalbe mulcted with a penaltie of tenn poundes sterlinge to the vse of the ffellowshippe and bee forced to restore or make good the thinges or goodes, Conveighed away, or otherwise shalbe arbitrarily punished at the discretion of the Governour or his deputie & the Court.

The Secretarie or sworn Clerke ffor the entrye of euerie folio 130. Action whatsoever shall have paid hym by the Enterer or plaintiffe eight stuyuers fflemishe and for takinge Inventorie of the goodes of anie persone shall have payd him tenn stuyuers fflemishe yf the said Inventorie exceed not halfe a sheet of paper Compressely written, yf yt doe he shall haue payd him twentie stuyuers and for a Copie thereof the halfe.

The Governour or his deputie for the tyme beinge takinge vnto him twoe of the Assistentes or Associates shall Immediately Call before him the partie in whose handes attachement shalbe made which partie shall there presently declare vpon his Corporall oathe what goodes or thinges he hathe in his handes of the defendants or had at the tyme of the Attachment makinge and shall foorthwith deliuer the same into the house or putt in suertye or Caution as well to take his oathe as also that the said goodes shalbe foorth Comminge, And this to bee performed at the next Court of Assistents or Associates ffollowinge which yf he refuse to doe he ys to bee dealt with all accordinge to the Order one this behalf made the 30th of August anno 1597 in stade.

The partie in whose handes attachement ys made at the suite of the Creditors or plaintiffe shalbe warned before the Court and Commaunded to declare vpon his oath without Concelement fraud or Couen, how muche and what monie goodes debtes or other thinge he had in his handes at the tyme of the Attachement makinge belonginge to the debitor of the plaintiffe or Creditor whereof dew notice shalbe taken and kept by the Secretarie or sworn Clerk and the said partie shall from the tyme of

the Attachement makinge stand charged and aunswearable for the monie goodes etc^a attached in his handes
which shalbe lyable to bee disposed of in suche order as
by the Governour or his deputie and the Court shalbe
taken or found meet in equitie & Conscience to apperteyne.

Yf the plaintiffe Call not vpon his Action within twoe
Court dayes of Assistents or Associates held after the
entry thereof suche Action shalbe held as voyd and the
defendant discharged in his persone & goodes of that
Instance.

Yf by means of Arbitrators appointed by the Court the
parties Contendinge cannot or will not agree between
themselues reporte shalbe made to the Court by the Arbitrators as in suche Cases apperteyneth to the end that the
said Court may proceed & take order one that behalf accordinge to equitie and reasone.

folio 131.
The declaration of the plaintiffe and the aunswear of
the defendant therevnto the Wyttnesses depositions
proofes specialtyes and reasons of bothe partyes havinge
been throughly debated examined heard seen and Considered as apperteyneth definitiue sentence of Court shalbe
Enacted or written and then plainly pronounced by the
Governour or his deputie and accordinglie bee put in execution & fullfilled.

Sentence of Court beinge passed against pawn goodes
ete^a there shalbe foorthwith four honest and Indifferent
persons ffreemen of this ffellowshippe Chosen and sworn
before the Court to estimate and appraise the said goodes
pawn ete^a Justly and vprightly as near as they can to
their best knowledg to the valew or pryce thereof to bee
solde for redie monie of which estimatinge or apprays-
inge the Secretarie or sworn Clerke shall take and keep
notice.

Yf either before or within fyfteen dayes after the appraysement the debitor or some other for him lawfully Authorised doe Content the Creditor, the goodes pawne etc* shalbe released the Charges to bee awarded by Court or the debt and dutie dew to the house yf there bee anie owinge by the said debitor or the Creditor beinge first aunsweared and discharged. But yf the debitor or some other for him lawfully Authorised come not within ffyfteen dayes after the appraisement and Content his Counter partie, the thinges Condempned and appraysed shall foorthwith bee solde by a candle burninge in the sighte of so manie of the ffellowshippe as wilbe present at the said sale for the highest pryce and most value that can be made by Crye of the Beadles before the goeinge out of the Candle ffor redie monie, And yf that suche sale shall bringe out more then the appraisement the same shalbe to the advantage and benefyte of the debitor, but yf yt bringe out lesse the losse shall lighte one the Creditor, to whome the said goodes shalbe reconed for so muche in monie or value as they were appraysed at, and that accordinglie so muche of his debt ys paid.

The Beadles for lookinge toe and Cryinge out of the said goodes solde by Candle or Execution shall haue paid them by the Treasurer vpon euerie pound fflemishe twoe pence lyke monie, And the Secretarie or sworn Clerk for taking notice & keepinge Register of matters shall have paid him vpon each pound fflemishe one penny lyke monie accordinge to auncient Custome, except the goodes solde be verye Costly by means whereof the said salarie or ffees might prooue excessiue great in which Case the Court may moderate the said Salarie or ffees.

The persone or persons in whose handes Attachement folio 132. ys made shall foorthwith after that difinitiue Sentence ys passed bee warned foorthwith to bringe in vnto the Treasurer (yf he or they have not brought them in before) the monie goodes etc⁴ attached and Condempned to the ende that execution may bee donne vpon the same as aforesaid.

A Creditor havinge pawn in his handes for the Assurance of his debt yf yt fall out that the debitor becomme Insolvent before the pawne be solde (althoughe he have Consent and Authoritye of the debitor to sell the said pawne) yet he shall not secretely sell or make away suche pawne but bringe the same to bee solde publickly by a Candle to the end that so muche as shalbe found over and aboue his debt may remain in the house for the aunswearinge of some other Creditor that may haue right therevnto.

As well monie Attached as that which shall proceed of sale made by a Candle shalbe sequestred and brought into the handes of the Treasurer to bee distributed to and amonge the Creditors accordinge to Sentence of Court and the orders of the ffellowshippe.

Yf there bee anie dutie or debt owinge to the ffellowshippe by anie persone Condempned the same shalbe first satisfyed and payd next shall the Charges of the execution saufe keepinge of the goodes and distribution thereof with reasonable Charges of buryall and Churche dutie bee aunsweared And then before all other shalbe preferred debtes dew for Victuaile meat & drinke house or Chamber hyre, Packhouse seller and servants hyre or lyke wayes for paynes taken, And then afterwardes the Creditors each one in order accordinge to the Enteringe of his Attachement in order and tyme before, or after one another shalbe paid, so ffarre as the monie in the said Treasurers handes will goe or reache, And yf there

bee anie remayner the same shalbe reserved and kept in
the house for the defendant or for his Executors or lawfull assignes.   And yf ffinally anie Creditor remayn in
whole or in parte vnpaid, he may otherwise seeke his
payment by Lawe against the debitor or his goodes yf he
comme to knowledg of anie.

Attachement made of debt in the hands of some debitor
shall goe before the bill of debt of the said debitors
attached in Generall termes except suche bill of debt be
first seen and viewed by the Treasurer & Secretarie or
sworn Clerk & be written or noted vp to aunswear the
first attachement & that before the other attachement of
the debt in the hands of the debitor of the defendant be
made.

Yf the plaintyffe shalbe found and so prooued to Claym folio 133.
by his Action more then ys dew vnto hym he shall forfeict
to the ffellowshippe vpon euerie pound so wrongfully
Claymed twelue pence of lyke monie as the Action or demaund ys.   And yf the Action bee whole disprooued he
shalbe Condempned and pay suche somme and sommes
of monie as the Court shall awarde towardes the Charges
and damages of the defendant for his repair or sendinge
over into these partes or stay here to aunswear the Action
Commenceth against him, And besydes shalbe bound
foorthwith to restore vnto the plaintiffe that which he
may have gotten or wrongfully reconed with Intrest and
reasonable charges as aforesaid at the taxation and order-
inge of the Court.   Lykewise yt shalbe lawfull for the
Court to allow or award vnto the partie grieved or
wronged vpon Action of debt or other Action suche
damages or Amendes as in equitie and Conscience shalbe
found reasonable and Convenient.

Yf at anie tyme the defendant hauinge put in suertyes

to aunswear to Action or Complaint made against him
shall refuse and will not stand to Sentence of Court but
shall appele decline from or not fulfill the said Sentence
in euerie point, then in suche Case the goodes of suche
persone or of his suertyes which first or best may bee
comme by, shalbe attached sequestered and executed ffor
the fullfyllinge of the said Sentence. But yf he or they
shall Closely Conueighe priuily transporte or make away
his or their goodes so that they Cannot bee found out or
bee comme by to be attached, then the persone or persons of such defendant or of his suertyes which of them
may bee first met with shalbe arrested and Committed to
saufe keepinge or warde till he or they have fullfilled the
said Sentence and payd the damages and Charges Inci-
dent and besydes a ffyne of tenn poundes sterlinge to the
vse of the ffellowshippe, savinge to the suerties their re-
couerie and amendes against the defendant for whome
they vndertooke & became bound. And yt ys to bee
vnderstood that in lawe all arrestes and attachements or
persons and goodes are dischargeable and may bee released vnder sufficient Caution or Suertie to stand to the
tryall of the lawe and to fullfill the Judgment or Sentence
of Court, except in Case where Sentence alredie ys passed.

The partie one whose syde Sentence ys pronounced in
matter of Incombrance or attachement of monie goodes
etc[a] and all suche as shall receiue monie or other matter
out of the Treasurers handes by awarde or Sentence of
Court shall put in twoe sufficient suertyes brethern of the
ffellowshippe whoe shall stand bound with him to save
folio 134. the Court harmles for a year and a day against all persons
whatsoever for the foresaid awarde or Sentence and for
all future Claym or demaund for that Cause or for suche
monie or thinge receiued.

Yf by reasone of the doubtfullnes of anie Cause Action or matter in question or for want of sufficient lighte or proofe the Court Cannot proceed to Judgment then by licence of the said Court yt shalbe lawfull ffor the plaintiffe to take his advantage of lawe elswhere and otherwise not vpon the forfeicture of as muche to the ffellowshippe as his Action shall draw or amount vnto.

Yf anie straunger or vnffree Englishe persone or subiect of the Kinges Maiestie one this syde the Seas where the ffellowshippe ys Resiant and Priuileged haue question difference or demaund with or against anie persone of the said ffellowshippe and shall as plaintiffe desyre Justice of the Governour or his deputie and the Court submittinge himself to the order and determination of the same and puttinge in twoe sufficient suerties brethern of the ffellowshippe to vndertake for him one that behalf and never after to decline from the said order or determination but to stand Contented therewith without further suyte Appele or provocation, In suche Case suche brother or persone of the ffellowshippe shall as he ys bound in lyke sorte submitt himself put in suerties and abyde the order and determination of Court without all declination prouocation or Appele.

Yf anie pawn pledge or distresse shalbe taken and be in the handes of the Treasurer or in the house for debt or dutie owinge to the ffellowshippe the partie Indebted (yf he bee present) shalbe warned once twice and the third tyme by a beadle vpon his perill to appear at the next Court of Assistentes or Associates, and yf the partie bee not present but be elswhere one this syde the Seas he shalbe warned by letter from the Court to appear and make aunswear within the verye same marte, And yf he bee in England he shall also have a letter of warninge

11

from the Court sent him by a Brother or beadle of the
ffellowshippe and presented vnto him before Wyttnes
willinge him to appear by himself or his lawfull
folio 135. Atturneye beinge a ffree Brother of the ffellowshippe at
the next marte ffollowinge, And suche partie beinge
Condempned for makinge default or none appearance
accordinge as he was Enioyned ffour honest and Indifferent men Brethern of the ffellowshippe shalbe foorthwith
named and appointed by the Court vpon their oathes before the said Court taken openly to estimate and apprayse
the said pawne or distresse taken to the valew and pryce
thereof to their best knowledg as the same are worthe in
redie monie which appraisement shalbe Registred by the
Secretarie or sworne Clerke to the Intent that the partie
Indebted payinge the Condempnation with the Charges
within ffyfteen dayes after the appraysement may haue
his pawne or suche distresse restored or else the same to
remayn for to bee solde by a Candle to the best advantage
or benefyte of the partie Indebted for the payment of the
dutie or debt owinge to the ffellowshippe And yf there
bee anie ouerplus the same shalbe payd to the partie Indebted or his lawfull Assignes or Executors demaundinge
the same.

Yf the Court for Consideration or Cause movinge shall
take a sparinge or Respyte or deferre for a tyme payment
of debt dew to anie of the ffellowshippe he shall not arrest
vexe or trouble or Cause to bee arrested vexed or troubled
for that Cause in the Court of Admiraltie anie shippe or
goodes Charged or laden into the partes one this syde the
Seas where the ffellowshippe ys Resident or returninge
from thence in anie porte or haven within the kinges
dominions vpon pain of forfeicture of the demaund or
value thereof together with disfranchisement except vpon

declaration made to the Governour or deputie and ffellowshippe in open Court he first bee licenced so to doe.

Yf anie persone shall witholde anie Impositions debt or
dutie to the house or shall refuse to make payment of
anie fyne forfeicture or broake wherein he ys Condempned
yt shalbe lawfull for the Treasurer for the tyme beinge
or lyke Officer with Consent of the Governour or his
deputie for default of payment vpon demaund by him
made or for disobedience one this behalf foorthwith by a
Beadle and yf need bee with the ayd of an Officer of the
place to arrest and attache aswell the bodie as the goodes
of suche persone or his suerties & the same to retayn and
keep Irrepleinsable till the Doble of the Impositions debt
or dutie fine or forfeicture or broake dew & owinge bee
by hym payd, or that the Court be satisfyed for the same
one this behalf.

Yf anie persone of the ffellowshippe havinge foreign folio 136.
processe or suite he shalbe bound vpon the penaltie of
ffyve poundes sterlinge to bringe note of the same to the
Secretarie to be perused. and afterwardes recorded by him
payinge him for the same.

Yf the Beadle (whose Office this ys) shall haue order to
arrest attache or lay holde one the persone or goodes of
anie man, shall refuse so to doe or after he shall have
Attached or layd holde one any man or anie goodes shall
lett him or them goe or be Conveighed away without
puttinge in suertye or sufficient pawne to the Creditor or
plaintiffe or without his Consent he shall aunswear and
pay the debt himself for the which the arrest or Attachement was made or else shalbe arbitrarily punished at the
discretion of the Court.

Yf yt shall happen that anie persone of this ffellowshippe doe decease in these partes or that anie persone

void or absent him or yf anie apprentice or other persone
shall Committ anie fault or Offence by reasone whereof
his Charge or the goodes in his handes were by anie Act
or Ordinance to bee seized or sequestered, in suche Case
the Treasurer takinge with him twoe of the Assistentes
and the Secretarie shall seal vp and sequester into his
handes all suche monie billes bookes of Accomptes papers
goodes specialtyes and all other thinges whatsoever as he
shall fynde in the Chamber Counting-house, pack-house
or anie other place of the said persone, to the vse of him
or them that shall have best righte therevnto, the ffellowshippe beinge first satisfyed and payd suche debt or dutie
as may bee owinge to the same, And yf anie persone
straunger or other shall make Clayme to the said monie
goodes debtes etc⁑ or anie parte thereof and shall proove
his said Clayme to bee iust and true lawfully by Wyttnes
or other sufficient proofe without fraude or Malengine the
said persone shall haue deliuerie made hym and possession of the said monie goodes billes etc⁑ or of so muche of
the same as shalbe found belonginge vnto him puttinge
in twoe sufficient suerties of the ffellowshippe to saue the
Court harmles in Case anie other persone shall Challenge
and recouer the said monie billes, goodes etc⁑ or any parte
thereof by lawe, to restore the same or the valew thereof
to bee foorthwith rendered there where as of verie righte
folio 137. yt belongeth And yf the Treasurer doe make deliuery before suche suertye sett, or in any other sorte then as ys
abouesaid yt shalbe at his owne perill.

INIURIES IN WOORD OR DEED QUARRELLINGE FIGHT-
INGE MISDEMEANOUR EXCESSE AND PLAYE.

No persone of this ffellowshippe whatsoever shall Call
anie other of the said ffellowshippe not beinge his servant knave false knave or any other vile or approbrious
name in despyte or malice for anie matter or Cause whatsoever vpon pain of fourtie Shillinges sterlinge.

No persone of this ffellowshippe shall stryke beat or
wound or attempt to stryke beat or wound anie other
persone of the said ffellowshippe vpon pain of tenn
poundes sterlinge.

No persone of this ffellowshippe shall of malice or In-
iuriously or wrongfully doe or speake anie thinge or
wryte or give out or Cause to bee written or given out
anie Ryme letter or libell to the slaunder Infamie or dis-
credite of anie other persone of the said ffellowshippe
takinge the same to hart and Complaininge thereof in
Convenient tyme vpon pain to bee Arbitrarily punished
for suche his misdemeanour at the discretion of the Court,
havinge regard to the qualitie of the fact of the persone
doeinge or sufferinge the wronge or Iniurie.

Yt shalbe lawfull for the Court to allowe or awarde to
anie partie grieued or wronged by woord or deed vpon
Action of debt or any other Civile Action of trespasse or
other suche damages or amendes as to the said Court
shalbe found reasonable and in Equitie and Conscience to
apperteyn.

Yf anie persone of this ffellowshippe offendinge in heat

169

of blood against another Rashly or vnadvisedly in woord
or deed he shall obey and submitt himself to the Order
appointment Arbitrement or determination of the Governour or his deputie and the Assistents or Associates
and Refusinge so to doe shalbe Condempned in a ffyne of
tenn poundes sterlinge and pay the same to the vse of the
ffellowshippe.

The Counseillors devysers persuaders or provokers of
others to the breach of the Orders ffor private lucre or
profytte or for anie other Corrupt Indirect or Sinister
Respect. Lykewise Abetters Complyces and ayders in
anie misdemeanour euill or vnlawfull Action Concealers
and Conveighours away of fugitive or Bankrupt persons
folio 144. or other offenders or evill doers or of their goodes to the
hurt and wronginge of others and hinderance of lawfull
and orderly proceedinge and Justice shalbe held as guiltie
as the principall offenders or euill doers themselues and
accordinglie bee Corrected and punished, or in suche
manner as to the Court they shalbe found to have de-
served.

INIURIOUS DEALINGE, QUARRELLINGE ETC.

Yf anie Brother of this ffellowshippe shall by Craftie or
Iniurious dealinge Couen fraude or fault of his Indirectly
Endamage beguile or Circumvent anie other persone
whatsoeuer in his goodes or substance he shalbe Compelled to Restitution amendes or satisfaction or bee otherwise punished at the discretion of the Court.

No persone of this ffellowshippe shall seeke or willinglie
give occasion of Quarrellinge or fightinge or willinge
quarrell or fight (except in his owne defence) with anie
straunger in the place where the ffellowshippe ys Resiant
one this syde the Seas vpon payn, yf suche persone bee a

ffreeman to forfeict twentie poundes sterlinge to bee levyed vpon his bodie or goodes and to bee suspenced from the libertyes of the ffellowshippe for twoe yeares, And yf suche persone bee a Covenant servaunt or an Apprentice to bee foorthwith sent away or shipped for England and not to bee Employed in the trade of a merchant Adventurer one this syde the Seas where the ffellowshippe ys Privileged in three yeares after vpon pain of one hundred poundes sterlinge to bee forfeicted to the vse of the ffellowshippe and to bee levyed vpon the persone and goodes as well of him as of his maister or of anie other that shall Employe or sett him one worke.

Yf anie persone of this ffellowshippe shall of Malicious or Euill Intent Intercept or break vp the letters of anie other of the ffellowshippe yf suche persone bee his owne man he shall forfeict fyftie poundes sterlinge and bee expelled the ffellowshippe for three yeares tyme, but yf suche persone bee a Covenant Servaunt or apprentyce he shalbe foorthwith sent away or shipped into England and not to return and bee Employed in or about the Trade of a Merchant Adventurer in three yeares after vpon pain of fyftie pounds sterlinge doeinge to the Contrarie to bee levyed vpon his persone & goodes or vpon the persone and goodes of his Maister or suche other as shall sett hym one worke, And yf the said fact shalbe Committed against anie straunger or foreign persone The Court vpon Com- folio 145. plaint shall doe lyke Justice as yf the trespasse were donne against a brother of the ffellowshippe.

No persone of this ffellowshippe shall interrupt or lett another in his bergain buyinge or Sellinges or by anie means devyce or signe by himself Broker or other persone shall attempt to lett or hinder anothers proceedinge in buyinge bergayninge or sellinge vpon pain of ffyve poundes sterlinge.

No person of this ffellowshippe whatsoever shall take his Chamber or Pack house in anie suspected house or place or shall haunt to or lodge in anie suche house or place vpon pain of ffyve poundes sterlinge for euerie tyme he shalbe found faultie in the premisses, Neither shall anie persone of this ffellowshippe lodge in Taverne Inne or Victuaillinge house or have his Pack house or sett his wares in anie suche place to bee solde vpon pain of ffyve poundes sterlinge a month for so longe as he shall so lodge etc[a].

No maryed man of this ffellowshippe shall keep or holde anie harlot lighte or euill disposed woman or abuse himself with anie suche, vpon pain to forfeict for the first offence ffourtie poundes sterlinge for the second offence one hundred markes ster: and Offendinge the third tyme to bee Clearly dismissed of and from the liberties of the said ffellowshippe. And yf anie vnmaryed persone (not beinge an apprentice) shalbe found and prooued Culpable of the foresaid offence, he shall forfeict and pay for the first tyme tenn poundes sterlinge for the second tyme twentie poundes sterlinge and for the third offence ffourtie poundes sterlinge, and bee further punished at the discretion of the Court, a third parte of the Broakes to the ffellowshippe a third to the presenter and the other third to the poor.

Yf anie Apprentyce or Covenant servant in qualitye of an Apprentice shall Commonly and Inordinately vse dauncinge mumminge or walkinge abroad in the night seasone at vndue houres and after warninge or admonition given him by the Governor or his deputie shall not surcease suche yll rule, or yf anie apprentyce shall keep any strumpett, harlot or lighte woman or abuse his bodie, With anie suche or shall by gaminge, Exces in apparaille

ryot or other misrule Consume his maisters his own or
other mens goodes, he shall foorthwith either haue his
Charge or busynes taken from him by the Court be folio 146.
shipped home to his maister and banished the ffellowshippe one this syde the Seas for twoe yeares tyme, and
then also not to return but at the Request of his maister
and vpon Suertyes sett for his honest and good behaviour
thereafter or else he shalbe dealt withall and punished
otherwise at the discretion of the Governour or his
deputie and the Assistentes or Associates.

MISDEMEANOUR, EXCES.

No persone of this ffellowshippe being his owne man
shall vse vnreasonable or excessive drinkinge or to the
occasioninge of drunknes in himself or others shall vse
quaffinge or great draughtes of Wine or other drinke
forcinge or provokinge others to pledge, or to doe the
lyke he shall forfeict and pay for suche his offence tenn
shillinges fflemishe to the poor to be Collected by the
wardens, And yf after admonition given him by the said
Wardens or by the Conseirge or freehoste to forbear he
will not forbear & surcease but Continueth his disorder,
he shall forfeict and pay twentie shillinges fflemishe and
euerie tyme after the doble of the said somme to the vse
of the poor, and shalbe further rebuked and punished at
the discretion of the Court, And yf the Wardens shalbe
Negligent in demaundinge of the said penalties they
shalbe Compelled to pay the said penalties themselues,
And yf they will not demaund the penalties aforesaid
they shall forfeict and pay to the vse of the ffellowshippe
ffyve poundes sterlinge.

Yf anie apprentice shall use excessiue quaffinge or
drinkinge provokinge also others therevnto or shall playe

openly or Covertly at Cardes tables dyce or anie other
game for above 6ᵈ a game or shall by vsinge vauntinge
bettinge partinge or by anie other means or wayes exceed
the said valew, or shall bee out of his lodginge after tenn
a Clock in the summer and nyne a Clock in the winter
seasone he shalbe punished at the discretion of the Governour or his deputie and the Assistentes or Associates.

Yf anie persone of the ffellowshippe shalbe present
where excessive quaffinge and drinkinge ys vsed by
others and shall not Informe the Wardens (beinge absent
and knowinge of anie suche excesse) of the vsers Causer
or Causers thereof, he and euerie one in that Companie or
at the table where suche excessiue drinkinge as aforesaid
ys vsed, and not Informinge thereof shall forfeict and pay
tenn shillinges fflemishe to the vse of the poor, And yf
he or they shall refuse to make payment of the said
Broake beinge demaunded by the Wardens or by anie of
them, he or they so refusinge shall forfeict and pay ffyve
poundes sterlinge a man for their disobedience to the vse
of the ffellowshippe.

folio 147.

An Apprentice makinge a sett Bankett dinner or supper
shall Enforme the Governour or his deputie or the Treasurer or Secretarie thereof, and shall not make anie sett
Bankett dinner or supper in anie other place then the
Conseirge or ffree hostes houses for the furtherance and
advancement of his maisters busynes onely or by the
order of his maister, and not otherwise vpon pain of
suche punishment as shalbe found meet by the Governour or his deputie and the Court.

PLAY, GAMINGE ETC.

No persone of this ffellowshippe beinge his owne man
shall playe either at dyce Cardes or tables in these partes

one this syde the Seas, or shall sett or give out anie
monie or monies woorth to bee played or shalbe partner
in play with anie that doe playe at dyce Cardes or tables,
upon pain of twentie poundes sterlinge, for the first tyme
offendinge herein, the second tyme after One hundred
poundes sterlinge. And yf anie persone of the ffellowshippe whatsoever shall offend by anie other kynde of
gaminge not aboue mentioned and Contrarie to the true
meaninge of this Order against all vnlawfull gaminge, he
shalbe by the Governour or his deputie first warned to
surcease and then yf after suche warninge he shalbe
found to offend in that or anie other matter of gaminge
whether he bee a ffreeman or an Apprentice he shalbe
punished for euerie suche Offence with the order aboue
sett downe against gaminge. Provided notwithstandinge
that yt shalbe lawfull for anie not beinge an apprentice to
play at Cardes tables or other game so as he doe not exceed 12^d by vauntinge, lyinge bettinge partinge or other
lyke manner in anie one game.

No persone of this ffellowshippe shall playe at anie
game of Cardes tables etc^a in the Conseirges or ffree hostes
houses one the saboth daye vpon payn of ffyve shillings
fflemishe and the Conseirge or ffree hostes sufferinge anie
suche playe or gaminge shall forfeict & pay ten shillings
ffiemishe to the vse of the poor.

BERGAYNINGE ONE DAYES PROHIBITED.

When anie Brother of this ffellowshippe shall leave of
or forbear occupyinge or trade in these partes beyond the
Seas or shall by Expresse woordes declare to the letters
or owners of his Packhouse or Chamber that he will not
keep or have the same anie longer but that they may lett
out or hyre the same to some other at their pleasures for

their moste advantage or suche lyke woordes, then and from thencefoorfh suche Chamber or Packhouse ys and shalbe vnderstood to bee given over, so as yt shall and may bee lawfull for anie other persone of the ffellowshippe to hyre the same and not before or otherwise vpon pain of twentie poundes sterlinge and besydes to bee disposessed or depryved of the said Chamber or packhouse.

No Brother of the ffellowshippe shall sell shew or deliver anie Clothe Kersye or other Commoditye or ware whatsoever in the week dayes in tyme of sermoon or divine exercyse vpon pain of twentie poundes sterlinge. Neither shall anie persone sell shew or deliuer or buy, barter or bergain in way of Merchandise vpon the Saboth day, or other day, (althoughe otherwise one of the ordinarie shew dayes) sett a parte for a Generall faste or thankesgivinge vnto God, by order of the superiours or Magistrate vpon the same penaltie of twentie poundes sterlinge, to the vse of the ffellowshippe without favour or pardone.

Whoesoeuer of the ffellowshippe shall seperate himself ffrom the Ordinarie Churche or Congregation established by the Common Consent of the said ffellowshippe one this syde the Seas and Especially of the Governour or his deputie and Assistentes or Associates, suche persone vpon his seperation plainly discerned shalbe first Called before the Governour or his deputie and the Assistentes or Associates in the presence of the Minister then in place. And yf after admonition by the Court given him, he shall not revnite himself to the Churche and behave himself as a member thereof ought to doe, order shalbe foorthwith taken ffor the sendinge away into England or shippinge home of suche persone.

DECEIPT IN WARES ETC. NOYSOMNES, BY DOGGES.

No persone of this ffellowshippe shall by himself or by folio 149. anie other to his knowledg falsely or deceiptfully mingle vse or pack or handle hoppes peper or anie other wares whatsoever neither shall buy anie suche mingeled or falsefyed wares, which aforehand he knew to bee falsefyed or mingeled vpon pawn of ffourtie poundes sterlinge.

Yf anie persone Clayminge the ffreedome of this ffellowshippe either Patrimonie Seruyce or anie other Tyttle or pretence shall before or at suche his Claym bee found or prooued of vnhonest behaviour or not the Kynges true liegeman and subiect, or a Coosener felon or suche lyke Infamous persone, or bee iustly attainted of anie heynous Cryme, he shall not in anie wise bee admitted or receiued into the liberties or ffreedome of the said ffellowshippe. And yf anie persone after his Admission into the ffreedome of this ffellowshippe shalbe found guiltie of anie the abouewritten or other Capitall Cryme he shalbe ipso facto disffranchised and put out of the said ffellowshippe and never after bee receiued to the same again.

To avoyde much noysomnes besydes sundry daungers displeasures and Quarrelles that may fall out by keepinge of dogges vsed for sundry games and pastymes, yt ys Ordayned that no brother of this ffellowshippe or other persone resortinge vnder the same, shall without licence of his Excellencie or suche as have Righte or power to give leave keep anie dogge servinge for game vpon the Water or Lande, vpon payn of ffyve poundes sterlinge. And yet notwithstandinge lycence or leave so obtayned to keep dogges of game and hunt, yt shall not bee lawfull to keep anie suche dogge or dogges within the Englishe house or to lett them Comme into the said house or into the Church vpon the same penaltie of ffyve poundes sterlinge to bee levyed vpon the maister or owner of suche dogge or dogges as aforesaid.

IMPOSITIONS, ASSESMENTES CHARGES AND DUTIES TO THE HOUSE.

The Governour of this ffellowshippe of merchantes Adventurers or his deputie or deputees and the Assistentes or the greateest parte of them whereof the Governour or his deputie to bee one shall have ffull power and Authoritie to Impose and Taxe as also to take and levye accordinge to the Charters and Privileges one this behalfe all reasonable Impositions and sommes of monie whatsoever as well vpon all persons tradinge into the lowe Countries or Germanie or the partes neare adioyninge as also vpon the wares and merchandises transported or Caryed or to bee Transported and Caryed either into the said Countries or anie parte thereof either to Calais in ffraunce either by Water or by land or to be brought by anie subiect of the Realms of England or Ireland or of Wales from thence as to the said Governour or his deputie or deputees and the said Assistentes shalbe found necessarie and Convenient for the supportation mayntenance and good Government of the abouesaid ffellowshippe and to the vse benefyte and Commoditie of the same.

All white Clothes of eight and twentie yardes and vnder all short suffolke Blewes kersyes Bridgwaters Pennistones doosens Bayes Cottons etc* shall pay viii^d ster: per Clothe Impositions. And all fyne Clothes exceedinge eight and twentie yardes in lengthe and all Coloured Clothes (except short suffolke blewes) shall pay

178

xii^d sterlinge Impositions per Cloth and this Imposition to Continew vpon the abouesaid wares and all other woollen and other Englishe Commodityes reduced to the rate of a short Clothe, duringe the ffellowshippes pleasure and that otherwise bee lawfully Ordayned.

Euerie persone beinge his owne man and an ordinarie shipper of Englishe Commoditye shall pay for personall Impositions four shillinges sterlinge To Wytt when he shippeth no wares to the marte, or yf he doe when the Impost of the same amounts not aboue the said personall Impositions that marte otherwise he ys to pay accordinge to his doeinges.

Item Euerie Brother from tyme to tyme present in the folio 156. marte Towne or Townes having one or more partners in his Trade shall by himself his factor or servant martly sett downe in the booke of Impositions the name or names of euerie suche his partner and partners vpon pain for omittinge the same to pay fourtie shillinges sterlinge for a fyne to the vse of the ffellowshippe without favour or pardone.

Item euerie Partner or partners Brethern of the ffellowshippe althoughe they bee two or three or more in Companie and that but one of them bee in the Marte Towne, whose doeinges in the Marte shall not exceed their severall personall Impositions shall pay for each of their Impositions a parte fower shillinges sterlinge a man for so manie as they are.

Item. Euerie Brother of this ffellowshippe Refusinge or havinge his beinge in the Marte Towne or Townes or anie of them, althoughe yt shall not appear that he for the tyme shipped Commodityes thether or bought Commodityes there yet shall he pay euerie Marte wherein he shalbe present personall Impositions To Wytt fower shil-

linges sterlinge, And all brethern passinge but throughe
the Marte Townes as Trauaillers shall pay the same personall Impositions.

Item. Euerie Brother shippinge Englishe Commodytie
to the Towne of Embden shall not onlye first give Notice
of the iust qualitie & quantitie thereof vnto the deputie
or Appointers in Londone, But also bee holden and bound
not to Transporte the same from the said Towne where
the sale thereof ys to be made and elswhere except in the
Marte Towne vpon the penaltie of fourtie shillinges sterlinge per Clothe and vpon all other Englishe Commodities
after the Rate. Lykewise that the said deputie and Appointers in Londone vnto whome suche notice ys given
shalbe holden vpon the penaltie of ffyve poundes ster:
to send advertisement thereof with the first Conveniencie
vnto the place of Authoritie one this syde the Seas for the
better gatheringe of the Impositions dew for the said
Clothes etc. which shalbe dewlie paid and aunsweared in
one of the Marte Townes in the verie same Marte that
the goodes were shipped out or in the verie next Marte
followinge.

folio 157. Item Euerie persone Tradinge to the Towne of Calais
in ffraunce shalbe Bound to give true and iust notice of
suche Clothes Kersyes and suche other Englishe Commodityes as he purposethe to shippe from tyme to tyme or
shall shippe thether to the Governour or his deputie in
Londone although the said Clothes etc are to bee passed
without licence and to paye the Treasurer of the ffellowshippe there for the tyme being the Impositions dew for
the same. And that before the shippinge out thereof or
at the furthest before the end of the Marte wherein the
said Commodityes are shipped out vpon the penaltie Ordayned for misshippers.

When anie Brother shall send over sonne or Servaunt to bee made ffree he shall procure and present in orderly Certificate that he ys not indebted to the house for Impositions of Clothes or other wares shipped out of the Realm of England to the Towne of Embden or into anie other place in Germanie or the Lowe Countries synce the eight and twentith day of January anno 1597 or to the Towne of Calais in ffraunce synce the fourth day of December anno 1599 and yf he be found Indebted he shall pay or give satisfaction for the same before suche his sonne or servaunt shalbe admitted.

Item   Euerie Brother vsinge his trade and dealinges only in Wares and no woollen Commodityes or tradinge not at all or verie seldom in these partes shall pay twentie shillinges sterlinge a marte for his personall Impositions.

Item   whatsoever Brother at the makinge ffree either of his sonne or servant shall not bee found to have borne Charges to the house within four yeares before to the valew of eight and fourtie shillinges sterlinge he shall pay for personall Impositions at the Admission of suche his servaunt or sonne the somme of 48 shillinges ster: and that in regard of his seldom bearinge of Charge to the house & that nevertheless the number of the ffellowshippe ys by him Encreased.

Item   Euerie Brother bound to serve for wages beinge no trader himself shall pay but half personall Impositions but beinge a trader shall pay accordinge to his shippinges at least whole personall Impositions, But yf anie brother bee bound to serue without wages & bee none occupyer he shall for that tyme be free of all payment of personall Impositions.

Item   Euerie Brother of the ffellowshippe takinge ffac- folio 158.
torie of more then twoe men thoughe he have no doeinges

12

for himself shall pay whole Impositions, And yt ys to bee
vnderstood that factorie taken of standinge partners in
one Companie ys but taken of one man.

Item Euerie Brother of this ffellowshippe that shall
have anie trade or doinges in anie marte Towne shall
martly declare vnto the Treasurer or lyke Officer appointed by the Court vpon his Corporall oathe the name
and names of all suche persone and persones absent from
the Marte Towne as he hathe had anie doeinges for
thoughe it were but in receiptes and paymentes or suche
lyke matter, because that for the doeinge thereof suche
absent brethern would and should otherwise haue his or
their owne servaunts and thereby bee lyable to pay his or
their Impositions, And for euerie Brother absent to pay
his Impositions severally, vpon pain of Refusinge to take
suche oathe, or not duely discharginge euerie absente
brothers severall Impositions personall or accordinge to
his doeinges to forfeict and pay the somme of fourtie
shillinges sterlinge without favour or pardone.

Item ffreemens sonnes Admitted into the ffreedome of
this ffellowshippe havinge no doeinges of their owne but
for their fathers and takinge no factorie shall pay but
half personall Impositions, but ffreemens sonnes kept at
shoole in the Marte Townes and dealinge not at all for
themselues or others shalbe freed of all Impositions dur-
inge·that tyme.

An apprentice having served seaven yeares and tradinge within tearmes by licence shall pay but halfe Impositions personall except the Clothes Shipped that Marte
doe amount to more.

And yf Euerie Brother of this ffellowshippe by himself
his factor or servant shall refuse neglect or omitte to pay
his Impositions orderly and euerie Marte as the same ys

dew and ought to bee payd vnto the Treasurer or the
Collectors of Impositions in parte or in whole accordinge
to the true & seuerall qualitie and quantitie of the goodes
by himself or accordinge as ys before prescribed euerie
suche Brother shall forfeict and pay the doble of that
which he ought by this order to pay restinge vnpaid without favour or pardone.   And moreover yf anie Brother folio 159.
factor or servant beinge Commaunded by the Court or demaunded by the Treasurer or lyke officer for the tyme
beinge refuse payment of the said doble Impositions he
shall not only bee Compelled to pay the same but also bee
further punished at the discretion of the Governour or
his deputie and the Court, Prouided that for as muche as
the Impositions are sometymes Collected in twoe severall
places and that throughe Ignorance sometymes of that
which ys shipped to the one place & there paid for the
personall Impositions are not fully or not at all paid.   In
suche Case the Single Impositions only shalbe taken yf
in the Marte next ffollowinge after suche omission so yt
proceeded not of willful negligence the same bee orderlye
paid otherwise the doble shalbe levyed as abouesaid.

Moreouer yt ys further Ordayned that the Collectors of
Impositions shall within fourteen dayes at the furthest
after the begyninge of the new Marte make vp and subscribe the booke of Impositions dew in the Marte before
to the end that the Treasurers Accomptes for the same
Marte may bee in dew tyme, perfected and Audited as
apperteyneth, vpon the penaltie of ffyve poundes sterlinge
to bee forfeicted and paid by the said Collectors without
favour or pardone, And the Treasurers from tyme to
tyme shall haue their Accomptes in readynes to bee
Audited within tenn dayes after the makinge vp of the
said booke of Impositions, vpon pain of ten poundes sterlinge without favour or pardone.

Item all and euerie the vntradinge brethern of this ffellowshippe in the year 1588 shall accordinge to an Assessement then made vpon them pay at the makinge ffree of his or their first sonne or servaunt the said Assessement or an Assessement at the discretion of the Court where suche sonne or servaunt ys to bee admitted, yet so that none bee sett at lesse then three poundes nor none aboue twelue poundes sterlinge, And for all such Brethern as haue paid or sometymes pay personall Imposition beinge in that respect accompted traders yf from and after the ffyve and twentith daye of Marche anno *1592* vntill the end of three yeares next after suche their Impositions personall or real or accordinge to their doeinges shall not bee found in the whole to amount vnto the somme of three poundes sterlinge then euerie suche Brother shall lykewise at the makinge ffree of his first sonne or servaunt be assessed at the discretion of the Court & none to be assessed at lesse then 3 £ or more then 12 £ ster: as aforesaid.

folio 160. Item all fynes Broakes forfeictures prest monie pole monie Enhansements by Admissions into the liberties of this ffellowshippe and all other duties or Incommes whatsoever due or that ought to bee paid vnto the ffellowshippe shalbe payd Continually in sterling monie To Wytt in Germanie after the Rate of 25ˢʰ the pound sterlinge and in the lowe Countries after the rate of 33ˢʰ 4ᵈ the said pound sterlinge, Provided alwayes thatt all and euerie the Brethern of this ffellowshippe which before the ffyve and twentith day of March anno 1588 were and yet are Indebted to the house for anie Cause whatsoever shalbe at libertie to make payment of his debt or dutie in suche monie as he then ought either in Germanie or the lowe Countries to have paid or stood Charged ffor, Pro-

vided also that all pettye ffynes or Broakes as for absence
ffrom Courtes and late Comminge with suche lyke due or
payable to the poor shalbe from tyme to tyme payd in
suche monies as are Current in the places where the said
fynes or Broakes fall out and are to be levyed.

Yf this ffellowshippe shalbe, Indebted or owe vnto anie
persone or persones of the same ffellowshippe anie somme
or sommes of monie whatsoever yt bee, yt shall not bee
lawfull for anie suche persone or persones therefore to
retayn or stoppe in his or their handes anie Impositions
or anie other dutie or debt owinge to the said ffellowshippe, but shall pay the same when yt ys demaunded
vnto the Treasurer or other appointed for the receipt
thereof and of his dew shall make orderly demaund (yf
he so thinke good) at a Generall Court or Court of
Assistentes or Associates as the Case shall Requyre vpon
payn of suche witholdinge of his Impositions dutie or
debt to forfeict and pay the doble thereof without all
favour or pardone.

The Impositions for Clothe Kersye and other Englishe
Commodityes shipped for Stoad or anie parte of the
Highe Countries as also by Tolleration to Calais in
ffraunce there and in the Archdukes Countries at Antwerp to bee put to sale shall by provision bee Collected at
Londone, But whereas yt ys Requyred that all Impositions whatsoever may bee there Collected yt ys not found
meet to assent therevnto but Resolued that as hetherto
hathe been accustomed the Impositions of Clothe and
Englishe Commoditye as also personall Impositions of
the Martes shalbe still Collected at Middelbrough.   And
yt ys for auoydinge of fraude Ordayned and Enacted that
no brother of this ffellowshippe reconninge Clothe or Englishe Commoditye in the said Towne shall withold his folio 161.

Impositions for the same vnder pretence that the said Impositions are paid at Londone the Cloth etc havinge been entered for Stade or some other tolerated place, but shall pay the same orderlie vpon pain of payinge doble, And whereas there are diverse Indebted for this Cause they are foorthwith or before the end of Sinxon Marte anno 1605 to make payment or giue satisfaction to the house one that behalf vpon pain of payinge doble without favour or pardone. Actum 5th of September anno 1605. Middelburgi.

To make tryall whether that benefyte will redound to the bodie of the Companie which yt should seem the Brethern of Londone are persuaded of, namelie the Remedyinge of all the Inormities of disordered shippinge so muche Complayned and so smally hetherto redressed by anie other Course heretofore taken. Yt ys Provisionally Consented and agreed that accordinge to the desyre of the said Brethern in Londone and the order by them there devysed the Impositions of all Clothe and woollen Commoditie shipped out from the porte of Londone shalbe there Collected to the vse of the ffellowshippe in manner and forme ffollowinge To Wytt that euerie tradinge Brother hereafter before the shippinge out of anie Clothes or other Commodityes wherevpon Impositions are dew to bee payed shall bringe a true note from the Treasurer there for the tyme beinge vnto the Companies Secretarie or to suche as shall have the passinge of Entries vnder the Companies seale. That the said Treasurer ys satisfyed and paid the Impositions dew to the house for the Clothes and other Commodityes entended to bee shipped foorth by the Entrie which he shall requyre to be passed and that vpon pain not onlie to loose the benefytt of his ffree licence till the said Treasurer bee payed. But also

to bee debarred from havinge anie Entrie passed either
for Clothes vpon anie other lycence or ffor anie other
Commodities that vsually passe without licence till satisfaction be there given in that behalf.

Yt ys by Authoritye of the deputie Assistents with
Assent of the Generalitye ordayned and Enacted that yf
anie persone of this ffellowshippe doe lade or lay into anie
shippe boat bottome or Vessell or shall Cause to bee laden
or layd into anie shippe boat bottome or Vessell bound
for Stoad or anie other place one this syde the Seas, anie
Clothe Kersie or other Englishe woollen Commodityes,
which before was Entered in the Custome-house vpon the
Appointed shippe or vpon anie of them bound for Middel- folio 162.
broughe and doe not pay to the Treasurer in Londone for
the tyme beinge, before he shall so lade his Clothe
Kersye or other Woollen Englishe woollen Commoditye
for Stade or anie other place one this syde the Seas, the
full Impositions or duties due to the ffellowshippe for
them, he shall forfeict and pay to the vse of the said
ffellowshippe 6^{sh} 8^{d} sterlinge for euerie Clothe and all
other woollen Commodityes after the Rate so shipped
laden or layd into anie shippe boat bottome or other
Vessell And Moreover shalbe debarred of all benefyte
and vse of the ffree licence vntill he have satisfyed and
payd the said penaltie without favour or pardone.

For[1] the raysing of moneys for the necessary occasions

---

[1] Change of handwriting. The remaining orders of this chapter
belong to the period of the great disorder in trade under James I.,
and are therefore of especial interest.   It was during this period
that the society was compelled to hand in its charter and for several years make way for a new company promoted by Cockayne.
In 1617, however, the Adventurers were restored to their privileges.   Proclamation, Aug. 12, 1617, S. P. Dom. 187, 50.

of the ffellowshipp It is agreed that an ymprest of ij^s viii^d vpon a short Cloth and iiij^s vpon a long Cloth shalbe lent by the trading breathren of this ffellowshipp vnto the house, to be collected vpon all suche cloth as shalbe shipped for or vnto any the parte of the priviledges of this ffellowshipp beyond the Seas before Christmas next. And that the husband of the house shall keepe a perfect Accompt of the said ymprest moneys: to the end the ympresors maybe repaid as shall apperteyne. Generall Court at London the xixth of March Anno 1616.

The xviijth of May anno 1617 it was ordered that the ymprest money vppon a Coloured cloth dressed shalbe but ij^s and the ymposicon vppon the same but xij^a.

At a Generall Court holden in London the xiiijth of January 1617, It was agreed, That for the discharging of the great debtes [1] of the ffellowshipp, the Imprest raysed to iiij^s vpon a short white cloth, and vj^s vpon a long: and the Imposicons to xij^d vpon a short Cloth, & xviij^d vpon a long.

At a Generall Court holden in London the xxvjth of January anno 1617 It was further agreed that after the Continuance of the Collection of the Imprest money for some iij or iiij yeares whereby the debts of the ffellow-shipp may in the mean tyme be in some good measure discharged: then a fitt order and Course shalbe set for the repayment also of the said Imprest moneys.

folio 163. At a Generall Court holden in Londone the xvjth of September anno 1618. It was agreed that Clothes deyed and dressed out of whites shalbe passed for the Imposi-tions of xij^d the short, and xviij^d the long Cloth without any imprest money.

---

[1] The debts of the Fellowship at a somewhat later date appear in a petition to Parliament as amounting to £80,000. Cf. Newcastle Merchants Adventurers, II., 116.

ORDINANCE TOUCHINGE MARIAGE WITH FOREIGN BORNE WEMEN AND PURCHASE OF LANDES ETC OUT OF THE REALM OF ENGLAND.

Yf anie persone which now ys or hereafter shalbe ffree of the ffellowshippe of Merchantes Adventurers of the Realm of England shall at anie tyme or tymes take to wyfe anie women borne out of the said Realm or the dominions thereof though Endenised or even naturalized by Judgment of Sir Henry Hubbard the Kynges Atturnye Generall or shall at anie tyme or tymes purchase obtayne gett or have to himself or anie persone or persons to his vse or vpon anie Confidence or trust anie landes Tenementes or hereditamentes in anie these partes or places beyond the Seas out of the Realm of England or the dominions thereof suche persone shall then and from thencefoorth Imediately after suche mariage or purchase so to bee had or made be (ipso facto) disfranchised of and from the said ffellowshippe, and shall not anie tyme hereafter be reputed receiued accepted accosed as one of the said ffellowshippe or ffree of the same, but shall from thencefoorth in all and euerie place and places be'e vtterly excluded of and from all libertyes Trade of Merchandise preeminences Jurisdictions and voyces belonginge to the said ffellowshippe or to anie persone beinge ffree of the same, neither shall anie suche persone as aforesaid in anie wise duringe so longe tyme as he or anie persone or persones to his vse or vpon anie Confidence or trust shalbe seised of anie Landes, Tenementes or Hereditaments in

189

these parties out of the Realm of England, or duringe so
longe tyme as he and his wyfe shall Enhabite out of the
said Realm of England or the dominions thereof assembled amongst the said ffellowshippe or be present at anie
Consultation Conference Court or Counseill to be had by
or amongst the said ffellowshippe.

Yf anie Brother of this ffellowshippe shall purchase
obtayn gett or have to himself or to anie other persone or
persones to his vse or vpon anie Confidence or Trust anie
Landes Tenementes or hereditamentes in anie these partes
or places beyond the Seas out of the Realm of England or
the dominions thereof or shall Intend to marye with a
Straunger or foreign borne woman though Endenized or
euen Naturalized by Judgment of the Kyngs Atturny
folio 168. Generall he shall declare and signifye suche his purchase
or Intention of Mariage at a Generall Court and Craue
licence to sue for letters Patents ffor Remission of the
Statute made in the year anno 1564 whereby he ys (ipso
facto) disfranchised by reasone of suche his purchase or
maryage agreable also with this Ordinance one that behalf for the obtayninge whereof (yf he gett licence of
Court) tyme may bee graunted him, and withall have
duringe the said tyme at the discretion of the said Court
to Continue his Trade, yf so yt shall seem good vnto the
Court, without which leave or licence he shall not vse the
Trade of Merchaunt Adventurer, but forbear the same
wholie till he haue licence or that by virtue of the aboue
mentioned letters Patents he bee Readmitted vpon pain
never to be receiued into the ffreedome of the ffellowshippe by anie way or means whatsoever but to bee held
and reputed as an vnffree persone for euer after.

And suche persone as aforesaid havinge tyme graunted
him to procure the said Letters Patents and beinge withall

licenced duringe the tyme to ffollow and vse the Trade of
a Merchant Adventurer yf he doe not present the said
letters Patents at or within the tyme appointed no further
or longer tyme or respyte shalbe given him, nor licence
to trade graunted, but he shall foorthwith forbear and
leave the Trade of a merchant Adventurer till he haue
presented the said Letters Patents and be readmitted in
open Generall Court by Virtue of the same, and licence
of the ffellowshippe as aforesaid vpon pain never to bee
receiued into the ffreedome of the said ffellowshippe by
anie means whatsoever but vtterly to bee Excluded from
the same.

But yf anie persone disfranchised for foreign purchase
or mariage doe as abouesaid present his letters Patents of
Remission and grace he shalbe Readmitted into the ffreedome of the ffellowshippe vpon the same Haunce that he
was first ffree of payinge all duties to the House, And a
gratification suche as the Court shall thinke meet to impose vpon him, Except suche persone duringe the tyme
of his disfranchisement bee found and prooued to haue
donne and Committed anie thinge or trespasse against
the Ordinances of the ffellowshippe by means whereof he
ought not to be received into the ffreedome of the said
ffellowshippe.

And suche persone beinge receiued into the ffreedome folio 169.
of the ffellowshippe again shall have Convenient tyme
sett and appointed him by the Court to make sale of
suche landes Tenementes or hereditaments as he hathe
purchased or otherwise obtayned or gotten in righte of
his wyfe and to dispose of his other affaires, the which
tyme beinge he shall foorthwith remoue with his wyfe
and familie into England or some parte of the dominions
thereof there to remain and dwell except for some vrgent

Cause he shalbe licenced by the Court to return into these partes. But yf before or by the tyme appointed he shall not make sale of his Landes Tenementes, hereditamentes aforesaid remoue into England or the dominions thereof with his Wyfe and familie and there remain and dwell as aforesaid he shalbe held and reputed an unffree persone and disfranchysed neuer after to Enioye anie Liberties Rightes Priuileges or benefytes of the said ffellowshippe his said former Readmission by Letters Patents which in this Cas eorrespect ar voyd and of none effect by the tenour thereof Nothwithstandinge.

And yf anie persone shall obtayn leaue to Continue his Trade for a tyme or to dispose of his affaires by or within a Certain tyme or shalbe licenced to return with his wyfe and familie into these partes, he shall not duringe the said tyme of his abode deale as factor for anie man, nor doe the busynes of anie other then of himself and his partner and partners in Joinct Companie vpon pain to forfeict after the Rate of four poundes sterlinge per Clothe vpon all woollen Commodityes by him solde and tenn poundes sterlinge vpon euerie hundred poundes sterlinge woorth of all other wares or Commodityes by him bought sold or handeled, the one half to bee paid by suche persone himself and the other halfe by him or them that shall employ or sett suche persone one worke yf there bee anie suche, yf not the whole penaltie aboue written shalbe paid by the Offender alone.

Provided that suche persones as are in publicke seruyce of the ffellowshippe or are ffree brokers havinge procured their Letters Patents & otherwise performed the Contentes of the same may dwell and remain in these partes duringe suche their publicke service or vocation. Provided also that euerie Brother whoe hathe been so maryed

or ys alredie knowen to have been precontracted before
the seaventeenth day of Julie anno 1564 may Enioye
suche ffreedomes and liberties as by an Act made before
that tyme and yet in force they might haue enioyed. folio 170.
And whatsoever graunt hathe been heretofore made by
the ffellowshippe vnto anie persone in respect of his
abode or dealings for himself one this syde the Seas,
otherwise then by this Ordinance ys permitted shalbe to
suche persone Respectiuely holden and performed so that
he deale not in trade of a merchaunt Adventurer for anie
else then he did deale for at the tyme of the abouesaid
graunt anie thinge herein to the Contrarie Notwithstandinge.   And no brother of this ffellowshippe shall
procure, solicite or Consent by woord wrylinge silence or
otherwise the violation of the abouewritten ordinance or
of anie Clause Article or sentence thereof vpon pain to
forfeict to the vse of the ffellowshippe yf yt bee the
Governour ffourtie poundes sterlinge yf his deputie
ffourtie markes sterlinge yf an Assistent or Associate
twentie poundes sterlinge and yf one of the Generalitie a
ffreeman or havinge voyce in Court twentie markes sterlinge to bee levyed without favour or pardone or in
default thereof the partie Offendinge one this behalf to be
disfranchised and dismissed of and from the ffreedome of
this ffellowshippe.

No persone disfranchised for maryinge or doeinge
Contrarie to this Act or Ordinance or anie parte thereof
shall take anie apprentice to be ffree of this ffellowshippe
duringe the tyme of suche his disfranchisement albeyt
that he haue leaue to trade vpon pain that suche apprentice shall not enioye anie ffreedome in the said ffellowshippe.   But yf anie apprentice haue been taken before
the disfranchisement of his maister for the abouesaid

Cause thoughe his said maister be Readmitted but be still vnffree yet he shall and may bee admitted into the liberties of the ffellowshippe the maister payinge for a fyne at the Admission of suche apprentice over and aboue all other duties the somme of ffyve poundes sterlinge.

As well all suche Brethern of this ffellowshippe as are alredie maryed, as also all those that shall hereafter marye with anie Endenized or Naturalised straungers borne shalbe vnderstood to bee and shalbe ipso facto disfranchised exempted and fallen from the ffreedome liberties, trade of merchandise preheminences Jurisdictions and voices belonginge to the said ffellowshippe and folio 171. accordingly shall not bee suffered to vse the trade of a merchant Adventurer by buyinge, sellinge, shippinge vpon licence or without anie other means whatsoeuer, Except, they shall by leaue of Court first had and obteyned accordinge to the Orders of the ffellowshippe bee permitted so to doe; or have sued out by lyke leave and procured Letters Patents of Remission and bee Readmitted, as hathe been the Custome in the Case of foreign mariage vpon the forfeictures and penalties provided by the said Orders, accordinge to which Orders in euerie point they are to bee vsed and dealt withall by the Court, as also to frame and demean themselues, Enacted the 28th Decembris anno 1609 In Middelbroughe.

THE BYE LAW OR AGREEMENT BETWEEN THE   folio 200
RESIDENCES OF LONDON & HAMBURGH
DATED 22^d OCT^r 1688.

Forasmuch as the Charter of the Fellowship of merchants Adventurers of England is to be Renewed and the Residence of London hath thought it convenient to have the vse of some particular Priviledges secured to themselves.

Viz^t

That the Residence of London shall have the Sole 1 Choice of the Deputy and All other Officers used in & for that Residence.

That no By Laws shall be made or Ratifyed hereafter 2 with out Concurrence of the Residence of London and that those already made shall be revised and either confirmed or Altered by joint consent of the Residences of London & Hamburg.

That no Imposition Rates or Duties shall be assessed 3 relating to Trade without the Consent of the Residence of London.

All which being communicated to the Residence of Hamburgh wee are contented therewith in manner Following And therefore Wee the said Residence of Ham-

[1] For obvious reasons this by-law is appended to the general body of the laws instead of being introduced under one or other of the chapters of Wheeler's Digest, as is the case with the shorter orders of the later period. For a discussion of the agreement here arrived at by the two Residences, see the paper on the "Organization of the Merchants Adventurers," Transactions of the Royal Historical Society. Vol. 15.

burgh by our Publick letter to the Residence of London dated the sixth of December 1687. Have Amply Signifyed our Willingness to Sattisfye the said Residence of London and to secure their Interest in the particulars mentioned in all Brotherly affection And Sincere Intentions faithfully therein Promising them Neuer to impose on them in any of the said particulars and to ratifye the same by a Publick Act of our Court here. In as Strong & binding words as they themselves can devise so as the said Alterations might be settled between us and the said Residence of London And not by any Alteration in the Charter which Offers the said Residence of London by their publick letters dated the 20ᵗʰ day of January last haue accepted & Agreed to.

folio 201. In pursuance of which agreement for the Settleling an Intire Peace and Union Between us the Said Residence of Hamburgh and the said Residence of London & for securing the said Residence of London and their Successors in the enjoyment of the said Priviledges for time to come.

It is now hereby Voted & Declared Enacted and Ordained by the Deputy Assistants and Fellowship of merchants Adventurers of England in this Residence of Hamburgh at Our Generall Court held here this Two and Twentieth day of October 1688. That notwithstanding the Clauses in all or any of the Charters of the said Fellowship heretofore Granted or hereafter to be granted whereby the Governour Assistants & Fellowshipp of merchants Adventurers of England or any of them Resiant beyond the Seas are or shall be empowered to choose a Governor and all the Officers Committees and Associates of the said Fellowshipp as well in England as beyond the Sea And to make Laws, Statutes and Ordinances for the Government of the said Fellowship and to Tax Impose take and Levy Impositions Rates Sums of Money for the Suport thereof And Notwithstanding the usage of Us the said Residence of Hamburgh in Exercising the said severall Powers.

Wee the said Deputy Assistants & Fellowshipp in the said Residence of Hamburgh doe hereby Enact Ordain and Establish in manner and form following

Viz'

That no Governour of the Fellowshipp shall be chosen 1 hereafter without the foreknowledge & Consent first had of the Residence of London And that the Governour of the Fellowshipp or his Deputy in the Residence of London togeather with the Generality of the said Residence shall have and Wee doe hereby give them free liberty Lycence Sole Power & Authority from time to time and at all times hereafter to Elect & Choose & appoint a Deputy and soe many Other.

13

THE RISE AND STATE OF THE FELLOWSHIP OF MER-
CHANT-ADVENTURERS OF ENGLAND.[1]

Br. Mus. Stowe MS. 303, fols. 99-108.

The English Nation after the conjunction of the Hep-
tarchy of the Saxons before all Hiemo[es] could be settled
were first so suddenly invaded, and att last for some
years suppressed by the Danes, & afterwardes so totally
broken & Conquered by the Normans, that there can noe
footsteps be found of any fforeign Trade driven by the
Natives of the Land in those times.

And thence till Edward the 3[d] they were so engaged in
ffrance to maintain that interest on the other side the sea
which the Norman ffamily brought along with it to this
crowne, and afterwards in the Barons wars for their
libertyes, and then in the Conquest of Wales Ireland and
Scotland, that there was little provision in all that time
made to civilize the nation and lead the people into a

---

[1] This account belongs to the early 17th century. The strong
pleading for a regulated trade and the special privileges of the
Fellowship stamps it at once as belonging to that voluminous mass
of controversial writing called by Schanz, "*Flug und partei-
Schriften*," on trade and monopolies, during the period of Elizabeth and the Stuarts. During James I.'s reign the Adventurers
were for several years deprived of their charter privileges, and
throughout the entire period they were forced to fight vigorously
for their rights. The above account must therefore be read as a
source more or less partisan in character. For a similar account
see p. 210 of this volume; also the "Petition of the Merchant Adventurers before Parliament against the Act of 12 Henry VII.,
c. 6, Br. Mus. Harl. MS. 597, fol. 211, published by Schanz,
Handelspolitik, II., p. 582.

likeing of fforeign traffique or the attempting of any manufacture att home, which might lay the foundation
thereof. But first the jews and the Lombards and then
the Easterlings and the Hanses of Germany and Merchants of the Netherlands under the House of Burgundy
had obtained such interest in the princes throughout
those times, that they were invested with the highest
priveleges that could be demanded farre above the
natives, possessed of the whole trade of this land, and
transported the fatt thereof into their own countries and
in effect had made such a greater conquest upon the people and estates of the English then either the Dane or
the Norman. All that was attempted in this time of
darkness was by some few mercers of London then called
the Brethren of St. Thomas of Beckett[1] who towards the

[1] The origin of the Fellowship of Merchants Adventurers, and
their connection with the Brotherhood of St. Thomas is still very
obscure. Modern writers accept an intimate relationship between
the early Adventurers and the Mercers, but they are all inclined to
treat the claims of the Society to origin in a Brotherhood of St.
Thomas à Becket as invented. Gross, *Gild Merchant*, I. 149;
Schanz, *Handelspolitik*, I. 336; Green, *Town Life*, I. 94. On the
other hand the statements of the Adventurers are definite and
emphatic on their early existence as a Brotherhood under the
name of St. Thomas à Becket. Wheeler, *A Treatise on Commerce*, 10; Act, 12 Henry VII, c. 6, Stowe (cited above), etc. No
evidence bearing on the question that is at all definite in character
has been known to exist. Quite recently, however, there came to
my notice an historic fact which establishes St. Thomas à Becket
beyond a doubt, as the patron saint of the Adventurers at a comparatively early date. In the charter to the Adventurers in 1462
provision is made for the use of certain fines to maintain two
chapels in honor of St. Thomas à Becket of Canterbury (Hakluyt,
I. 208). This is clear proof of a practice, on the part of the Fellowship, in harmony with the later claim.

end of the yeare 1200, did sometimes repayre into the
Netherlands there to seek the commodities of their trade
which in two days were brought thither over the moun-
tains through Germany by land where as they quickly
found better advantages to furnish themselves for their
oune occasions, soe they as soone observed what infinite
riches the people of those Countries did acquire by endraping the woolls of this Land, & venting the same into
all Nations, Serving the English *alsoe* wth Clothing of that
materiall wch they could have noe where, in those days,
but hence, & all supported and maintained by that
Excellent polity of Government, which was observed
both by Maker & M^{e}chant, in their severall callings,
ffrom all wch therefore they were stirred up to try if they
might, after they were known in those countries, obtain
that countenance from some of the princes, In those
provinces which for the favor and power of the Easterlings and others with the Kings of England they did dis-
payre of att home and at last A° 1296 [1] they were as a
governed body entertayned by John Duke of Brabant,
and endowed with many great priveleges.   Under this
p^{o}tences the English first began the trade of fforeign
Commodities imported hither, & together therew^{th} had

---

[1] Compare with this date that of 1248 in the extract from Wheeler,
p. 210.   In a petition of the Adventurers to Parliament in the time
of Elizabeth there is still another date.   "For in the tyme of
John, Duke of Brabant, Earle of Flanders, successor to the said
Ferdinande in the yeare of our lord god 1216 . . . for continuance
of trade, priveleges were given to the said Englysh Marchants to
come and returne to and from those partes, to choose a capytayne
or counsell there, to examine determine and punish all trespasses
whatsoever (offences towchinge mutulation of member and life only
excepted)." Br. Mus. Harl. MS. 597, fol. 211.   Printed in Schanz,
Handelspolitik, II., Urk. Bei. 134.

the opportunity to incline & invite divers Clothiers of those Countries to repayre for England, & sett up the manufacture of Clothing here, wherein alsoe they p°vayled. And afterwards when Edward the 3ᵈ came into those Countries, where he first assumed the tittle & Armes of ffrance, He beinge eye witnesse of the fflourishing of those people upon the operation of English woolles alone, was the first Prince of this Land that put him self forth to advance Clothing in England, as the many wholesome Lawes made in his Reigne doe fully manifest. Upon those foundations Hen. 4ʰ, his Grandchild, though not next successo°, knowing well upon what tittle he gott the Croune, did Seek to divert the warlike people of this Nation upon the Making of cloth, & other Woollen Manufactures, & finding from experience that from the fruits of Government already begun by the English in fforeign parts, they had not only obtayned a Considerable trade inwards, but had soe farre advanced the Clothing in England in the interim, that their was noe need of fforeign Drapy, & all this notwithstanding all the troubles for 110 years before both abroad & att home, did first incorporate the English Mᵉchnts here in England a' 1406, 8° Regni, which Chres were likewise confirmed, & enlarged as there was occasion by all succeeding Kings, except Edward 5ᵗʰ till Henry 7ᵗʰ, & severall Nationall Intercourses made betweene this Realme & the House of Burgundy wᶜʰ exceedingly p°moted ye Trade in England even during those long bloudy warres betweene the Branches of Yorrke and Lancaster. When Hen. 7ᵗʰ had p°vayled, he having the same cares & motives as Hen. 4ᵗʰ pursued the same designe, & as in his Reigne ye Charters of the said ffellowshipp were often renewed, soe they were as often enlarged wᵗʰ divers wholesome Laws for

Goverm᙮. Ye effect whereof was such as that to his time it is justly asscribed that the English Clothing first obtayned its renoune, both abroad & att home, and then first this State durst adventure upon Lawes for restraining what Clothes should be exported undyed & undressed, & so to give a Law to the Stranger ffrom whence have arisen the ffraternityes & Crafts of Cloth workers & Dyers, and so the full Manufacture of the English Drapery.

The Reignes of Hen. 8ᵗʰ, Edw. 6ᵗʰ & Queen Mary still cherished ye sᵈ ffellowspp, each Prince severally & successively confirming and renewing the same Grants unto them, by wᶜʰ countenance as the Trade still proposed & fell more & more into the hands of the Natives, soe the Mᵉchnts of the Steelyard & those of the Intercourse did both in those tymes forfeit their priviledges, & have ever since bene contayned wᵗʰin the just bounds of Strangers, yett still consistent wᵗʰ all mutuall & neighborlly correspondence.

Queene Elizabeth in her Reigne, did find the maintaininge of the ffellowspp, & the inlarging of their Chres, & reducing of their Govᵉmt to more exact Rules, wᶜʰ tho thrice passed under Lʳᵉˢ Patents, to be the only remedy against ye proscription of ye English both out of Germany & the Low Countryes, wᶜʰ had that success that still Clothing increased & ye sᵈ ffellowspp again recovered footing both in Germany & the Low Countryes notwithstanding all the opposition of the Emperor, & the King of Spain. And, whereas before the troubles, this Nacon vented not above 30000 Cloths into the Low Countryes, & 6000 Cloˢ into Germany by the Hanses or Steelyard men, they where advanced to 60000 Cloˢ yearly exported.

The 12ᵗʰ & 13ᵗʰ years of King James brought up the

Clothing of this Land to ye greatest height & glory that ever was seene in any nation, in somuch that for divers years together ye ffellowspp alone, besides all other Mchnts, trading Spayne, Ffrance, Italy, Turky, the East Lands, Muscovia, & other pts., did transport for Germany & the 17 Provinces of the Netherlands 80 & 90000 Cls. yearly, besides a greate Number of Coloured Clo[s] & other Wooll[n] Manufactures made & p[e]fected in England.

This deduccon is brought thus farre doune, p[r]ly to show that w[th] the ffellowspp[s] the Clothing of this Land first began, but especially to demonstrate that by & in Govemt, the same was first planted, that as this Goverm[t] was still from tyme to time rectified, & a well regulated Trade maintained, all Traffique & Clothing ever grew up more & more, & while the State held constantly to this Goverm't, this Nation fflourished in all Trade & encreased in all manner of Clothing to the emulacon if not Envy of their neighbo[es].

The ffellowspp cannot deny but that since ye year 1613 many very good concurrent reasons might be given of the decay of Clothing of this Land and the Trade of their Company, but w[th] all doe Humbly declare their opinion. That ye maine, chiefe & principall cause of all was, & still is the want of p[e]serving & upholding the ancient Government in w[ch] their ffellowspp was & is constituted, and that the rest are for the maine pte but ye naturall effects & consequences of ye dissolution, discountenancing & discontinuance thereof . . . [1]

[1] The remaining thirteen pages of the manuscript deal with the much discussed question of the advantages or disadvantages of a trade regulated and controlled by companies, particularly that of the Merchants Adventurers.

THE STATUTE OF 1497, RESTRICTING THE JURISDIC-
TION OF THE FELLOWSHIP AND LIMITING THE
FINE FOR ADMISSION TO TEN MARKS.

Statutes of the Realm, 12 Henry VII., c. 6.

MERCHAUNTIS ADVENTURERS.

To the descrete Comens in this (present) Parliament assembled; shewith unto
your (discrete) Wisedomes the Marchauntes Adventurers inhabite and dwelling in diverse parties of this Realme of
Englond oute of the Citie of London, that where they
have their free passage resorte cours and recours with
their goodis wares and merchandises into divers costis
and parties beyond the See, aswell into Spayne Portyn-
gale Britaign Irland Normandye Fraunce Civile Venyce
Danske Estland Friselond, and other divers and many
places regions and contres being in leage and amytie with
the Kinge our Sovereign Lord, there to bye and sell and
make their exchaunges with their seid godes wares and
marchaundises accordyng to the lawe and custume used
in every of the seid regions and places, And there every
persone frely to use theym self to his moost avauntage,
withoute exaccion fyne imposicion or contribucion to be
had or taken of theym or of eny of theym to for or by any
Englisshe persone, or persones; And in semblable wise
they before this tyme have hadde used and of right owen
to have and use theire free passage resorte and recours
into the costes of Flaunders Holand Seland Braband and
other places thereto nygh adjoynyng undir the obeisaunce
of the Archeduke of Burgoyn, In whiche places the uni-

Petitions of the Merchants Adventur-ers, dwelling out of London;

204

versall martes be comenly kepte and holden iiij tymes in
the yere, to which martis all Englisshe men and dyvers
other nacions in tyme passed have used to resorte, there
to sell and uttre the commoditees of their Contreies and
frely to bye ageyn suche thinges as semed theym moost
necessarie and expedient for their profite and the weale
of the Contrey and parties that they be comme from; till
nowe of late that by the feliship of the Mercers and
othre merchauntes and adventurers, dwellyng and being
free within the Citie of London, by confederacie made
amonge theym self of their uncharitable
and inordinate covetise for their singuler   Ordinance of Mer-
profite and lucre, contrarie to every Eng-   chants Adventurers of
lisshemans libertie and to the libertie of   L o n d o n, imposing
                                               Fines on Persons deal-
the seid Marte there, whiche is that every   ing at Foreign Marts :
persone of what nacion that he be of shuld
have their free libertie there to bye sell and make the
commutacions with the wares godes and merchaundises att
theire pleasure, have, contrarie to all lawe reason charite
right and conscience, amonges theym self, to the prejudice of all Englisshemen, made an Ordinaunce and Con-
stitucion, that is to sey, that noe Englishman resortyng
to the seid Martes shall neither bye ne sell any godes
wares or merchaundises there, excepte he first componde
and make fyne with the seid feliship merchauntes of London and their seid confederatis att their pleasure, upon
payn of forfeiture to the seid feliship Marchauntes of London and to their seid Confederatis of suche Merchandises
godes or wares so by him bought or sold there; whiche
fyne imposicion and exaccion at the be-
gynnyng when it was first taken, was   First Pretext of
demaunded by colour of a fraternite of   such Fines;
Seynt Thomas of Caunterbury, att which tyme the seid

fyne was but the value of halfe a olde noble sterling, and
soe by colour of suche feyned holynesse it hath be suffered to be taken for a fewe yeris passid, and aftirward it
was encreaced to Cs. Flemmysh; and nowe
it is soe that the seid feleship and Merchauntes of London take of every English
man or yonge merchaunte beyng there att
his first comming xx li. sterlinge for a fyne, to suffre him
to bye and sell his owen propre goodes wares and merchaundises that he hath there: By occasion wherof all
merchauntis, not beyng of the seid feliship and confederacie, withdraw theym self from the seid Martis; wherby
the wollen Clothe of this Realme, which is oon of the
great commodities of the same, by making whereof the
Kingis true Subjectis be put in occupacion, and the pover
pepull have most universally their leving, and also other
divers comoditees of diverse and severall parties of this
same Realme, is not sold ne uttered as it hath be in tyme
passed, but for lacke of utteraunce of the same in diverse
parties whare suche clothes be made, they be conveied to
London where they be sold ferre undir the price that they
be worthe, and that they coste to the makers of the same,
and at some tyme they be lente to longe daies and the
money thereof att divers tymes never paied; And over
that the comodities and merchaundises of that parties,
whiche the seid feliship marchauntis of London and othre
their confederatis bryng into this lande, is so solde to
your seid complaynants and othre the Kinges true sub-
jetts, att so dere and high exceding price that the bier of
the same cannot lyve therupon; by reason wherof all the
Cities Townes and Burghs of this Realme in effecte be
falle into great povertie ruyne and decaye, and as nowe in
maner they be withoute hope of comforte or relief, and

(marginal note:) Increase, Abuse, and ill Effects of such Fines;

the Kingis Customes and Subsidies and the Navie of the land greatly decreased and mynysshed, and daily they be like more and more to decaye, if due reformacion be not had in this behalf; Be it therefore enactid by the Kinge our Sovereign Lord by thadvyse and assent of the Lordis spuall and temporall and of the Comens in this present parliament assembled and by auctorite of the same, That every Englisshman, beyng the Kingis true liegeman, from hensforth have free passage resorte cours and recourse into the seid coostis of Flaunders Holand, Seland Braband, and othre places thereto nygh adjoynyng undir thobeisaunce of the seid Archeduke, to the Martes there hereaftir to be holden, w^t his or their merchaundises goodes and

Englishmen may resort to the Marts in Flanders etc. and deal there without any Exaction from Englishmen exceeding Ten Marks.

wares, there to bye and sell and make their eschaunges frely at his or theire pleasure, withoute exaccion fyne imposicion extorcion or contribucion to be hadde levied taken or perceyved of theym or of any of theym to for or by any Englissh persone or persones to his or their owne use, or to the use of the seid fraternite or feliship, or of any othre like, excepte onely x marc sterling: And that noo persone Englissh as is afore reherced hereaftir take, to his own use or to thuse of the seid fraternite or feliship there, of any other Englissh persone of what estate degre or condicion that he be of, soe alwey that he be the Kinge our Sovereign Lordis true liegeman, any fyne exaccion imposicion or contribucion for his libertie or fredome to bye and sell any goodes wares or merchaundises in or at any of the seid Martes, more or above the some of x marcs sterling oonly; upon payn of forfeiture to our seid Sovereign Lord for every tyme that he dothe the contrarie of this acte xx li. and also to forfeite to the partie greved in this behalf x tymes so moche as he contrarie to this present acte takith of hym; and that the seid parties so greved shall have in this behalf an accion of dette for the seid forfeiture of x tymes in any of the Kings Courtes within this Realme by wrytte playnte bill or informacion, and suche processe to be made in the same as is or ought to be made in or upon an accion of dette att comen lawe, and the triall therof to be hade in suche Shire Citie Towne or place, where the seid accion is commenced or sued, and that the defendaunt in any suche accion be not admytted to wage his lawe, nor that noon esson or proteccion be for suche defendaunt admytted or allowed in that behalf.[1]

Penalty £20 to the King, Ten Times the Sum taken, to the Party.

[1] A petition to Parliament in the time of Elizabeth by the Adventurers for the repeal of this act is published by Schauz: *Handelspolitik*, II, Urk. Bei. 134. It contains a brief historic sketch of the Fellowship. The act was repealed through the efforts of Sir Thomas Gresham, whose attitude toward the reduction of the fines and the influence of the adventurers on the rate of exchange, appears in a letter by Gresham to the Duke of Northumberland, published in Burgon's *Life and Times of Sir T. Gresham*, I, App. No. 7.

Wheeler: A Treatise of Commerce, pp. 9-13, 19 and 57.

OF THE FIRST INSTITUTION OF THE FELLOWSHIP OR COMPANIE OF
MERCHANTS ADVENTURERS, AND THE CAUSES THEREOF.

MARCUS CATO, a prudent Counsellour, and a good
husband in deed, saith: *Quod oportet Patremfamilias vend-
acem esse non emacem :* And who knoweth not, that we
haue no small need of many things, whereof foreigne
Countreys haue great store, and that wee may well spare
many things, whereof the said Countreys haue also need?
Now to vent the superfluities of our Countrey, and bring
in the Commodities of others, there is no readier, or better
meane then by Merchandize: and seeing we haue no way
to encrease our treasure by mynes of golde and siluer at
home, and can haue nothing from abroad without mony,
or ware, it followeth necessarily that the abouesaid good
counsel of *Cato*, to be sellers and not buyers, is to be

[1] Wheeler's *Treatise of Commerce*, is an elaborate defence of
the Adventurers, but furnishes also a great deal of valuable
historical information. The author was secretary to the Fellowship at the beginning of the seventeenth century, and of all its
members, the most intimately acquainted with its history. Without his admirable work, the story of the Adventurers would be still
wrapped in obscurity. The compilation of the *Laws and Ordinances* together with the little volume on Commerce, not only first
revealed the importance of the Society, but until the discovery of
the Records, they must remain the principal source for its history.
A Treatise of Commerce was published in London in 1601, in 4to,
125 pages. In the same year an edition, also in quarto, appeared
in Middleburg. The work is now quite rare.

followed, yet so, that wee carry not out more in value ouer the seas then we bring home from thence, or transport things hurtfull to the State, for this were no good husbandry, but tendeth to the subuersion of the land and diminishing of the treasure thereof, whereas by the other wee shall greatly encrease it, the trade being carried and managed under a conuenient gouerment & orders, and not in a dispersed, loose, and stragling maner: the practice whereof we may see in this Realme almost these 400 yeeres together: First in the Staple and Wooll trade, and next in that of the Merchants Aduenturers and Cloth trade. And King *Edward* the third thought it not enough to bring the working and making of the Cloth into the realme, except, when the same was indraped, he withal prouided for the vent thereof in forreigne parts, to the most benefit and aduancement of that newe begun Arte, and therefore whereas the abouesaid Company (though then otherwise termed then now) in the yeere 1248, had obtained Priuiledges of *John* Duke of *Brabant*, the said King confirmed the same for the substantial gouerment of the said Company in their trade.

The brotherhood of Saint Thomas Becket of Canterbury.

In the yeere 1399. The Arte of making of Cloth being growen to good perfection within this Realme, King *Henrie* the Fourth first prohibited the inuection of forreigne made Cloth, and gaue unto the said Company a very beneficiall and ample Charter of Priuiledges, confirmed by Acte of Parliament for the same purpose and intent, as his Predecessor King *Edward* the Third had done before him: whose example the succeeding Kings, *Henrie* the fifth, and sixt, *Edward* the Fourth, and *Richard* the third followed, ratifying and confirming their Predecessors doings on his behalfe: the next in order following King

Henri the seauenth, like a wise and Prouident Prince, well
marking and considering howe necessary and seruiceable
the state of *Merchandise* was vnto this Realme, not onely
liked and confirmed that which the aboue rehearsed
Kings had done before him, but also greatly enlarged and
augmented the fame by three seuerall Charters, and by
other his gracious and royall fauours from time to time,
not onely towards the said Company in generall, but
withal to diuers Merchants in particular: *Mercatores ille
saepenumero pecunia multa data gratuito inuabat, vt Mer-
catura (Ar suna omnium cunctis aeque mor-*
talibus tum commoda, tum necessaria) in Polidorus in vita
Henrice septimi.
suo Regno copiosior esset.   And when vpon
a variance fallen out betweene him and the Archduke
Philip, he had drawen as well the said Company as
that of the Staple out of the low Countries, and placed
them at *Calice*, hee gaue vnto them within the said Towne
as large and beneficiall Priuiledges, as they before had enjoyed in the said lowe Countries, which were very large
and fauourable, intituling them by the name of *Merchants
Adventurers*.   And albeit in this Kings dayes, as also in
the raigne of King *Henrie* the fourth, the like complaint
as of late, was made by the Clothiers, Wooll growers,
Dyers, &c. against the Company of Merchants Adventurers: yet after due examination of the said complaint,
the issue procured great favour to the said Company, &
gaue occasion of the inlarging of their former Charters,
with an expresse restraint of all Straglers and Entermed-
lers, that might disturbe or impeach their trade: and
whereas also the *Easterlings* at this time had entered into
the same trade, the aforesaid prudent Prince King *Henrie*
the seuenth, did not onely straightly inhibite them so to
doe, but also tooke Recognizance of twenty thousand

Markes of the Aldermen of the Steelyarde at *London*, that
the said *Easterlings* should not cary any English cloth to
the place of Residence of the Merchants Adventurers in
the lowe Countries, or open their Fardels of cloth in the
said Countries, to the preiudice of the said Company, by
putting the same to vent there, which they were not wont
to do. In the time of the reigne of K. E. the 6, *Iohn
Tulle*, *Iohn Dimock* & others, brethren of the said Company, enformed the Bishop of Elye, at that time L. Chan-
cellor, of matter against the Company, but their bil
brought to the Councel boord, and examined, it was
finally ordered, that the said Complainants should submit themselves vnto the obedience of the Companies
orders, and pay certaine fines, which the Lordes then laid
vpon them, besides that two of the principallest found to
be the Ringleaders of the rest, were committeed to the
Fleet, there to remaine, till such time as the Company of
M. M. Adventurers should sue for their release. And
albeit the said persons renewed their complaints, in the
first yeere of Q. *Maries* raigne, and did put vp a bill to
the Parliament house, against the Company, yet the same
being answered by the said Company, was reiected, and
cast out of the Parliament house. Since the time of King
Hrnrie the seuenth, the succeeding Princes, King *Henrie*
the eighth of famous memorie, King *Edward* the sixth, and
Queene *Marie* have continued, confirmed, and enlarged
the abouesaid Charters and Priuiledges, but aboue all
other, our most gracious Soueraigne, that now raigneth,
Queene *Elizabeth*, hath shewed her gracious and fauourable affection towardes the said Companie, in not onely
confirming the letters Patentes, and Charters of her
most Noble Grandfather, and of other her Highnesse
Predecessours aboue mentioned, but also in adding there-

unto other more large, and beneficiall Priuiledges of her owne. For whereas the M. M. Aduenturers about the beginning of her Maiesties reigne, by diuerse restraints, Edicts, and Proclamations, made and set forth by the Gouernours and Commanders of the Low Countryes, were empeached and prohibited to trade in the said Countries, contrary to the ancient Entercourses, and the Priuiledges to the said Company granted of old time, and consequently were occasioned to seek, and erect a Trade in the partes of Germanie, which they did with their great charges and trauaile for the vent of the Commodities of the Realme, her Highness calling to remembrance this and other faithful & acceptible seruice at sundrie times done by the sayd M. M. Aduenturers in diuerse great and and weighty affaires of her Maiesty and realme, and minding the encrease and aduancement of the said Merchants, as much as any her Progenitours, (as her Highnesse professeth in the said Charter) it pleased her said Maiestie in the sixt yere of her reigne, to giue and grant vnto them those gracious and ample priuiledges, which the said Companie now enjoyeth, and afterwards vpon new occasion, the trade of the said Company being much impeached by wrongfull entermedlings of vnfree persons in the same, it pleased her Maiesty by a new Charter, and Letters Patents under the great, seale of England, in the eight & twentith yeare of her reigne, to prouide against such iniurious, and vnorderly intrusion, acknowledging the seruices done to her Highnesse by the said M. M. Aduenturers, and pronouncing them to have beene, & to be verie beneficiall members to the generall state of the realme and common wealth of England:

14

The Company of Merchants Aduenturers consisteth of
a great number of wealthie, and well experimented Merchants, dwelling in diuerse great Cities, Maritime
Townes, and other parts of the Realme, to wit, London,
Yorke, Norwich, Exceter, Ipswitch, Newcastle, Hull, &c:
These men of olde time linked and bound themselues together in Companie for the exercise of Merchandize and
sea-fare, trading in Cloth, Kersie, and all other, as well
English as forreigne Commodities vendible abroad, by
the which they brought vnto the places where they
traded, much wealth, benefite, and commoditie, and for
that cause haue obtained many verie excellent and singular priuiledges, rights, iurisdictions, exemptions, and
immunities, all which those of the aforesaid Fellowship
equally enioy after a well ordered maner and forme, and
according to the ordinances, lawes and customes deuised
and agreed vpon by common consent of all the Merchants,
free of the said Fellowship, dwelling in the abouenamed
Townes and places of the land : the parts and places
which they trade vnto, are the Townes and ports lying
betweene the riuers of *Somme* in France, and the *Scawe* in
the Germane sea: not into all at once, or at each mans
pleasure, but into one, or two Townes at the most within
the abouesaid bounds, which they commonly call the
Mart Towne, or Townes; for that there onely they
stapled the commodities, which they brought out of England, & put the same to sale, and bought such forreigne
commodities, as the land wanted, and were brought from
far by Merchants of diuerse Nations and countries flocking thither, as to a Faire, or market to buy & sell.   And

albeit through the troubles and alterations of times, the Merchants Aduenturers haue beene forced to change and leaue their olde marte Townes, and seeke new, (as hath been partly touched before) yet wheresoeuer they seated themselues, thither presently re-paired other Strangers, leauing likewise the places whence the English Merchants were departed, and planting themselues where they resided: so that as long as the Company continued their Mart, or Staple in a place, so long grew and prospered that place; but when they for-sooke it, the welfare and goode estate thereof seemed withall to depart, and forsake it, as in olde time hath beene seene in *Bridges*, and in our time in some others, and no maruell; for diligent inquiry being made in the yeare 1550, by the commandement of the Emperour *Charles* the fifth, what benefite or commoditie came to his state of the low Countries, by the haunt and commerce of English Merchants: it was found, that in the Citie of Antwerp alone, where the Companie of Merchants Aduenturers was at time residing, were at least twenty thousand persons fed and maintained for the most part by the trade of the Merchants Aduenturers: besides thirtie thousand others in other places of the low Coun-tries likewise maintained and fed partly by the said trade, partly by endraping of cloth, and working in wool, and other commodities brought out of England. . . .

The Companie of M. Aduentures is able to make and diuert a trade.

THE NUMBER OF "FREEMEN OF THE COMPANY OF M. M. ADVEN-
TURERS" AND THE STINT OF TRADE.

For it is very well knowne, that the Company of M. M. Adventurers is sufficient and able enough, and ouer many to buy vp, and vent all that Cloth, and those sortes of woollen commoditie, made and endraped within the Realme, wherewith they vsually deale, and which are vendible in the Countries, whither they trade beyond the seas; for they are not so fewe as 3500 per-

3500 Freemen of the Company of M. M. Aduenturers.

sons in number enhabiting London, & sundry Cities and partes of the realme, especially the townes that lye conueniently for the sea, of which a very great many vse not the trade for that it sufficeth for al, but are constrained to get their liuing by some other meanes; and to the end that those which are traders may be equally and indifferently cared and soried for, and that the wealthie or richer sort with their great purses may not engrosse the whole Commoditie into their owne hands, and so haue all, and some neuer a whit, there is a stint, and reasonable proportion allotted, and set by an ancient order & manner, what quantitie either at once, or by the yere euery man may ship out or transport which he is not to goe beyond nor exceed : which whole stint and proportion, if it were shipped, or transported out of the lande, would amount unto yerely the double quantitie of al cloth of those sorts made in the Realme, which the Merchants Adventurers deale in. . . . . [1]

[1] Compare the following statement by an opponent of the Society in 1622, with the above: "All the Trade of the Merchants of the Staple, of the merchant Strangers, and of all other English Merchants, concerning th' exportation of all the Commodities of Wooll into those countries where the same are especially to bee vented, is in the Power of the Merchants Adventurours only ; and it is come to be managed by 40 or 50 persons of that Company, consisting of three or foure thousand." Malynes : *Maintenance of Free Trade*, 50.

EXTRACT FROM "THE DEBATE BETWENE THE HER-
ALDES OF ENGLANDE AND FRAUNCE COMPYLED
BY JOHNN COKE."

Societe des Anciens Textes Francais, xxxvii, 114, 115.

Concerning your marchauntes of Fraunce, we have
also marchauntes in England, who frequenteth all partes
of the world for traffique of marchaundyse. And especially II. Companyes, that is to say, the ryght worshypful
Company of Marchauntes adventurers, and the famous
felyship of the Estaple of Calais, by whom not only the
Martes of Barowe and Andwarpe be mayntened, but also
in effect al the townes of Brabant, Holand, Zeland and
Flaunders. These II. Companies do more feates of marchaundises then al the marchauntes of Fraunce; and for
somoche the worlde knoweth this to be trewe, I pass them
over.[1]

[1] The writer, John Coke, belongs to the middle of the 15th century.

The following was omitted on page 197 :

The text comes to an abrupt stop at this point, but beginning
between folios 202 and 203 is a continuation by another hand. The
rest of this sentence reads: "officers in the said Residence of London as to the s^d gov^r Dep^{ty} & generality there shall seem meet,"
and the entire continuation consists of seven paragraphs, the remainder of the act. Besides confirming what has already been
granted, the other provisions asked for by the London Residence
are agreed to. The act is signed by Saml Free Dep^{ty}.

THE CHARTER[1] OF 1407.

Rymer: Foedera, IV, Pt. I, 107 (Hague Edition).

IN BEHALF OF THE MERCHANTS (TRADING) TO HOLLAND.

Henry, by the Grace of God, King of England and France and Lord of Ireland, to all to whom the present letters come, greeting.

Be it known that, as we have heard that through lack of good and sane rule and government, divers losses, dissensions, troubles and difficulties have been too frequently brought about in times past among the merchants of our kingdom of England and of our other dominions, in the regions of Holland, Zealand, Brabant and Flanders, and in whatever other parts beyond the sea which are in friendship with us, where they live and trade, and that in all probability still greater losses than these (which God forbid) may be feared to come to pass in the future,

---

[1] Translated from the Latin text in Rymer. This is the earliest charter mentioned in the *Inspeximus* of the Society's charters, R. O. State Papers, Dom. Chas. II, Vol. 27. In the inventory of the papers of the Company made in 1547, it is designated as "furste letres patentes graunted unto the said felleshipp of marchauntes adventurers by Kinge Henry the 4 of Noble memory." Schanz, *Handelspolitik*, II, Urk. Bei., 133. Too much importance has been attached to this charter as marking the beginning of the society. There is nothing in it specifying that it is to a special organization of merchants, and it does not differ materially from the grants made at a still earlier period to English merchants. The fact that it is the first grant mentioned in the *Inspeximus* does not prove that it is the first. The grant by Henry VI, in 1462, is omitted entirely from that document.

218

unless for the sake of better government among all the same merchants we quickly turn our protecting hand.

We, earnestly desiring to take precaution against these losses and dangers threatening both these same merchants and others from the said kingdom and dominions of ours, about to frequent the aforesaid parts, and that they be ruled and treated justly, wish, and by the tenor of these presents grant to these same merchants that they may assemble themselves and come together as often and whenever they please, in any suitable and proper place, and elect and maintain among themselves at their pleasure, freely and without danger certain sufficient and fit persons for their governors in those parts.

We grant further and concede in as far as possible to these governors thus to be elected by the merchants aforesaid, the special power and authority of ruling and governing each and every merchant our subjects, who live in those regions, and those moreover who come and go into these same parts; of doing full and speedy justice, either themselves or through their deputies, both to them and to any one of them in any of their causes and quarrels which have arisen or may arise among them in the aforesaid parts, and of adjusting, of enforcing adjustment, of restoring, quieting and bringing to a peaceful settlement whatever contentions, quarrels, discords and disputes have arisen or may arise between the same merchants our subjects and the merchants of the regions aforesaid,

And to redress, repair, make restitution and correct whatever transgressions, harms, seizures, excesses, acts of violence and injuries have been done or may be done through the aforesaid merchants our subjects to the merchants of the said regions,

And of requiring, seeking and receiving similar restitutions, reparations, satisfaction and amends from the merchants of the aforesaid regions or their deputies,

And by common agreement on the part of the merchants our subjects before named to make and establish
statutes, ordinances and customs as shall seem expedient
for the better government of the affairs of the same merchants our subjects in these regions,

And to punish reasonably each one in proportion to the
amount of his wrong, all merchants our subjects, who
oppose, rebel against, or are disobedient to the aforesaid
officers thus elected or their deputies, or any of them, or
against any of their statutes, ordinances and laws aforesaid,

We will, furthermore, that all just and reasonable
statutes, ordinances and customs be made and established
in the aforesaid manner by the said governors, so elected,

And that all just and reasonable ordinances of the
said merchants, our liege subjects, made and established with the common consent of these merchants for
their government in the aforesaid places, according to
the privileges and authority given to them by the lords
or rulers of the said regions, collectively or individually, or to be made and confirmed by the aforesaid
governors, who shall from now on be elected as prescribed, according to the aforesaid privileges, or other
privileges to be granted to these merchants our lieges by
the said lords or rulers, collectively or individually, that
they be observed firmly and inviolably as in force, firm
and accepted.

We give also as a firm command, to the merchants
aforesaid, to each and every one our subjects, by right
of the present letters, that they shall pay attention to,

consult, obey and assist as is becoming, the same governors thus to be elected and their deputies in all and everything aforesaid, and in due reason preserving the government and rule, each in his own part without exception.

Given in our palace at Westminster, witness our great seal, the 5th day of February in the year one thousand four hundred and six [1] and the eighth of our reign.

EXTRACTS FROM THE CHARTER OF EDWARD IV. IN 1462.

Hakluyt: The Principal Navigations, Voyages, etc., I, 208. [2]

"A large Charter [3] granted by k. *Edward* the 4 in the second yere of his reigne, to the marchants of England resident especially in the Netherland, for their chusing of a master and governor among themselves, which government was first appointed unto one William Obray: with expresse mention, what authority he should have.

[1] The date, 1406, in the text is based on the style of reckoning in England after the 13th century, according to which the year began on the 25th of March. Giry, *Manuel de Diplomatie*, 125.

[2] Richard Hakluyt: The Principal Navigations, Voyages, Traffiques and Discoveries of the *English Nation . . .* London . . . 1599. 3 volumes.

[3] This important charter is not found in the *Inspeximus* of the Charters (R. O. State Papers, Dom. Chas. II, Vol. 27) by Howard. The omission is striking, and were it not for direct evidence to the contrary, might justify the suspicion that the charter is spurious or that it had reference to another group of merchants. Its genuineness and the Adventurers' claim to it are, however, clearly seen by a comparison of its contents with the list of documents in the possession of the Company in 1547. Br. Mus., Sloane MS. 2103, fol. 2, published by Schanz: *Handelspolitik*, II, Urk. Bei., 133, Items 5, 34 and 35.

Edward by the grace of God king of France, & of England, & lord of Ireland, to al those which shal see or heare these letters, sendeth greeting, & good wil. Know ye, that whereas we have understood, as well by the report of our loving and faithfull Counsellors, as by the common complaint and report of all men, that many vexations, griefs, debates, discords, annoyes, dissentions, & damages, have heretofore bene done, moved, committed, and happened, and do daily fal out and happen among the common marchants & mariners, our subiects of our realmes of *France* & *England*, & our lordships of *Ireland* and *Wales*, & of other our dominions, seigneuries, and territories, because that good discretion and authority hath not bin observed among our saide subiects, which abide, frequente, converse, remain, inhabit, & passe, aswel by sea as by land, into yᵉ parts of *Brabant, Flanders, Henault, Holland, Zeland,* and divers other countreis & seigneuries belonging aswell to the high and mighty prince, our most deere and loving cousin yᵉ Duke of *Burgoine,* of *Brabant,* earle of *Flanders,* &c. as being in the obedience & dominion of other lords, which are in friendship, alliance, & good wil with us: and that it is to be doubted that through the saide inconvenience and occasion, many discommodities may ensue & fal out in time to come (which God forbid) unles we should provide convenient remedie in this behalfe for our subiects aforesaid: wherefore we desiring most effectually and heartily to avoide the mischiefe of the said inconveniences & to provide convenient remedy for the same, to the end that the said common marchants and mariners and others our subiects of our said realms & dominions, which at this present and hereafter shal haunt and frequent yᵉ said countreis, may be iustly & lawfully ruled, gouverned, and intreated by right & equity in the countreis aforesaid, and that equity, reason & justice may be ministered unto them and every of them, according as the cases shall require, we being wel assured and having ful confidence, in the discretion, faithfulnes, wisdome, experience & good diligence of our most deare and welbeloved subiect *Will. Obray* our servant, & in regard of the good, faithfull, and acceptable services, which he hath done us in our realm —& among our subiects in times past, & hoping that he wil do also hereafter, we have made, ordained, consti. tuted, committed and established, and by the tenour of these presents, of our special grace, ful power, & authority royall, we ordaine, appoint, commit, and establish, (during our pleasure[1]) to be gouvernor, judge, warden of iustice, and the appurtenances & appendances thereof, which we have or may have over our said common subiects the marchants travailing hereafter as wel by sea as by land, and abiding in the said countries of *Brabant, Flanders, Henault, Holland, Zealand,* and other countreis beyond the sea, as is aforesaid, together with the wages, rights, profits, and emoluments heretofore accustomed & as the said *Will. Obray* at other times hath had and received of our said subiects when he hath had, used, and exercised the said office of gouvernor, & also with other such rights and profits, as hereafter shal more plainly be declared.   And furthermore for our parts we have given

[1] Among the list of documents of the Fellowship made in 1547 is one noted as follows: "Item a discharge of one William Overey from the rome of governor, dated the 24 day of June anno 1462." Br. Mus., Sloane MS. 2103, fol. 22. Schanz: *Handelspolitik*, Urk. Bei., 133, Item 34. Unfortunately the document itself has not been found, and there is no means of determining by whose authority Obray was discharged.

him, and by these presents do give him, as much as in us lieth, during our pleasure, ful power, authority, and special commandement, to governe, rule, and cause to be governed and ruled with good iustice by himselfe, or by his sufficient lieuetenants or deputies, all and every our foresaid subjects the common marchants & mariners comming, remaining, frequenting, passing, & repairing from henceforth into the said countreis of *Brabant, Flanders, Henault, Holland, Zealand,* and other countreyes beyond the sea, as it is said, and to keep and cause to be kept, to exercise and maintein, for us and in our place, the said office of governour, and to doe all such things which a faithfull governour ought to do, and to take knowledge and administration of the causes of the said common marchants and mariners, our subiects, and of every of them, and of their causes and quarels moved, or hereafter to be moved in the countreis aforesaid, or within the limits & borders thereof, and to doe them full and speedy iustice. And to reforme, cause reformation, governe, appease and pacifie all contentions, discords, questions or debates between those our said subiects moved, or to [be] moved: and to right, redresse, repaire, restore, and amend all transgressions, domages, enterprises, outrages, violences and iniuries committed, or to be committed: and likewise to require, to aske, demand and receive, restitutions, reparations, restaurations, and amends of our said subiects the common marchants & mariners, or of their factors in the countreis aforesaid. And that, whensoever and as often as it shall please the said governor or his deputies, they may in some convenient and honest place within the said countreis make or cause to be made, somon, and hold in our name, iurisdictions, courts, and assemblies: and in our said name

take administration and knowledge of causes, as it is
aforesaide, and to hold and keep pleas, for and in our
behalfe, and to make agreements, mediatours, and um-
pires, to iudge, and to make decrees, and to minister
iustice, to ordaine, appoint, censure, and constraine our
saide subiects to sweare and take all kind of oathes,
which order of iustice and custom require and affoorde,
and to enjoy our authoritie, and to use, execute and
accomplish, by way of equitie and iustice, and to doe, or
cause to be done all execution and exercise of law and
iustice; and to ordaine, appoint & establish sixe serjeants
or under, to doe the executions & arrests of our said
court. . . . . . Moreover wee will, and by the tenour
of these presents wee give and graunt unto the saide
governour, and to our saide subiects the common marchants and mariners, that as oft and whensoever it please
them, they may meet and assemble in some honest and
convenient place, and by the consent of the said governour to choose and appoynt among them at their pleasure,
freely and without danger, certaine sufficient and fit persons to the number of twelve or under, which we wil
have to be named Justicers, unto the which Justicers so
elected by the saide governour and our saide subiects, as
it is said, and to every of them, we give and graunt
especiall power and authoritie to sitte and assist in court,
with the said governour or his lieutenants, for their aide
and assistance. . . . And furthermore we wil, that all
just and reasonable statutes, lawes, ordinances, decrees,
and constitutions made and established, or to be made
and established, in the countreys aforesaide, by the consent of the saide governour, and of the saie [sic] Justicers,
shalbe corrected, amended, and made, as they shall see to
bee expedient in this behalfe, for the better government

of the estate of the common marchants and mariners our saide subiects, and shalbe held as ratified, firme, acceptable and approved, . . . kept and obeyed. And also, of our farther favour and grace wee will and we grant, that by the consent of our said governour, our said subiects the common marchants and mariners may make and set downe in the said countreis, by their common consent, as often as they shall thinke good for their better government and estate, such iust and reasonable lawes, statutes, ordinances, decrees, constitutions, and customes, as they shal thinke expedient in this behalfe: which we comand to be kept as ratified, confirmed, allowed, & approved, available, and established. Provided alwaies, that they do not seeke anything preiudicial to this present power and authoritie given and graunted by us to the saide governour. . . . And likewise . . . we have ordained and do ordaine, have consented & doe consent, and by these presents have given & do give ful power & especiall authority to our said servant *Will. Obray* governour aforesaid, that at al time and times when he shal think good, he may ordaine, elect, chuse, and appoint in the countreis aforesaid, such ministers, officers, and servitours as hereafter shalbe named,[1] and

---

[1] The officers named are correctors or brokers, alnagers, weighers, folders and packers. The merchants are expressly charged to make contracts only in the presence of a broker, who may "present, report and testifie the said contracts or bargains before the said governor," and not to employ alnagers, weighers, etc., that have not been appointed by him. "That it may duely appeare" that the customs have been paid, unlading and unpacking is ordered to be done in the presence of the governor or his lieutenants. Violation of this regulation is to be punished by fines, "the fourth part of which forfeitures and confiscations shall be employed to the repairing and maintenance of two chapels

such others as he shal think necessary, and to discharge
them, and to change them, & set others in their roomes,
at his good will and pleasure, unto such a number as he
shall thinke good and reasonable for the time being to be
and receive of our sayd subiects from henceforth yearely,
during our pleasure, all such and like wages and profits,
as he had and received of our said subiects, in the yeare
1458, when hee held and exercised the said office of governour, without diminishing or rebating anything thereof,
notwithstanding this present augmentation made, increased, and done unto him, of our grace and favour: and
that hee shall gather, take, and receive the same in such
forme and manner, as the other money above mentioned
is to be gathered.   And to the ende that the sayd *William
Obray* may have and take possession, season, and en-
terance of the said office of governour in our name we
have and doe place him, by the delivery of these presents,
in possession, season, and entrance of the said office, and
of the rights, profits, stipends, wages, and moneis aforesayd, to begin to exercise the sayd office of governour in
our name, the first day of May next ensuing after the
date of these presents, for the sayd *William Obray* to

founded to the honour of *Saint Thomas* of Canterburie by our
saide subjects in the townes of *Bruges* in Flanders, and of Middle-
borough in Zeland." Compare p. 199, n. 1, of this volume.

The governor, Obray, is to receive a fee of "two pence of grosse
money of Flanders" for the seal on goods imported from the Low
Countries, "one pennie of our money of *England* of the value of a
liver of grosse money of Flanders, upon al and singular the goods,
wares and merchandises of our sayd subjects frequenting the sayd
countries," and "yearely during our pleasure, all such and like
wages and profits as he had and received of our said subiects, in
the yeare 1458, when he held and exercised the said office of governour."

hold and exercise, practise and use the same, during our pleasure, with the sayd wages, moneys, rights, and profites above mentioned, without any contradiction or impeachment. . . . And you our subiects, the common marchants and mariners, so behave yourselves, that you may receive commendation of us for your good obedience, knowing that such as shall be found doing or to have done the contrary, we will see them so punished without redemption, that they shall bee an example to all rebellious persons. We pray and most instantly require in the ayde of equitie, all others our friends, allies, and well-willers, aswell princes and potentates, as their iusticers, officers, lieutenants, deputies, commissaries, and subiects, and every of them in regard of equitie; that they would vouchsafe, and that it would please them to give, doe, and lend comfort, ayde, assistance, and prisons if neede require, to our sayd governour, his lieutenants, commissaries, deputies, iusticers, & others our officers and ministers aforesayd: and herein wee pray them on our behalfe, and in our owne name. And it may please them herein to doe so much, that we may have occasion to thanke them, and to accompt our selves beholding for the same: and as they would that we should do for them in the like matter, or in a greater: which we will willingly doe, if we be required thereunto by them. In witnesse whereof we have caused these our letters to bee made patents. Witnes our selves at *Westminster*, the sixteenth of April, in the second yere our reigne.

EXTRACTS FROM THE CHARTER BY QUEEN ELIZABETH,
INCORPORATING THE FELLOWSHIP AND MAKING
IT A "BODY POLITICK." JULY, 18, 1564.[1]

R. O. State Papers, Dom., Charles II., Vol. 27, pp. 33-69.   (Howard.)

. . . We therefore . . . at the humble suite and
petition of the said governor and Merchants Adventurers, and in consideration of the faithful and acceptable service at sundrie tymes done by the said
Merchants Adventurers unto us sithence we came to our
crowne in diverse the great and mighty affairs of us, and
our realm and for more quietness and surety of our said

[1] Space does not permit printing the entire charter; the following
abstract, from the Br. Mus. Cott. Ms. Tib. D., viii, fol. 43, will give
an idea of its scope : 1. The name and freedom of the company
incorproated. 2. The governor and assistants named. 3. The
Company incorporated. 4. The Company to choose a governor and
assistant in the Low Countries. 5. Admission of freemen. 6. Jurisdiction to rule and govern the whole Fellowship. 7. Keeping of
Courts. 8. Punishment or fine of disobedience in non-appearance
at Courts. 9. Marriage of foreign women or having lands in foreign countries. 10. Such as were married before these Patents.
11. Making or frustrating of laws. 12. Making laws for such as
are not free. 13. Execution of Acts, rules and ordinances. 14.
The subjects trading into those countries to be obedient to the
governor. 15. Jailors to receive prisoners. 16. Authority to dis-
franchize offenders. 17. Appointing of officers. 18. Weighers,
porters, ployers and packers. 19. A confirmation of all former
privileges by kings of England or foreign potentates before
granted. 20. Proviso for the privileges of the Merchants of the
Staple. 21. A comanndiment to all officers to assist and aid the
Company. 22. The Queen's Majesty may revoke the grant or so
much of it as shall please her highness.

merchants in avoiding and taking away said doubts[1] questions and ambiguities, and for other good causes and considerations us specially moving, are pleased and contented and of our special grace certain knowledg and mere motion, Doe by these presents, for us our heirs and successors will ordain and grant that the Fellowship or Company of the said Merchants Adventurers, by whatsoeuer name or names they be or at any tyme or tymes have been incorporated united, established named, called, or known, in or by any charters letters, patents, or grants of our said grandfather or of any other our noble progenitors or by force of any Custome usage or prescription shall be from henceforth by force and authority of these presents, made, ordained, incorporated, united and established one perpetuall fellowship and comminalty and body Body Politick and Corporate in Name and in deed and shall have perpetuall succession and continuance forever and shall be named, called, known, and incorporated by the name of Governor Assistants and Fellowship of Merchants Adventurers of England; and that the said John Marth, Emanuel Lucas, Sir Thomas Leigh, Sir William Gerrard, Sir William Chester Knight, Richard Mallorie, Richard Champion, Thomas Rowe, Roger Martin, Richard Chamberlain, Rowland Hayward, Edward Jackman, Richard Lambert, Aldermen Sir Thomas Gresham Knight, Lawrence Withers, Richard Fowlkes, Lionel Duckett, William Gifford, William Beswick, Richard Springham, Nicholas Wheeler,

[1] The doubts here referred to are explained in the preamble, where it is stated that since the Company's enforced departure, owing to the recent edicts, from its former marts in the Low Countries to the ports of Germany, questions have arisen as to the validity of its Charters and privileges.

George Bafford, John Gresham, John Traves, Thomas
Heton, Thomas Rivett, Matthew Field, Henry Vinier,
Edward Castlynne, John Rivers, Francis Robinson, John
Quartes, John Bodeley, William Gravener, John Violet,
Thomas Turnbull, Henrie Beechat, Thomas Blancke,
William Peterson, Jeffry Walkden, Thomas Sharkey,
Richard Hills, John Wilner, William Eaton, Edward
Bright, Edmond Burton, Richard Pipe, Thomas Walker
and William Hewett, and all and every other person or
persons, our subjects which heretofore have or hath been
admitted and allowed and now remaine and be free of the
fellowship or company of the said Merchants Adventurers
lately trading into the said countries of Holland, Zealand,
Brabant, Flanders, and other places nigh adjoining or
any of them for Merchandize and all and every other
person or persons which at any time hereafter by reason
of patrimony or apprenticeship should or ought to have
been admitted received or made free of the said fellowship
or Company by the Orders and Rules of the same, bee and
shall be in such sort free of the said Fellowship of Governor Assistants and Fellowship of Merchants Adventurers of England, and with such diversity and distinction in
Freedom and in such manner form and condition to all
intents and purposes, as they be should or might have
been free of the said Fellowship of Merchants Adventurers lately trading the said countries of Holland,
Zealand, Brabant, Flanders and other places nigh adjoining or any of them commonly called the Merchants Adventurers by and according to the Rules and Ordinances
of the same Fellowship and in no other maner, forme,
sort quality or conditions. And that the said John Marth
Emanuel Lucas . . . be and shall be one perpetual fellowship or Commonality and Body Corporate in deed and

in name and shall have succession perpetual, and continuance for ever and shall be called and known from hence for ever by the same name of Governour Assistants and Fellowship of Merchants Adventurers of England. And further we do ordain, create and make the said John Marth the first and present governor of the same Fellowship of Merchants Adventurers of England, to have and continue the same room and office of governor of the same Fellowship of Merchants Adventurers of England until such a time as the said Fellowship of Merchants Adventurers of England shall elect and chose any other of the said Fellowship or corporation to be governor of the same, in manner and form hereinafter mentioned. And alsoe we by these presents doe ordeyne, create and make the said Sr William Gerrard knight, Richard Champion, Thomas Rowe, Richard Lambert, Thomas Heton, Thomas Rivett, Mathew Field, Henry Vinier, John Rivers, John Quartes, William Gravenor, Thomas Turnbull, Henry Preacher, Thomas Blancke, William Peterson, Jeffrey Walkden, Thomas Starkey, Richard Hills, John Millner, Edward Bright, Edmond Burton, Richard Pipe and Thomas Walker and every of them the first and present assistants to the said governor and his Deputy and Deputies, to have and continue the same office roome or stead of Assistants to the said governor and his Deputie and deputies until such time as the said Fellowship of Merchants Adventurers of England shall elect and chose others of themselves to have and exercise the said office, roome, and seat of assistants in manner and form hereinafter mentioned . . . We for us our heirs and successors doe really fully and perfectly incorporate, name, create, establish and declare by these presents unto the said Governor, Assistants and fellowship of Merchants Adventurers of

England and to their successors that they and their successors by the same name of Governor, Assistants, . . .
shall and may have perpetual succession and a common
seale, which shall perpetually serve for the affairs and
business of the said Governor, assistants . . . and their
successors, and that they and their successors by the
name of Governor, assistants . . . shall and may from
hence forth and for ever more be able and have full lawful and perfect power and ability and capacity in law to
sue and impleade to be sued and impleaded . . .

And moreover we grant . . . that they . . . may
from time to time forever hereafter assemble themselves
together beyond the seas in the countries and towns of
Holland, Zealand, Brabant, Flanders, East-friezland,
West-Friezland, and Hamburg, and the territories to the
same belonging or in any part thereof in such part of the
same where the said Fellowship of the Merchant Adventurers of England shall repayre and be resident and abiding for the sale of their Merchandizes, and that then and
there the said Fellowship of Merchant Adventurers of
England or the greatest part of them there then being
shall and may at their liberty and pleasures name chuse
and select of the said fellowship of Merchant Adventurers
of England one or more person or persons to be Deputie or Deputies to the said Governor so from tyme to
tyme to be elected the same Governor Deputy and Deputies to be and continue in the said office and offices and
to be removed from the same by the assent of the said fellowship or of the more part of the same Fellowship so
resiant as is aforesaid at their will and pleasure. . . .

And that the said Governor or his Deputie or Deputies and the said 24 Assistants or the more part of them
for the tyme being shall from henceforth forever have use

and exercise full jurisdiction power and authority lawfully
to rule and governe the same Fellowship of Merchants
Adventurers of England and their successors and all and
every merchant and member of the same in all their private causes and suits quarrels and demeanours, offences
and complaints amongst them in the same countries and
towns of Holland, Zealand, Brabant and Flanders East-
Friezland West Friezland Hamburg and the territories of
the same or in any of them rising moved and to be moved
and to reform decide and pacify all manner of questions
discords and variance, between themselves and between
them or any of them and other merchants in the said
countries and towns of Holland, Zealand, Brabant, Flanders, East Friezland, West Friezland Hamburg and in
the territories of the same or in any of them moved and to
be moved and all manner of tresspasses, hurts, misprisons,
excesses, violences, and injuries, to merchants strangers
in the said foreign countries or in any of them done by the
said merchants of the said Fellowship . . .

And further we for us our heirs . . . grant to the said
Governor Assistants of the Fellowship of Merchants Adventurers of England and their successors . . . to call,
assign, appoint and assemble courts and congregations of
all the said Fellowship of Merchants Adventurers of England as well at the place or places of old time accustomed
within the city of London and elsewhere within this our
realm as also in the said countries and towns of Holland
Zealand, Brabant, Flanders, East-Friezland, West Friezland, Hamburg, and the territories of the same . . . as
often and whensoever as to the said governor deputie or
deputies . . . it shall seeme and be thought expedient
for the weale of the said Fellowship of Merchants Adventurers of England. . . . [1]

[1] Power and authority is also given to the Governor Deputy and

And moreover we greatly minding that the discreet, honest and decent government heretofore used . . . should be kept . . . do grant to the said Governor Assistants and Fellowship of Merchants Adventurers of England and to their successors that the said Governor or his Deputy or Deputies or the said assistants or their successors for the tyme being or 13 of them which shall be resiant as aforesaid from tyme to tyme and at all tymes from henceforth shall and may enact, establish allow and confirm and also revoke disanull and repeale all and every Act and Acts Law and Ordinance heretofore had or made by the said Governor or Deputy and assistants of the said Fellowship of Merchants Adventurers of England lately trading to the said countries of Holland, Brabant, Zealand, Flanders, East Friezland, West Friezland, Hamburg, and the territories of the same or in any of them or in such part of the same where the said Fellowship of Merchants Adventurers of England shall repayre and be resient for the sale of their merchandizes, and shall and may from henceforth from tyme to tyme at all tymes hereafter forever enact, make ordain and establish acts Laws Constitutions and Ordinances as well for the good Government, Rule and Order of the said Governor Assistants and Fellowship of Merchants Adventurers of England and their successors and every Merchant and

Assistants to commit any man to gaol or prison for non-attendance after being duly summoned; also for "any other offence done or to be done against the Commonwealth of the said Fellowship or against any of the privileges to them heretofore or by these presents granted," without bail or mainprize, and to punish further by fines according to the quality of the offence. Marriage with a foreign woman, or the possession property abroad, involved disfranchisement.

particular member of the same Fellowship or body-cor-
porate.

As also of all and every other of the subject and subjects of our heirs and successors intermedling, exercising
and using the seate of Trade of the said Merchants Adventurers by any means in the said countries and Towns
of Holland, Zealand, Brabant, Flanders, . . .

So that the said laws be not hurtful . . . to the rights
of the crown . . .[1]

In witness whereof we have caused these our Letters
to be made Patents. Witness ourself at Westminster the
Eighteenth day of July in the six yeare of our Reigne.

[1] In the sections immediately following, the Governor, Deputy,
etc., are authorized to carry the laws thus made into execution
both among the members of the Fellowship and others exercising
the trade of the Merchants Adventurers. All Mayors, sheriffs,
bailiffs and constables are enjoined to aid the officers of the Society
in enforcing the laws.

Power is also granted to appoint one officer or divers officers
"as well within the city of London and in all other our Dominions
as also in the said countries and places beyond the seas . . . to
levy and gather all manner of fines, forfeitures penalties and mulcts
of every person and persons of the said Fellowship of Merchant
Adventurers of England or of any other person or persons not
being of the said fellowship offending or breaking any statutes
Lawes, Acts, and Ordinances." Said officer shall have power to
arrest body and goods in case of default of payment in all and
every place and places "within this our realme and Dominions and
in the said parts beyond the seas."

Power to choose and appoint porters, weighers, measurers,
ployers and packers in the part beyond the sea is also granted.
Then follows a confirmation of all that has ever been granted by
"our noble progenitors," and the proviso that "these our Letters
patents or anything in them contained shall not in any wise be
prejudicial or hurtful to the Mayor Constable and Fellowship of
the Merchants of the staple of England."

THE FELLOWSHIP'S FOREIGN GRANTS AND PRIVELEGES.

R. O. State Papers, Dom., Chas. II., 22, 6.

1. Of John the 2^d Duke of Brabant dated the 2^d of July 1296.

2. Of John the 3^d Duke of Brabant dated the 8th of Oct. 1315.

3. Of William the 5th Earl of Holland & Zealand the 13th of Dec. 1408.

4. Of the same dated Mar. 4th 1413.

5. Of the same dated Mar. 7th 1413.

6. Of John Earl of Holland & Zealand & dated August 9 1421.

7. Of Jaqueline Countess of Holland & Zealand &c dated June 24, 1434.[1]

8. Of Philip Duke of Burgundy & Brabant & Earl ot Flanders, Holland Zealand &c dated 28th of August 1445.

9. Of the same dated August 6 1446.

10. Of the City of Antwerp dated 12° Aug 1446.[2]

Of the Earle of the Citty of Berghen op Zoom in Brabant, dated 8th April 1458.

11. Of the same dated 17th September 1469.

---

[1] Compare the ordinance of Duke Philipp of Burgundy June 19th 1434, in which he prohibited the importation of all English Woollen cloths and wool yarn for all parts of the Netherlands. A part of this ordinance is published in Schanz, *Handelspolitik*, II., Urk. Bei., 171. Cp. also Urk. Bei., 172 & 173 consisting of extracts from ordinances providing for carrying out the prohibition.

[2] Published by Schanz, *Handelspolitik* II., Urk. Bei., 2, as are also those of Bergen op Zoom of 1470, Urk. Bei. 3.

12. Of the same dated 16th May 1470.

13. Of the city of Antwerp dated 7th of July 1474.

14. Of the citty and towne of Berghen op Zoom dated 18th April 1480.

15. By Intercourse between King Henry VII. & *Maximillian the Emperor* in behalf of his son Philip Archduke of Austria and Lord of the Netherlands, ult. ffebr. 1488.

16. By Intercourse called Magnus Intercursus in 26 Ch the late Treaty with the States General, is grounded & the same thereby confirmed between the same princes dated 24 febbr 1495.

17. By the same princes dated 25' of April 1499.

18. Of the Citty of Antwerp dated 20 January 1499.

19. Of the Citty of Antwerp dated 8 January 1501.

20. By Intercourse between King Henry VII & Philip King of Castile & Lord of the Netherlands dated ult° April 1506.

21. By Intercourse between King Henry VII & Maximillian the Emperor in behalf of his grand child Charles Archduke of Austria & Lord of the Netherlands dated 5' June 1507.

22. Of Middleburgh in Zealand dated 11 August 1512.

23. By Intercourse between King Henry VIII & Charles Prince of Spaine & Lord of the Netherlands dated 4 Jan. 1515.

24. Of the city of Antwerp dated 1st of June 1518.[1]

25. Of the city of Berghen op Zoom dated 16 May 1519.

---

[1] Br. Mus. Cotton MS. Galba, B. ix. 69, contains a list of these privileges, or " commercial articles " as they are called, "between the English merchants and the town of Antwerp." Printed in Schanz, *Handelspolitik*, II., Urk. Bei., 23.

26. By treaty of Intercourse between King Henry VIII & the L⁴ Charles the Emperor dated 11″ August 1520.

27. By Intercourse between the same princes at the Treaty of Windsor dated 19ᵗʰ June 1522.

28. By Intercourse at the Treaty of Cambray dated 5 Aug. 1529.

29. Of the Towne of Antwerp dated 8ᵗʰ June & 22 Decemb. 1537.

30. By Intercourse betweene the former Princes dated 11ᵗʰ Ffebruary 1542.

31. Of the Lord & Towne of Berghen op Zoom dated 19 of December 1543.

32. By Entercourse between the last mentioned princes dated 26 Ffebruary 1545.

33. Of Antwerp dated the 20″ of August 1548.

34. Of the Earl and Citty of Eastfriezland when the troubles began in the Netherlands 1564.

35. Of the Citty of Hamburgh in Germany, Embden being too near the Netherlands 1566.

36. Of Stade in Germany 1578.

37. Of the townes of Middleburgh in Zealand after the United States had renounced the King of Spain dated 5ᵗʰ October 1582.

38. By the States General dated 9″ January 1586.

39. By the same 14″ of July 1598.

40. By the States General dated 14 of June 1599.

41. Of Embden dated 9 November 1599.

42. Of Stade dated 18″ of November 1608.

43. Of Hamburgh 1611.

44. Of Middleburgh dated 10″ of March 1616.

45. Of Hamburgh 1616.

46. Of Delft in Holland 1621.

47. Of Embden 13 November 1630.

48. Of Rotterdam in Holland dat 5 Ffeb^n 1634.

50. Of Dordrecht in Holland dated Nov. 1655.

So their Marts at present are for Germany, Hamburgh,[1] for the Netherlands, Dordrecht.

ABSTRACT OF PRIVILEGES AGREED ON BETWEEN THE CITTY OF DORT AND THE COMPANY OF MERCHTS ADVENTURERS IN ENGLAND, RATIFIED 29 NOVEMBER, 1655.[2]

R. O. State Papers, Dom. Chas. II, Vol. 275, 82.

The City covenanteth

1. That the company shall freely securely and peaceably hold and continue their residence and Trade of importation, exportation, buying and selling all sorts of merchandize whatsoever within the said city paying the customs due for them, excepting the customes of all clothes, Kersies bayes and English beere, which they shall receive from England, Hamburgh or any other place of their residences, And promise to procure from the

---

[1] The privileges of the Adventurers in Hamburg granted in 1567, are printed in the Appendix to Ehrenberg, *England und Hamburg*. The text is in Latin, from a copy in the Lübecker Staats-archiv. The Hamburg original was destroyed by fire in 1842; that of the Adventurers has not been found.

[2] The Concordat between the city of Dort and the Adventurers was for fifteen years, but in 1666, as a result of the war with the Dutch, the privileges of the company were suspended both by the States General and the city. The following year the Society was re-instated. I have been unable to find the origiual of these privileges which consists of 58 articles. That of the city of Dordrecht had the seal of the Adventurers and of the municipality. It was preserved in the Stadt-archiv, Weeskamer, Lade, H, No. 7, in 1783, but at the time of the making of the new catalogue some years ago it could not be found, and it is apparently lost.

States Generall the like freedom of custome upon all other sorts of woollen manufactures.

2. That the citty shall from time to time procure for the company (when they shall demand it) shippes of warr to convoy their ships and goods from Dort to any port of England without any charge to the company.

3. That in case of shipwreck the Company shall enjoy the same privileges as the Burgers and to restore all that shall be saved, paying only the charge of salvage, and promise to procure the like for the company from the States of Holland for all parts of the Province.

4. That if any of the Company or their adherents be wounded or slain, within the liberties of the citty, that present apprehension shall be made of the offender and speedy execution of Justice.

5. That if any damage be done to the company's ships by cutting or stealing any of their Tackle or apparell, the offenders shall make full restitution of damages.

6. That if any goods shall be stolen from the Company, either secretly or by force, if they can be found they shall be restored to the owner; whether they be found in the hand of the thief or upon the markett, and the officers of the city shall be bound to make search for them wherever the owner shall direct, and restore them if they be found.

7. The citty grant to the Company the Church named [1] to exercise their own religion in, and to maintain it in reparation at the citties charge, with liberty to ye company to bury their dead; and that no other use shall be made of it, either for divine service or burial without consent of the Company.

[1] The Court Church at Dort was known as the "Wynkoopers Kapel," and was sometimes called the "Ijzeren Waag."

8. That the citty shall provide for the Company a privileged House and Gardens[1] to their contentment as long as they shall reside in the citty, and to fit it for the habitation of their Deputy Governor, chaplain, secretary, two hosts of the Company and three Beadles, and a reader for the church, and therein the Company have free liberty to assemble and keep courts—for the exercising of their government and privileges and if all the officers of the Company cannot be accomodated within that ground with convenient houses, they shall be provided otherwise at the citties charge and both one and the other be kept in good repair at their charge.

9. That the Company and all their adherents shall as well in ye said publique House, as in their private habitations, take in all sorts of Beer and wine and other house provisions without payment of Excise, provided that the publick Hosts of ye Company nor any private person shall not sell any of it to any but the members of the said Company and their adherents,—and that every single member of the Company living in a private House may take in every year fourty Tonn of Turfe and a pportion of wood clear of excise, and that the widows of the members shall enioy the same freedome of Excise as long as they remain in that citty, provided that every member of the said Company shall exhibit a Ticket into the Excise Office under the hand of the Deputy or Secretary of what provision he takes therein.

10. That the Company and their adherents shall be freed from all watch and ward, charge of garrisons and all contributions personall or real whatsoever, that are

[1] The buildings and gardens occupied by the Fellowship were known in Dort as "Het Hof." They are now used by the city as a school.

already laid upon the Burgesses and subjects of ye citty
or shall hereafter be laid, either by the States Generall or
the citty, and that all the members residing in England,
or in any parts beyond the seas, shall enjoy the same
freedome within the citty.

11. That no English or Scotch soldiers shall be quartered within the citty, nor any officers or soldiers of any
nation whatsoever shall be quartered within the Publique
English House or ye houses of any of the members of
the Company or in the House of any Burger wherein any
of the members of the Company lodge or have their
warehouses.

12. The Citty grants to the Company to settle their
government according to their charters, in such persons
as they shall see fitt, and that they may exercise and administer civil jurisdiction to all of their own nation—
definitively according to their own customs and constitution and to execute the same according to their own
charters; and that the magistrates of the town shall assist in the execution of the sentences of the Company, and
that the Company shall administer the goods and estates
of all their members and adherents that shall die or become insolvent, within the citty and liberties thereof, and
likewise of all the English subjects, and to give such pre-
ference and concurrence for payment out of the estate as
they shall see fitt, and that all the Burgers and inhabitants of the citty, that have any pretense to any debts
due from the party so dying or becoming insolvent, shall
submit to the judgment of the English Company.

EXTRACTS FROM THE COURT REGISTER OF THE ADVENTURERS.[1]

Br. Mus. Pamphlets, $\frac{712, g, 16}{2}$

AT A COURT HOLDEN MARCH 4, 1603.

The brethren of this Company assembled together, doe hold it very requisite for the better carriage of their Trade, that suite shoulde be made unto the kings Majesty, by the means of my Lord Chancellors to be preferred that in the confirmation of the Companies Charters of Privileges, this also might be added and inserted, that the Company in their Courts as well in England as beyond the Seas to be holden, may impose reasonable fines and penalties upon such subjects of this Realme, not free of this Company, that shall ship woollen commodities into the countries and Places where they are privileged, thereby to cause such intruding subjects to desist from that trade, which properly appertains to the Company of Adventurers. In consideration whereof, and in hope of

[1] The records of the Merchants Adventurers have not been discovered. Apart from the *Lawes, Customes* etc., published in this volume, only the most scanty extracts from the private books and registers of the Fellowship have appeared. Even in the few cases where such has been found, no absolute proof of their authenticity can be established. These extracts from Court proceedings are taken from a pamphlet which came to my notice in the British Museum. It is entitled "A Discourse of Motives," etc., and was written by an opponent of the Society. He concludes his excerpts with the statement "The transcript of this oath and orders were truly extracted out of their own Register and is concordant with the original."

the more favor in some other suites they meane to move hereafter, they are pleased that the kings majesty may have and receive the one moity of all such fines and penalties as shall be imposed upon such intruders; and further they agree to yield unto his majesty in respect aforesaid, an annual rent of 50£ or 100 Marks per annum.

AT A COURT HOLDEN OCTOBER 11, 1606.

Letters from the Brethren at Middleburgh of the fourth of October 1606 were made publique, they gave knowledge that they have agreed to the augmentation of the general stint, and of the yearly and monthly number of clothes to be shipped out upon the free licence, referring us to the specifications of every man's proportion of stint sent with their letters, and now read; which proportion of stint all the trading brethern are enjoyned not to exceed within the compass of any one year, upon penalty of 40 s. per cloth, and to prevent abuse they ordain every brother that shall ship any woollen commodity shall be yearly purged upon his oath, the form whereof was now sent and read also; and in case any should refuse or neglect to take the said oath by the last day of August every yeare, then he to pay 20£ sterling and to have no benefit of the free licence until he hath taken the said oath.

AT A COURT HOLDEN NOVEMBER 16, 1623.

The Court had consideration according to the season o the yeare, of their yearly presents to such honourable persons as they have received favours from; and first forasmuch as they have been extraordinarily bound to the favours of the Lord Treasurer, the remembrance is now to be enlarged at New Yeares tide, and that they shall

16

present his Lordshipe with 200 pieces of 22s. in gold and a piece of plate as an acknowledgement of his lordships especial favors.

Moreover to the Lord Duke of Buckingham.

To the Archbishop of Canterbury.

To the Lord Treasurer { To Mr. Secretary Calout.
To the Lord Keeper { To Mr. Comptroller &c.

AT A COURT HOLDEN APRIL 19, 1634.

"Master Withers did exhibit two severall Papers to this Court to be considered of, concerning what abatements should be made for all defects of Cloth whether in weight, length or breadth, as also some points for the ordering of tarre which he desired might be commended to the courts at Hamburg and Delfte, that they might consider thereon and further advise of any other course thereon and it was accordingly ordered; but the Court of Hamburg is to be desired to make no act in this business till they have acquainted this court with opinion thereon. As for that Mr. Withers desired that no brother should buy any white cloth that is made in Gloucestershire, Wiltshire, Oxfordshire, and the Eastern limits of Somersetshire, without abatements for all faults in which they shall be found defective, etc.[1]

---

[1] It was so ordered upon pain of 20 s. forfeit, but nothing was to be done till the Lords of the Privy Council gave their consent; notwithstanding it was done without, on May 21, 1634. On this the author comments as follows: "It is worthy the observing when this order was made, even about the time when they had by their often gifts at news years tide, and other left handed means, got their authority to be proclaimed for restraining all merchants, not free of the Company, of transporting any woollen commodities, or to pay 100£, and come into the company; then they make this order to curb the poor Clothier to abate for defects as much as they please."

THE ORDINANCE OF 1643.[1]

Br. Mus. Pampblets, 669, f. 7 (50).

An Ordinance of the Lords and Commons in Parliament Assembled, for the upholding the government of the Fellowship of Merchants Adventurers of England to the better maintenance of the Trade of Cloathing and woollen manufacture of the Kingdome.

For the better encouragement and supportation of the Fellowship of Merchants Adventurers of England, which hath been found very serviceable and profitable unto this State; and for the better Government and regulation of Trade, especially that ancient and great Trade of Cloathing, whereby the same will be much advanced to the common good, and benefit of the people: The Lords and Commons in Parliament doe ordaine that the said Fellowship shall continue and be a corporation, and shall have power to levy monies on the members of their Corporation, and their goods, for their necessary charge and maintenance of their government: And that no person

---

[1] This ordinance, passed on October 11th, 1643, affords a definite indication of the side espoused by the Fellowship in the Great Civil War. It is not likely, that the Adventurers were all of one mind concerning the great national questions, but from reliable evidence I am satisfied that the great body of the Society was on the side of parliament ; frequent loans from the Fellowship of large sums are made to parliament during this period. (Cf. p. x, n. 2.) It is also worthy of note that the attempt to force the kingship on Cromwell emanated from men high in the councils of the Adventurers. Sir Christopher Packe, the prime mover in the ordinance of 1656, was also the Governor of the Society. Thurloe, *State* Papers, vi., 74.

shall Trade into those parts, limited by their Incorporation but such as are free of that Corporation, upon forfeiture of their goods. Provided, that the said Fellowship shall not exclude any person from his Freedome and
admission into the said Fellowship, which shall desire it
by way of redemption, if such person by their custome be
capable thereof, and hath been bred a Merchant, and
shall pay one hundred pounds for the same, if he be Free,
and an Inhabitant of the City of London, and Trade from
that Port, or fifty pounds if he be not Free, and no Inhabitant of the said City, and Trade not from thence;
and that the said Fellowship shall have power to imprison
Members of their own Company in matters of government, and to give such an oath, or oathes to them, as
shall bee approved by both Houses of Parliament. Provided, that all Rights confirmed by act of Parliament or
Ancient Charters, shall hereby be saved, and the said
Lords and Commons do further ordaine, That with all
convenient expedition, a Bill shall be prepared in order
to an Act of Parliament to be passed in this present Parliament for the further setling and full confirming of
Priviledges to the said Fellowship, with such other
clauses and provisions as shall be found expedient by
both Houses of Parliament: This Ordinance to remaine
in full force, untill a Bill or Act shall be prepared and
passed, according to the intent and true meaning of this
Ordinance. And it is ordered, that this Ordinance be
forthwith Printed and published, that all persons concerned therein may take notice thereof, as appertaineth.
JOHN BROWNE, Cler. Parliamentorum,
H. ELSYNG, Cler. Parl. Dom. Com.

EXTRACT FROM THE ACT OF 1688 "LAYING OPEN" THE
TRADE OF THE MERCHANTS ADVENTURERS.

Statutes of the Realm, 1 William and Mary, c. 32.

AN ACT FOR THE BETTER PREVENTING THE EXPORTATION OF
WOOLE AND ENCOURAGEING THE WOOLLEN MANUFACTURES
OF THIS KINGDOME.[1]

And for the better Encouragement of the Manufactures as well as the Growth of Wooll, Be it further enacted
by the authority aforesaid, That from henceforward it
shall and may be lawful to and for any person or persons
whatsoever, to buy any cloath, Stuffs, Stockings or other
Manufactures of Wooll made in the Kingdom of *England*
Dominion of *Wales*, or the Town of *Berwecke* upon *Tweed*
and the same freely without Molestation or Trouble whatsoever, to Export into any parts beyond the Seas, paying
the usuall Customs.

Provided, that nothing contained in the Act, shall be
construed to avoid the Charters and Grants made to the
Levant Company, to the *Eastland* Company, to the *Russia*
Company, to the *African* Company, or the Priviledges
granted to them, or any of them.[2]

---

[1] The first nine sections of the Act make provision for the prohibition of the export of wool, wool-fels, mortlings shortlings yarn
made of wool, wool-flocks, fullers-earth, fulling-clay and tobacco-
pipe clay. Section ten contains the clause affecting the trade of
woollen manufactures here given.

[2] In these two paragraphs the Merchant Adventurers are deprived of their privileges. Why they alone are thus disfranchised
and the other companies specially excepted I have been unable to
ascertain.

EXTRACTS FROM THE CORRESPONDENCE OF MR.
RYCANT, THE ENGLISH RESIDENT AT
HAMBURG.

R. O. State Papers For. Off., Ham. No. 8.

A "LETTER FROM PAUL RYCANT (THE RESIDENT AT HAMBURG) TO RT. HON. EARL OF NOTTINGHAM HIS MAJESTIES PRINCIPAL SECRETARY OF STATE." AUG. 2, 1689.

I can now give y^r Lord^{shp} the newes of my arrivall at this place on the 18th Inst. with the five ships belonging to the Comp^a of this place laden wth cloth, and other woolen manufactures of England. . . . . . I was both on my way from Gluckstadt heither, and at this place, received by the English merchants wth the same respect and honour which is usually paid to his ma^{ties} Resident and I am now lodged at the English hous, untill I can be provided with a hous of my owne. . . .

LETTER OF PAUL RYCANT HIS MAJESTIES RESIDENT.

. . . . I finde the trade of the Hamburg Company in this place to be very great in the woollen manufactory of England, have exported in the five last ships above the value of $\frac{m}{200}$ ster., but that which gives our merchants here great discouragement is the surprising news, that the parliament is laying their trade open and give liberty to whomsoever, that will to export cloth and other woolen manufactory into these parts. If such an Act, my Lord, as this should passe in general terms, without providing for the safety of the company's charter and privileges abroad and that free trade in the woollen manufactory of

250

our nation be granted to all persons whatsoever, as well to the River of Elbe, as our mart towns in Holland, the Comp* will loose their great privileges, they now enjoy in this place, and which have always been esteemed of great advantage, not only for the sale of our woollen manufactory but also upon many accounts to the nation in generall; and if the same be once lost, they will ever hereafter be irrecoverable. Upon the rumor of this intended libertie of trade, several foreigners already discourse to the Comp* disadvantage. . . . .

LETTER FROM PAUL RYCANT. SEPT. 6, 1689.

In my former letters I presumed to acquaint your Lordship with my thoughts of the great prejudice and damage which would attend the trade of our woolen manufactory, in case that the Companie of Merchant Adventurers should be laid open. But since, I understand, that the act has been passed nothing but time and experience will be able to verify and confirme the truth of my arguments: untill. which is done I desire to know, in what manner I am to comport and behave myself in case the government of this city should repeale and make void the priviledges and immunities granted to the Company of Merchant-Adventurers which were no longer to continue in force, then the companie remained a body corporate which being now disfranchized in England; I know not how I should answer in case I should be asked the reason, why our priviledges should not terminate with our charter in England, on which all our priviledges are grounded. But I cannot of all things in this world comprehend, why and for what reason the trade of Turkey and Africa, &c should be continued in their usnal regulations and that only of the Merchant-Adventurers be laid open to all forraigners and Traders whatsoever, . . .

I have now before me your Lordships of the 24th of September which is very full of reason and satisfactory in the great matter relating to the subsistence and priviledges of the Hamburg Comp^a for which both I and they and all relating to that society are much obliged to the favours of your Lordship. [1]

I have for sometime had a contest with the government of this city, touching some points in the concordat relating to the affairs of the Merchants: which is now reduced to this issue that a conference is appointed to be held (which I design to have at my hous) and in case it succeeds not according unto right, and the privileges granted to our Companie, I shall then appeal unto Majesties favour and discretion therein, intending to follow the commands of his Majesty to maintain the rights and privileges of this Companie, notwithstanding the late act of parliament opening the trade to all such as shall export the woolen manufactories of England, without any other abatement or diminution of the other privileges to the Companie.

Yesterday my Lord Hyde came to this city, where I and the Merchants received him with the respect due to the sonne of a Nobleman of England, and of the Govenor of the Hamburg Companie.

[1] In a letter of the 18th, Rycant tells of his having submitted his Lordship's letter to the *General Court* which desires him to thank his Lordship. In the meantime if the Senate desire to abrogate the Company's privileges he will demand their continuance in the name of His Majesty. They do not apprehend any evil effects from Englishmen coming into their trade; it is strangers whom they fear.

LETTER FROM THE STATES GENERAL OF HOLLAND
TO THE TOWN COUNCIL OF DORT, IN 1751.[1]

Resolutien van den Oudraad, 1751, blz. 25. Dordrecht.

Honorable, wise, thoughtful very discrete Gentlemen,

So we did at our meeting of the 30th December last approve and resolve that Samuel Jay, English Preacher,

Cornelia van Dorst, widow of Grès,

Johan Holterap, English reader,

Sara Notemans, sexton and Jan van Gelder, bell-ringer } of the English church at Dort,

in consideration that all the persons just named are survivors (left overs) of the English Court by whom they were chosen and appointed, should have and enjoy freedom of the country's imposts; but that those who might be called into their places and be appointed after them, should be held to pay the country's taxes the same as all other inhabitants. Thus we judged it necessary to inform your Honor by letter of the above, in order that, in the case of the appointment of other persons in their stead, you could regulate yourself according to it.

Wherewith honorable, Wise, Thoughtful very discreet Gentlemen we recommend you to the gracious protection of God.

Given in the Hague the 5th of Jan. 1751.

By order of the Committee of the Council

(sig)   A. v. STRATEN.

[1] Translated from the Dutch.

253

LETTER FROM LORD BUTE TO MR. MATHIAS.
JULY 28, 1761.

R. 0. State Papers For., No. 74.

Having received and laid before the king your dispatch of the 17th inst, wherein you mention the desire of the French Court to extort from the Senate of Hamburgh, by keeping on the Embargo upon their ships trading to France, the point which they have long had in view, of the Establishment of a French Company there, with the same privileges as those so long enjoyed by the British Society of Merchants; His majesty was glad to see, you was of the opinion that the minister of that town was not like to succeed therein, and as a grant of that kind in favor of France must be very prejudicial to the Interests of the kings subjects, His majesty depends upon your keeping a watchful eye upon what may pass, in regard to such a solicitation, and upon your doing your utmost to prevent the concurrence of the Senate in an Innovation that must give so just a subject of offence to the king.

I am &c. BUTE.

EXTRACT FROM THE FRENCH NOTE IN REGARD TO THE
ESTABLISHMENT OF A FRENCH COMPANY
AT HAMBURG.[1]

. . . And as this condition (the embargo) might

[1] The document from which the translation is made is a copy of the French solicitation sent to Bute in August, 1761. On Sept. 15th, Mathias writes in regard to it, " Your Lordship will observe by the contents of the said answer that there does not appear to be any apprehension that the Senate will ever condescend to any proposals made to them on the part of France for establishing a trading company in the city with the same privileges which the British Factory enjoy here . . . "

bring about that a French company of commerce would be established in your city, with the same privileges as those enjoyed by the British Society these two hundred years past; the establishing of such a company, as you are well aware gentlemen, the Court of France has had in view for a long time, and for which purpose it has caused proposals to be submitted by the late M. Poussin and to be continued, although without success by M. de Champeaux. . . .

EXTRACTS FROM THE CORRESPONDENCE OF SIR EDWARD THORNTON, MINISTER PLENIPOTENTIARY TO THE CIRCLE OF LOWER SAXONY AND RESIDENT TO THE HANSE TOWNS.

R. O. State Papers, For. Ham., No. 28.

THE SECOND PARAGRAPH OF THORNTON'S INSTRUCTIONS.
MAY 4, 1805.

2. You shall upon all occasions give countenance and protection to our subjects, as well merchants as masters of ships, and others trading in those parts and particularly to the Company of Merchants Adventurers; taking care that the privileges and immunities which they have time out of mind enjoyed, be not violated or encroached upon . . .

EXTRACT FROM A LETTER BY THORNTON.   JUNE 4, 1805.

I announced some days ago to the English Company of Merchant Adventurers residing in Hamburg my arrival with the character of His Majesty's Minister; and I was waited upon a few days after by a deputation from that Body to congratulate me upon this occasion, and to offer me the Freedom of their Society, which is to be presented to me on the 29th of this month.

(Right Honorable Lord Mulgrave.)

EXTRACT FROM A LETTER BY THORNTON. JULY 5, 1805.

The French have as I understand, frequently demanded of the Senate the establishment of a company with privileges similar to those granted to the English Company of Merchants Adventurers, so long ago settled in this Town, and although the privileges of the latter are in themselves little more than local Distinctions, and influencing in a very small Degree indeed the general Commerce of His Majesty's Subjects, yet the Town has hitherto very properly resisted a demand, which if conceded to the French now, would probably have much more extensive effects, than the obsolete concessions made to the English Company.[1]

[1] I have not found any clue to the fate of the Company after 1805. During the occupation of Hamburg by Napoleon, its activities were of course suspended, and it is quite possible that they were resumed after 1813. The prolonged continuance of the Fellowship at Hamburg down to a date so comparatively recent has been quite unsuspected; the accounts of the Adventurers by present day writers all conclude with a much earlier period.

CONTINUATION OF THE BY-LAW OF 1688.[1]

That no Governour of the Fellowshipp shall be chosen hereafter without the foreknowledge & Consent first had of the Residence of London And that the Governour of the Fellowshipp or his Deputy in the Residence of London togeather with the Generality of the said Residence shall have and Wee doe hereby give them free liberty Lycence Sole Power & Authority from time to time and at all times hereafter to Elect & Choose & appoint a Deputy and soe many Other[2] officers in the said Residence of London as to the s^d gov^d Dep^{ties} & generallity there shall seem meet for the dispatch of the business of the said Residence of London with such salaries & availes as they shall think fitt . . . and to amove put out and displace the same at their Will & pleasure . . and that the said gov^r or his Deputy in the Residence of London together with the generallity of the Residence shall also have and wee do hereby give them ful Liberty, Lycence sole Power & Authority to Elect choose and appoint out of the Members of the said Residence such Persons to be a special committee or associates in & for the said Residence of London as they shall think fitt & to remove & displace the same at their like will & pleasure.

[1] The introduction of the Continuation of the By-law at this place is due entirely to accident. It was deemed preferable to give it here than to omit it entirely. The first part of the order will be found on page 197, see also note on page 217.

[2] Up to this point this paragraph is a repetition of the last one on folio 201, the repetition occurring in the manuscript.

2. And it is hereby likewise enacted and ordered that no bye law Statutes Rules and Orders or Constitutions for the government of the said Fellowship shal at any time hereafter be made or established without the consent first had of the Residence of London—And further that those Bye Laws Orders Rules & Statutes & Constitutions which are already made and not repealed by this present Investment shall be delivered soe soon as conveniently may bee and in the meantime remain in full force until any alteration shall be agreed upon by the joint consent of the said Residences of London & Hamburg.

3. And it is hereby enacted and ordained that no Impositions Rates or Duties relating to trade shall be assessed taxed or imposed without the consent first had of the Residence of London—And for the more firm settling & securing unto the said Residence of London and their successors all and every the Lycences Powers & Privileges hereby intended them It is Declared noted enacted and ordained that this draught or Instrument shall pass and from word to word be truly entered and enregistered in our book of ordinances as a standing order and shall remain irrevocable without the consent of the said Residence of London first had to refer that purpose signified under their common seal and subscribed by the governor or Deputy of the said Residence of London for the time being.

And in case it should so happen that the said Residence of London should at any time hereafter find cause or think fitt to waive suspend or relinquish the privileges hereby given & intended them or any part thereof That it shall nevertheless be lawful for the said Residence of London at any time or times afterwards at their own Will & pleasure to Resume & take again to themselves the said priveleges so waived or suspended in part or in all in as full & ample manner as they are hereby granted and intended to be granted them and as if they had never been waived or suspended, Without the least contradiction opposition Lett or hindrance of this Residence of Hamburg—which accordingly shall take its full effect and force so soon as the said Residence of London shall at any time or times have signified their resolutions therein by any writings subscribed by the gov or Dep^ty of the said Residence under their common seal to the Residence at Hamburg.

And for the further satisfaction of the said Residence of London and for the sure making and securing of the Priveleges to them.   It is hereby declared noted enacted and ordained that if at any time hereafter *any member* or *members* of the said Fellowship residing in this Residence of Hamburg *shall attempt move insist* or *vote* or cause or procure any other person or persons to move, insist or vote for abrogating or making void or repealing or diminishing the Lawes & Priveleges hereby granted or intended to the said Residence of London without their consent first had in manner as aforesaid that such member or members and each and every of them shall *Forfeit* and pay to the use of the Fellowship *Fifty Pounds Sterling* without any favour or abatement Provided such member be first admonished or acquainted with the contents of this standing order which the Secretary of this Residence of Hamburg is and shall be obliged and bound to publish and make known from time to time to every member as occasion shall require on Penalty of *Fifty Pounds Sterling* to the use of the Fellowship & the loss of his place all which forfeitures shall be levied paid &

disposed of to such uses as the Residence of London from time to time to Direct and appoint.

Finally it is ordered and enacted that this Instrument being now ordained noted confirmed & established by the Deputy Assistants & Fellowship of the Merchants Adventurers of England in this Residence of Hamburgh a true copy thereof from word to word being fairly written and subscribed by the present Deputy at Hamburgh & ratified under the common seal of this Residence shall be transmitted to the Residence of London to be Enregistered in their Book of Orders and thereto remain upon Record.

Actum in Hamburgh at a generall Court held there the two and twentieth day of October A D 1688.

[L S]   SAM^L FREE Dep^{ty}.

www.ingramcontent.com/pod-product-compliance
Lightning Source LLC
Chambersburg PA
CBHW031945090426
42739CB00006B/86